Research Supervision for Supervisors and their Students

Dan Remenyi PhD

and

Arthur Money PhD

ISBN: 978-1-908272-48-5

Printed by Good News Digital Books

Published by: Academic Publishing International Limited, Reading, RG4 9AY, United Kingdom, info@academic-publishing.org

Available from www.academic-bookshop.com

Contents

Contents

Contents

Contents

About the Authors

Between them, Dan Remenyi and Arthur Money have more than 60 years experience in supervising research degree candidates. They have supervised and/or examined more than 100 research degree candidates.

They have worked at various Business Schools and universities where they have taught research methodology, research supervision, concepts of academic development and research degree assessment.

Dan Remenyi's original academic interest was in economics and political science and after his first degree he pursued a career in business before completing a doctorate 20 years ago. Since then he has been involved in information systems, knowledge management and project management. He currently specialises in research methodology and the sociology of research.

Arthur Money's first interests were in mathematics and mathematical statistics. After some years in the science faculty he moved to the business school environment where he has worked for more than 30 years. Besides teaching statistical techniques his interests extend to the application of statistical analysis to all functional areas in business and management.

Dan Remenyi holds a BSocSc, MBA and a PhD. He is a Visiting Professor at a number of different Universities and a member of the associate faculty at Henley Business School and Trinity College Dublin.

Arthur Money holds a BSc, BSc (Hons), MSc, PhD. He is a Professor Emeritus of Henley Business School, University of Reading.

Preface to the second edition

The past few years has seen a number of changes in the issues related to being awarded a doctorate and how the supervisor needs to support his or her research degree candidates (sometimes referred to as students or research students). These changes have impacted a number of different aspects of the relationship between supervisor and degree candidate but the most important areas are:-

1. There is an increasing demand for the product of the research to be shown to have practical value i.e. value in use as well as delivering a theoretical contribution. This has been referred to as Mode 2 research.

2. Appointing two supervisors has become the norm. Some universities are moving towards the USA style of having a committee, sometimes an informal committee, as a supervisory body. There will normally be one person who has primary responsibility for the degree candidate's performance.

3. Universities and business schools have become aware of the need to ensure that supervisors have acquired the necessary skills to be allowed to supervise. Individuals who do not already have a doctorate are now generally regarded as being ineligible to supervise. The primary or lead supervisor will normally have been a second supervisor at least once before taking the lead role.

4. Universities will look to finding examiners with suitable qualifications and the external examiner will be expected to have had a doctorate for some time and also to be a research active individual. Some universities seek to find examiners who have a track record of their research appearing in quality journals.

5. Obtaining approval for the research from the appropriate university Ethics Committee is now normally a requirement to commence the research. This introduces a new challenge to the degree candidate and an Ethics Protocol has become a sine qua non in academic research.

6. Universities have become more aware of the need for regular progress checks during the period of registration and the attendance by research students at formal colloquia is now routine.

At the same time some universities have legacy situations whereby degree candidates have been registered for long periods of time without adequate progress. In some cases individuals had been accepted who were not for one reason or another able to complete. Sometimes this is due to a lack of cognitive capacity on the part of the degree candidate. Sometimes this has occurred because the degree candidate has not been able to meet the challenge of writing in an adequately academic way. On other occasions the degree candidate is distracted from the research process by undertaking too much other work such as teaching or marking. Some of these situations were only terminated by the university informing the degree candidate that he or she had "run out of time". It is no longer permissible in some countries nor acceptable in others to have individuals registered for a degree for 10 or 15 or more years.

Different approaches to doctoral education have evolved. The professional doctorate is increasingly recognised. Although these degrees have been offered for at least 20 years they were sometimes considered not quite as good as the traditional academic doctorate. The professional doctorate degree, which will normally not be a PhD, but rather a Doctor of Business Administration (DBA) or a Doctor of Education (DEd) or a Doctor of Engineering (DEng) will have a material professional orientation as well as a strong academic focus. Of course the balance between the professional and academic content does vary from university to university, but it is clear that both professional and academic criteria are applied to the examination processes. Another approach is a doctorate by practice and currently this is referred to as a PhD by Practice. This is quite new and it will probably evolve over time. The rationale behind this doctorate is that universities have been awarding a doctorate in Fine Arts on the basis of a piece of art such as a painting or a sculpture or in Music to the composition of a piece of music, so why shouldn't a university award a doctorate on the basis of a piece of business or management activity. The regulations for these degrees point out that rigour and originality are required. It is too early to say if this type of doctorate will be regarded as equivalent to the other forms of doctorate.

A well known university took an unusual approach to doctorates in that it invited members of staff to submit a portfolio of work which they had produced over the past ten years or so for consideration for the award of a doctorate. The portfolio was accompanied by an Introductory Chapter and a Summary Chapter. This is similar to the publication route to a doctorate but there was a material difference. The works submitted in this case were not undertaken or produced during a period of supervised research.

The different routes to doctorates described above have the same objective of having the degree candidate add something of value to the body of theoretical knowledge which has some practical application and to do so through the production of a scholarly piece of work.

Each approach to acquiring a research degree requires supervision. Although the emphasis of the supervision may be different, the same basic principles will apply to each of these degrees.

Another dimension of the doctoral degree to mention is that those who hold doctorates should, in addition to being competent academic researchers and scholars, also be what Chris Golde of the Carnegie Foundation calls a *steward of the discipline*. The term a steward of the discipline suggests that a doctoral degree holder should be able to defend those aspects of the field of study which have already been researched and where there has been an agreement to the understanding thereof.

The doctoral landscape has indeed changed over the past decade. Many of us involved in doctoral education argue that the acquisition of a doctorate is now more challenging than before. Few, if anyone, would say that it has become easier. There is more choice available to prospective doctoral candidates and it is well known that more choice does not make decision making easier. It is important for prospective doctoral candidates to properly understand what is involved in obtaining a doctorate and to manage their degree processes as best they can.

In general there is today more structure in the way research candidates are helped to achieve the standard required for the degree to be awarded. In many ways these changes have been helpful to both the supervisor and the degree candidate, but they have of course introduced new layers of bureaucracy which means there is more work involved. However the intention is that the results should be better and that research candidates will have a better university experience.

This second edition has addressed the new circumstances in which doctoral candidates find themselves and offers advice to both these candidates and their supervisors.

Dan Remenyi
dan.remenyi@tcd.ie
January 2012

Preface to the first edition

Research should be fun rather than a grind and one should believe in its relevance and value
Keen P, (1980), 'MIS Research: Reference disciplines and a cumulative tradition', *Proceedings of the First International Conference on Information Systems***, Philadelphia, PA, December 8-10, pp. 9-18.**

There is little doubt that educational expectations have been changing. More people want to have a university degree and our society has been encouraging this trend. In fact talk of the knowledge society and its need for expertise has encouraged many people to follow advanced studies. This has resulted in more and more individuals attending university and a resulting increase in graduates. As the number of first-degree graduates has increased the demand for Masters degrees has also been on the increase. More and more universities have begun to take mature individuals without a first Bachelor's degree onto Masters programmes. The result of this trend has been that having a Masters degree is nowhere near as special as it used to be. Although these degrees, which are normally offered by course work, are available in a wide range of subject areas the most popular by far is the Masters of Business Administration (MBA). This in turn has lead to a major increase in the demand for doctoral degrees in business with the establishment in several universities of the Doctor of Business Administration (DBA) degree.

The number of individuals studying for MBA and DBA degrees has lead to a substantial increase in the demand for research supervisors. Unfortunately the quality of the supervision and supervisors has been mixed and this has sometimes lead to problems for both degree candidates and universities in that the completion rate is often not as good as it should be.

With a few noticeable exceptions universities have generally not paid as much attention to the quality of research supervision as they should have. It has been assumed that researchers would largely look after themselves. In general Deans of Research or Chairpersons of Advanced Degrees Committees have taken the view that if there have been no complaints, the provision made for supervision must be adequate. It has been the *no news is good news* philosophy. This has been compounded by the fact that there has not been a tradition of reviewing the competence or effectiveness of research supervisors. Supervision has been seen as a sort of additional activity which has generally not been included in the three common requirements for university work, i.e. teaching, research and administration.

This book has been written as a response to the need to improve the standard of supervision of research degrees in universities. In general the quality of research degree supervision is not good. Until recently there have been few courses on the subject of supervision and little published in this area. There has been no comprehensive textbook available covering the key issues involved in research degree supervision.

As mentioned this lack of quality in supervision is evidenced by the poor completion rate and by the fact that dissertations often only just meet minimum requirements or standards. However, funding bodies and Higher Education Authorities have become conscious of the need for better standards of supervision. Furthermore students who have not been appropriately supervised have been known to threaten litigation. There is now a much greater appreciation of the need for sound research supervision processes to be in place, which helps to ensure the quality of the educational experience as well as the standard of the output.

This book will make a contribution to improving the standard of research supervision. It is primarily intended for research supervisors, both experienced and as yet inexperienced. But supervision works best as a co-operative exercise, so this book should also be of use to prospective research students.

Dan Remenyi PhD
dan.remenyi@tcd.ie
March 2004

Who will benefit from reading this book?

As the title suggests this book will help both supervisors and their students. The book explains the nature of supervision and how to approach this activity with appropriate care and attention. The book highlights the pitfalls involved in supervision and offers advice on how to avoid them. It should be remembered that supervision is a skill much like a craft, which can only be learnt slowly with the help of an accomplished practitioner. Occasional reference to this book while learning to supervise will be helpful.

Students who would like to know what they could reasonably expect from their own supervisor/s will find this book invaluable. This is especially true for distance learning, e-learning and part-time students who do not have continuous contact with their supervisors.

This book will also be helpful to anyone who is conducting a course or a seminar for novice supervisors.

Becoming familiar with the information in this book will also benefit those who are considering whether or not to embark on a doctorate. The book points out the challenges as well as the great advantages to be had by undertaking a major research project for a doctoral degree.

The material in this book is primarily aimed at Social Scientists and especially those working in the field of Business and Management studies. However the principles of research and the supervision thereof are much the same across many academic fields of studies. Therefore supervisors and their students from a wide range of other disciplines will derive value from reading this book.

Acknowledgements

This book is the result of years of working with research degree candidates at a number of different universities. The material in the book has been drawn from many different experiences. Some have been a great success while others have been quite difficult. The book calls upon not only supervising experiences but also experiences from examining research degrees.

The authors would like to thank all the students and others from whom they have learnt how to supervise research over the years.

Research degree supervision is a skill that is best, and some would say can only be learnt by experience, with the help and advice of an accomplished practitioner. Becoming a really effective supervisor is indeed a trial and error experience. Everyone makes mistakes and supervising research degrees is an area where mistakes can be relatively easily made. It is however hoped that the experiences of others can help highlight situations to be avoided. We hope that everyone can learn from the experiences of others.

How to use this book

Research Supervision for Supervisors and their Students covers a wide range of topics and has not been written with a view that it should necessarily be read from cover to cover. Rather, it is more of a dip-in book to find information on a particular aspect of supervision.

We have provided a reasonably comprehensive range of references, including website addresses. We are sure that readers will appreciate that URLs often change, but we have checked their availability at the time of going to print.

Part One
Orienting the Supervisor

Chapter 1

Research degrees and supervision

If politics is the art of the possible, research is surely the art of the soluble. Both are immensely practical-minded affairs.
Medawar P, 'The Act of Creation', in New Statesman, London, 19 June 1964; repr. in The Art of the Soluble, 1967.

1.1   The range of research degrees

There is an increasing demand for Masters and Doctoral degrees in a wide variety of subject areas. This trend, which was probably initiated by the success of the famous or maybe even infamous[1] Masters in Business Administration (MBA), has seen an enormous increase in the demand for Masters of Science (MSc), Masters of Commerce (MCom), Masters of Economics (MEcon) to mention only a few such degrees. Furthermore these degrees, unlike the older form of Masters degrees, are now hybrid educational events involving both lectures and research projects. The level of the research required for these new degrees varies[2] a lot. Some universities require a simple research report, whereas others look for a more thorough dissertation. However, the student usually needs to be able to demonstrate competence in research.

Some universities describe the written report required at the end of the research degree process as a dissertation, while other universities will refer to this document as a thesis. In this book we have chosen to use the word dissertation. The problem in using the word thesis to describe the written work is that the same word maybe used to describe the theoretical contribution the researcher is claiming to have made in his or her field of study.

To a lesser extent, there has also been a large increase in interest in degrees at the doctoral level. Whereas only a decade ago doctoral degrees were seen as being accessible only to the few academically or intellectually inclined, today many more individuals are obtaining Doctorates, and they are finding the knowledge and the research skills acquired in so doing relevant in management consulting and business, or in government research jobs. Furthermore the title Doctor opens doors or opportunities that may otherwise be difficult to access.

---

[1] Over the years there seems to have been a love hate relationship between employers and those who have promoted the MBA as a special degree for would-be fast track executives. As the cost of this degree has soared there is a growing concern that it is not possible to achieve a return on the investment cost in a reasonable amount of time.

[2] Some Masters by course work allocate as much as 50% to the research project while others will allocate as little as 10%. Thus there is considerable variation in the weight given to the research element and this is reflected in the amount of work required for the research report or dissertation.

As well as the traditional Doctor of Philosophy (PhD) and the DPhil[3] degree there are many institutions offering other doctorates such as the Doctor of Business Administration (DBA) degree, which although requiring a major research project, also requires students to complete seminars or courses and other professional development activities. These degrees are sometimes incorrectly referred to as Doctorates by coursework.

The term professional doctorate, referred to by some individuals as the "Prof Doc", is now well established and this requires a balance to be struck between professional and academic objectives. Where this balance lies depends on the university or business school which is offering this degree. Sometimes these professional doctorates are referred to as taught doctorates but this is a misnomer as the essence of a university awarded doctorate is that research has been done by which something of value has been added to the body of knowledge.

There is another issue related to the "Prof Doc" which is referred to as the Mode 1 and Mode 2 question. This terminology has been in use for at least 10 years and refers to a change in attitude towards the manner in which doctoral programmes are set up and managed by a university or business school. A Mode 1 doctorate is best described as a traditional academic degree. The main characteristic of this degree is that it produces a contribution to the body of theoretical knowledge without much concern to its application or use within the business community. On the other hand a Mode 2 doctorate requires not only a contribution to the body of theoretical knowledge, but also a clear demonstration that the findings have direct use in practical situations. As society has become more concerned about the utility of university education so the emphasis on Mode 2 type doctorates is set to grow.

A more recent innovation in doctoral degrees, which is referred to as a PhD by Practice, involves the degree candidate presenting a description and a critical review of a substantial piece of work in which they have been involved. This written document needs to be accompanied by evidence that the work described has added something of value to the

---

[3] The DPhil is traditionally offered at Oxford University and a small number of other institutions in England and Scotland as well as in South Africa to mention only three locations. Other Universities offer doctoral degrees such as the Doctor of Commerce (DCom), Doctor of Technology (DTech), the Doctor of Engineering (DEng) etc.

body of theoretical knowledge. It is at present too early to be confident that the PhD by Practice degree will be accepted as being equivalent to the academic PhD or the professional DBA etc. Of course an honorary doctorate is an exception to this.

1.2   How a research degree changes the graduate

There are a number of ways in which the process of obtaining a research degree changes the individual as a direct consequence of the process through which the individual has to journey. A research degree requires working on one's own with much less detailed direction than the student will normally have had before. Research students will have to keep up his or her own curiosity and energy levels. They require a high degree of initiative as they will need to find for themselves interesting informants from whom to collect relevant data. They may have to seek out organisations in which to perform a case study or perhaps some action research. Obtaining access to individuals or organisations is often not easy.

A particularly important issue which the supervisor needs to impress upon the research student is that he or she has full responsibility for their own research. Whatever may happen it is not acceptable for the individual to say that he or she was not a success because of the inadequacies of the supervisor. Nor is it appropriate for the student to blame any other aspects of the facilities offered by the university, such as library, computer or laboratory access. This is a critical issue as the research degree candidate is about to make one of the biggest investments he or she will ever make in their lifetimes. Besides the fees, the living cost etc., the main investment is the time it will take to complete the degree. Thousands of hours of work are involved.

The final point that needs to be emphasised is that in obtaining a doctorate an individual is becoming a social scientist, as business and management studies is part of social science. In becoming a scientist an individual's attitude can change to a number of issues. First of all a scientist does not take data, evidence or propositions at face value. Science demands that evidence presented is carefully examined and that the implication of the evidence is thought about. Jumping to conclusions is the opposite of this and is not how scientists work. Scientists try to be objective and will usually ask for as much evidence as possible. But most of all scientists realise the paramount importance of communications. Great care and attention is given to listening and to picking up nuances in what is being said. Scientists are also aware of the value in understanding what is not being said. A scientist reflects carefully on how words are understood. In scientific discourse words which are indefinable should not be used. Commonly used indefinable words include *very, great, a lot, plethora, dearth, obvious, it is clear, easy, wonderful, fantastic* etc.

Of course, it is not simply the communication that needs to be transformed into a scientific idiom. Language represents the thinking behind it. If a research student says "I was not able to disprove my hypothesis", this is not simply a matter of pointing out that the word "disprove" is incorrect. The correct terminology is "I was not able to reject my hypothesis". There is in all probability a much deeper problem in that the research student may believe that it is possible to prove a hypothesis. Careless expressions are used continuously in TV programmes about science. A recent broadcast contained statements like, "countless experiments show that..." and "this experiment settled once and for all....". Such statements are not acceptable in scientific circles. Continuous care is required in the choice of each word.

One of the ways of explaining just how important it is to take "scientific care" with the dissertation is emphasised by the fact the examiners will read the document and will question the appropriateness of every word used. Thus if a research student says "At the end of the first interview my data were not sufficiently clear to warrant conclusions to be drawn", the examiner could challenge this by saying "Is the word comprehensive not a better way of describing the data situation"? No other educational experience prepares the individual for the closeness with which the dissertation can be examined.

By the end of the doctoral process the research degree candidate should have been through a voyage of discovery and be, in a number of respects, a different person. The supervisor needs to make this clear at the start of the voyage and help him or her to acquire the new scientific mind set required.

1.3 The 1 plus 3 doctorate

It has been thought by some that the traditional doctorate leads to a situation where the new graduate is too specialised in his or her problem and its answer to the detriment having a more general understanding of academic research. For this reason universities are now paying much more attention to what is being called transferable skills. Transferable skills are the generic skills which are required for successful academic research at degree level as well as for conducting research which will be published in peer reviewed journals or research undertaken for commercial purposes. These skills involve problem definition, data identification and collection, both quantitative and qualitative data analysis and methods for the interpretation of the results. Another important aspect of transferable skills is the acquisition of writing skills which many doctoral students find problematic.

It has been suggested that these transferable skills should or even will extend beyond matters directly related to research. Some universities offer modules related to setting up a business in which issues such as raising funds, registering patents, recruiting staff etc. are addressed.

Some universities have formalised the delivery of these transferable skills by creating a masters degree in research referred to as an MRes. This degree is undertaken in the first year of registration and is immediately followed by the doctoral programme. As the doctoral degree is designed to take 3 years the combination of these two degrees is referred to as a 1 plus 3 approach to the doctorate.

1.4   The need for supervisors

One of the major impacts of these educational developments and trends has been the increase in requirements for supervisors and in some instances this has presented substantial problems for universities. It was traditionally thought that if an individual had a Masters or Doctoral degree then they were qualified to supervise the degree that they had completed. Increasingly this type of thinking has been changed as it is being realised that just having a degree does not necessarily qualify one to help someone else get such a degree. Having a doctoral degree alone is an inadequate qualification and is certainly not sufficient of an experience to supervise others[4]. This attitude of *get the degree today and su-*

---

[4] This question of qualifications to supervise others for Doctorates is a very thorny subject as it has also been common, and is still the practice today in some universities that certain academics, even those without Doctorates will supervise doctoral degree candidates. The rationale behind this is that a Doctorate is actually an apprenticeship in research and thus a well-established and competent researcher can help anyone obtain a Doctorate degree. There is no doubt some truth in this. Another side of this debate was recently revealed when at a board of examiners' meeting it was said that a full professor is entitled to perform any function the university requires him or her to do. Although it would be no less than silly to challenge the competence of certain well established fig-

pervise tomorrow has lead to there being some truly awful supervisors. In fact some of these so-called supervisors have actually been quite counter-productive to their student's prospects of obtaining their degree. Some institutions now insist that all novice supervisors attend a course in research supervision. Other institutions will not allow anyone to supervise until they have first worked as a 'second' supervisor alongside a more experienced person as the 'first' supervisor. Also the concept of having a supervisory panel or committee[5], of say 3 to 5 people, is beginning to take root. This can be very useful to doctoral candidates as it gives them more access to individuals who have an interest in their success.

The research element of the Masters degree is seen by a number of the stakeholders, including businesses, as increasingly important. Not long ago research was perceived as only being relevant if the graduate wanted to pursue an academic or university career. However today the research component is considered as important evidence of the graduate being able to work on his or her own and thus be an independent researcher. A well-researched and well-written dissertation will also be evidence of innovation and creativity and skill at writing complex text which is understandable by others. Such a dissertation suggests that the graduate has been able to create his or her own intellectual capital, which is a cornerstone of what we now call the knowledge society. It is actually the skills mastered during the research process that are seen as practical tools for effectiveness in the knowledge society of the 21st century.

1.5   Why supervise?

Some universities virtually insist that all qualified members of the academic staff supervise students. These institutions will have quotas such as: everyone needs to supervise ten Masters and four Doctoral candidates. But this is not always a clever way of allocating supervisors as some academics are not good at supervising or just don't want to do this

---

ures in the academic community who without their own PhD have, in some cases, supervised 20 or 50 or even more successful doctoral candidates to completion, this practice is actually highly questionable. If nothing else it begs the question as to why the individual did not get a Doctorate him or herself. Currently attitudes are changing and it is unlikely that anyone without a doctorate would be appointed as a supervisor today.

[5] This approach has been practiced in the USA with considerable success and it allows for a wider range of skills being available to the student.

type of work. Supervising requires a particular type of mentality and not everyone is equipped with the required level of patience and concern for students.

In reality there is always some choice with regards to how involved an academic wants to become in supervising research work. Some academics will see supervising research degrees as an important opportunity for developing their careers while others may find it to be nothing more than a nuisance and a distraction from their own work. On the other hand supervising can directly support an individual's own personal research work. Some academics have research topics of their own for which they may find it useful to have students help with practical research issues or even fieldwork. Masters students, especially those doing degrees such as MBAs or MComs often do not have a research topic they feel particularly strongly about and which they wish to explore and are thus amenable to accept a suggested topic from an established academic. In fact sometimes the student may more or less take on the role of a research assistant for the supervisor. This is of course a delicate matter and needs to be handled carefully to ensure that the student's time is not actually exploited. It would be considered unethical to take too much of a research student's time if the work he or she was doing did not directly support the student's own personal interests.

In general the main reason an academic needs to make supervision an important part of a career is that it is expected that academics should be prepared to help others achieve the scholarly level they themselves have obtained. This notion is seldom articulated in quite these words, but nonetheless it is a fundamental principle or mind-set of academe. The creation and the dissemination of knowledge is of core value for academics. Research supervision is an important way in which academics pass on their learning to others and thus contribute to the continuity of knowledge, skills and talent in the university and to the wider community. Supervising is critical to the concept of *paying-forward* rather than *paying-back.* After all it is the whole community through their taxes that fund the expensive institutions[6], which are our universities, and society expects academics to continue the tradition of not only teaching but also developing others through supervision activities.

---

[6] There are of course private universities in many parts of the world that would fall outside government funding. Nonetheless, one would still expect faculty in these institutions to be motivated to pass on their knowledge to a wide audience.

Being a good supervisor can substantially enhance an academic's reputation and make him or her sought after as a member of faculty. This of course leads to greater employment opportunities and choices.

FINALLY ANOTHER IMPORTANT REASON INCLUDES THE FACT THAT SUPERVISION OF RESEARCH MAY HELP DEVELOP A PUBLICATION RECORD...

Being a supervisor can play an important role in creating an intellectual network and also business and public sector contacts that are evidence of an international standing which is often required for promotion especially to a readership, a chair or a professorship[7]. There is also a financial dimension. As the ability to raise funds for research continues to grow in importance the business and public sector contacts made by an academic during research degree supervision has become increasingly advantageous.

Finally, supervision of research may help develop a publication record, which is increasingly required for promotion. It is usual for the supervisor and the student to jointly publish on the work arising out of the dissertation and this, of course, counts as a publication for both the student and the supervisor[8].

By the way most individuals find supervising 3 or 4 students at doctoral level and 8 or 10 at Masters level very demanding and care needs to be taken not to overdo the number of students accepted by any one supervisor[9]. Becoming too stretched by a large number of students inevitably leads to problems. In recognition of this some universities have rules about how many students a supervisor can take on at one time and enquiries should be made about these rules.

---

[7] Increasingly universities want to be satisfied that an individual is a recognised member of an intellectual community which has an international reach before he or she can be considered for a full professorship.

[8] New rules about co-authoring are restricting how multi-authored papers are reported and limiting the number of researchers who may make a claim to a particular paper.

[9] These numbers for research candidates per supervisor are by no means accepted by all academics. There are examples of individual supervisors having 15 or 20 or even 25 doctoral candidates to look after. Although this is not recommended, 10 or maybe 12 Research candidates are in fact sometimes just about manageable by one supervisor. Another consideration is the maturity of the doctoral candidates. Working with 35 or 40 year old DBAs is an entirely different matter to looking after twenty something year olds, rather less mature and possibly less committed, PhD candidates.

1.6 Useful books and/or websites

University of Sheffield Post Graduate Degrees, Available:
  http://www.sheffield.ac.uk/postgraduate [09 Aug 2011].
Open University Business School, Available: http://www8.open.ac.uk/business-
    school/research/degrees. [09 Aug 2011].
Manchester Business School Research, Available:
    http://www.mbs.ac.uk/research [09 Aug 2011].
University of Bolton, Available
    http://www.bolton.ac.uk/AME/PostGradProvision.aspx
10 [October 2011]
Oxford Said Business School, Available:
    http://www.sbs.ox.ac.uk/degrees/dphil/Pages/default.aspx [09 Aug 2011].
Henley Business School DBA, Available:
    http://www.henley.reading.ac.uk/management/pg-research/mgmt-doctor-
    of-business-administration-dba.aspx [09 Aug 2011]
Harvard Business School Doctoral Programs, Available:
    http://www.hbs.edu/doctoral/ [09 Aug 2011].

Appendix 1 contains a number of other useful websites.

Chapter 2

Getting ready to supervise

The conscious world of a living individual is a cocooned and private thing. Each of us lives in his or her own cocoon and we have to imagine what it might be like to be someone else. The fact that another is conscious in the same way as I am, is an act of belief – one that philosophers have been known to care about.
Aleksander, I. (1997), *Impossible Minds – My Neurons My Consciousness***, London: Imperial College Press.**

2.1 University education

Degrees have been awarded in Europe since the 12th century. Tradition has it that the first university was established in Bolonga in Italy in 1088 and that this created an impetus which spread in a few hundred years all over Europe and then to much of the remainder of the world. Universities are sometimes said to be Europe's most successful export. Of course this is a highly Eurocentric view and other cultures would claim that there were early universities in many other places around the world which had no contact or association with Europe[10]. It is also sometimes claimed that the schools set up by Plato and Aristotle should be considered universities but this view is not well supported. One of the defining characteristics of a university is that there are well defined degree programmes leading to a recognised award. Neither Plato's Academy nor Aristotle's Lyceum would comply with this.

The early universities were created to satisfy the demand generated by the Renaissance for more priests, lawyers and doctors. Education at that time was dominated by the Roman Catholic Church. However in the following centuries education became more secular and with the advent of the Reformation the influence of the Roman Catholic Church declined. Scholars like Galileo found themselves in contention with Rome and of course, in those countries where there had been a change of religion such as England, men like Newton had little or no concern for the opinions of Rome.

The scope of university degrees spread into non-professional subjects and leading scholars in the university system became associated with research. Universities spread both in terms of their number and the number of students and faculty, but the university remained the domain for the gentleman scholar and scientist. University education was strictly a matter for the elite until well into the 20th century. It was only in the last quarter of the 20th century that the notion of mass education raised its head.

---

[10] It is claimed that there were university like institutions in both China and India in earlier times. A great university-like institution is said to have existed in Timbuktu in the 12[th]century, which is today in Mali, on the edge of the Sahara. http://www.youtube.com/watch?v=_4pJTaiev8k Hundreds of thousands of scrolls have been found in Timbuktu which are now in the process of being preserved. Thus Timbuktu was a great centre of learning in its day.

At about this time educators began to believe that teaching in the form of "talk and chalk" was not especially effective and that having students "finding out for themselves" was a much more satisfactory way of learning. The term "finding out for themselves" is a euphemism for research and as a result research has become a corner stone of education not only at university level but also in many schools.

2.2 The growth of supervision

Not long ago[11] it was possible for an academic to take a minimalist approach to research and to supervision. However in the past decade universities and business schools have become increasingly more serious about the importance of research and the needs for faculty to be research active and also to play a significant role as a supervisor. Of course the amount of research output varies substantially as does the number of research degree candidates a supervisor may be asked to supervise. It was once thought that a relatively small number of research degree candidates was adequate but today academics are being asked to undertake more and more supervision. Recently we have encountered academics to whom more than a dozen research degree candidates have been allocated[12]. At the same time we were informed by an academic acquaintance that he had 47 MBA research dissertations to supervise. This number is exceptional and we hasten to confirm that this situation is untenable. But it is indicative of the pressure which the trend of demanding more work from faculty members creates.

Under these circumstances it is important that supervisors have a clear picture of what to expect when supervising and it is equally necessary for research degree candidates to have the same.

2.3 Code of practice

The first step on the road to successful supervision is to establish if your Department or Faculty has a Code of Practice for Supervisors. Most Departments and Faculty now have such a document. The Code of Practice

---

[11] This is deliberately vague as a few academics are still taking a minimalist approach to research but fewer and fewer are getting away with it.

[12] It was once thought that one person could not be expected to supervise more than 6 doctoral degree candidates. Some business schools believe that somewhere about 7 or 8 full-time supervisions is equivalent to a full workload. But others claimed that a faculty member could look after considerably more.

will address many issues including how a new supervisor can get started. Frequently a new supervisor has to be part of a supervising team or attend a training course[13] before he or she will be permitted to supervise on his or her own. There are increasingly fewer universities that provide for only one supervisor per student. Two supervisors is seen as a much more satisfactory approach from both the student's and the supervisor's perspective.

Supervision does not necessarily come naturally to all academics. The work involved does not suit everyone. Supervisors need to be flexible and agile. Some students are not as easy to supervise as others. In fact sometimes research students are just plain difficult. They can be slow to learn and may not take the advice offered. It may require intensive contact with the student during which the advice is repeated again and again. Supervision can lead to confrontational situations and even sometimes to arguments. Where there are two or more supervisors involved the conflicts or disagreements may not only be between supervisor and student but also between the supervisors themselves. Thus supervision is not always a positive experience and academics that are not suited to it should avoid getting involved.

2.4   Are you likely to make a good supervisor?

There is little point in supervising a student unless the faculty member has a commitment to life-long learning for him or herself and is to some extent research active. A supervisor really needs to be a good listener, be able to generate and share new ideas, and to be constructively critical. These issues and some others are incorporated in the short light-hearted self test shown in Table 1 for the reader to assess if he or she is likely to be a suitable supervisor.

Referring to Table 2.1, rate yourself on a scale of 1 to 5 on the following personal characteristics[14], where 1 is low or poor and 5 is high or strong:

Table 2.1: The research supervision aptitude self-test

---

[13] Becoming a good supervisor is more like learning a craft than acquiring academic skills and thus a training course would only make a small contribution to a supervisor's development. The real learning in this arena will always be through the normally painful route of experience.

[14] The 10 characteristics described here are not intended to be exhaustive and this questionnaire may be extended to address several other skills if desired. But short questionnaires are often superior to long ones!

		Low				High
		1	2	3	4	5
1	Rate your ability to generate and share new ideas					
2	Rate your understanding of the main methodological options					
3	Rate your ability to help others find solutions to their problems					
4	Rate your commitment to life-long learning					
5	Rate yourself as a good listener					
6	Rate your ability to be constructively critical					
7	Rate your ability to keep confidences					
8	Rate your ability to read academic scripts					
9	Rate your ability to respond to students requests					
10	Rate yourself as an active researcher					
	Total score					

From this self-test it is possible to make a general assessment of how suited to the work of supervision an individual might be. It is by no means suggested that this is in any way a definitive test. It is actually as much for fun than anything else, but it should set you thinking as well.

2.4.1 Self-test scores and their implications

50   You appear to have all the characteristics you need to make a success of research supervision. Make sure that you have been really honest with yourself.

40 to 49   Being a research supervisor should be well within your reach.

30 to 39   You have quite a reasonable amount of potential for a research supervisor, but you will need to hone-up some of your personal characteristics.

29 or less   Think very hard before you embark on research supervision as you might just find the going tough.

15

In general any of the issues in the research supervision aptitude self-test for which you have scored less than 4 you may well need to improve. If you are going to make it as a successful research supervisor, and if you are going to have fun doing so, you need to be strong in pretty well all of these areas

Supervision is often a relatively long-term commitment ranging from one year[15] to three or four or even five years. Some supervision situations can extend even longer, although 10, 12 or 14-year degrees are largely a thing of the past[16]. Over a long period a supervisor and student can become *fed-up* or bored with each other. There is a potential for a variety of things to go wrong and the relationship can become confrontational. In fact the supervision experience can be really quite stressful. The consequences of failure can be unpleasant for both the student and the supervisor. It is hard for the student to be reaccepted at another institution for a research degree if a student 'fails' or just abandons his or her work. Having unsuccessful research students is not a good recommendation for an academic. So it is important for the novice supervisor to know what exactly is entailed in the supervision process.

There is always a unique relationship between the supervisor and the student in the sense that no two relationships will ever be exactly the same. It is not necessary that the student and the supervisor like each other, but it is important that there is a degree of mutual respect. At some stage during the course of the degree the researcher may well feel that he or she has not chosen well with regards to their particular supervisor. As learning the skills of a researcher is difficult[17] a number of prob-

---

[15] One year would be a fast track full-time Masters degree.

[16] Three to four years is currently the recommended duration of a Doctorate in most subjects. However this situation is relatively new. Previously Doctorates were allowed to take much longer periods of time. Most supervisors or examiners have encountered six or eight or ten year Doctorates. However there have even been examples of Doctorates taking nearly 20 years to complete. It has been said that this long period was due to the doctoral candidate wanting to do his or her best ever piece of work. In fact this is largely an excuse for individuals just not getting on with the research work due to their being distracted with teaching and other responsibilities in the department at the university. The notion of the Doctorate being the lifetime best piece of work was seldom, if ever a reality.

[17] In the same way that it is difficult to 'teach' anyone the skills of supervising, as this needs to be learned by working alongside an accomplished practitioner, it is equally problematical to 'tell' anyone what to do to get their doctorate. The doctorate is an intellectual apprenticeship whereby appropriate understanding and skills are acquired by

lems can arise such as the supervisor not being responsive enough or the supervisor being too directive. If the relationship breaks down then it is probably better that the student changes supervisor. However, this should never be done lightly as a new supervisor may be difficult to find and it may transpire that the same problems arise with the new person. The aphorism *the devil you know is better than the devil you don't know* applies here. From the supervisor's point of view it is just not worthwhile trying to hang on to a student who is unhappy. It is one of the functions of the Dean of Research to attempt to rectify these types of situation.

If it is the supervisor who is unhappy with the student then it is clearly his or her responsibility to make this known to the student. This is a fundamental aspect of the supervisor's duty of care. The exact nature of the unhappiness should be spelt out, preferably in writing. If the student cannot or will not rectify the situation then the supervisor needs to pass this matter on to the Dean or Director of Research.

But it is also important to note that the supervisor-student relationship will change throughout the duration of the research with the supervisor leading the relationship in the early months but with the student growing in confidence and competence until he or she leads the relationship in the later part of the degree.

The supervisor's role is complex. It is at least simultaneously an advisor, a mentor, a teacher, a confidant, a senior research colleague, a handholder, an assessor and an examiner (Mauch and Birch 1983). Actually the word supervisor does not describe well the relationship between the supervisor and student as this word implies a sort of authority which does not exist. The supervisor has virtually no authority as he or she can only advise the student. In continental Europe the word used to describe this relationship is sometimes promoter and this is in some ways better than supervisor.

The relationship between the supervisor and the research degree candidate evolves over time. This is shown in Figure 2.1.

---

the student or learner over a period of time through discourse and observation as well as by trial and error.

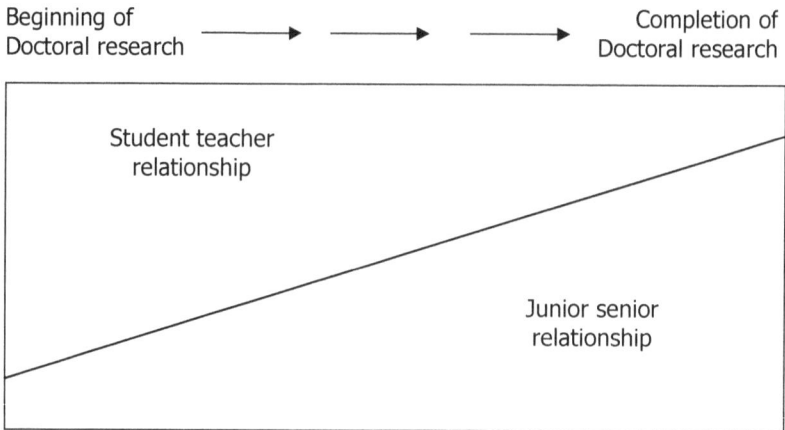

Figure 2.1: The evolution of the supervisor/student relationship

Figure 2.1 clearly points out that at the outset the supervisor is primarily a teacher but by the end of the doctoral degree process this has changed and the supervisor and the student are colleagues.

2.5　Key issues for good supervision

Before anyone should think of becoming a supervisor he or she needs to be familiar with a number of key issues including: -

- The standard required for the degree in question;
- The house rules of the institution and how they are implemented;
- The requirements of the ethics committee;
- How to access resources.

2.5.1　The standards required by the institution

Any individual who takes on supervision should have clearly in their mind the standard required for the degree concerned. If there is any doubt in his or her mind advice should be sought. Sometimes supervisors, especially those who do not have much experience, demand too high a standard of their students[18,19]. This can delay the submission of

---

[18] Many universities have dealt with the issue of inexperienced supervisors by having two. The lead supervisor will often be required to have been a second supervisor at least on one occasion before being appointed a lead supervisor.

[19] The point of inexperience also raises its head with respect to examiners. In a recent incident a very ugly situation arose when a young doctoral graduate was appointed as an

the final work or even cause unpleasant arguments. There is another important dimension to do with knowing the standards and the general requirements for the degrees being supervised which relates to gossip or even myths which develop in academic departments. An interesting example of this is the story often found in university departments in one form or another. The story has various forms, but it essentially states that *Jane Bloggins got her Doctorate a few years ago and she only did 10 interviews*. The other common variant of the story is that *Jane Bloggins finished the work on her Masters in two months, or maybe it is her Doctorate in seven months*. Of course, many of such stories are just distortions of what actually happened.

2.5.2   *The house rules and how they are implemented*

Every institution has its own rules for a research degree. These rules are often complex and interpreted quite idiosyncratically depending on precedent. It is useful if supervisors know something of these house rules and are aware of who in the organisation really understands them and knows how they will be interpreted.

Before agreeing to supervise a research student it is important for the supervisor to establish that he or she has the time to make this level of commitment. Having a full teaching load and then taking on supervisory work sometimes turns out to be just too much and this leads to problems for both the supervisor and the research student.

As mentioned above it is often assumed that just because someone has the degree they are qualified to supervise someone else. This is not always true; in fact, it is probably seldom true. Besides an understanding of the research supervision process, which may be learnt from others or from reading a book such as this one, a key qualification for supervision is a high degree of patience, an ability to listen and being prepared to respond in a timely way to the needs of the student. In addition it is essential that the supervisor keep up with the tools and techniques of current academic research. For example, today a thorough knowledge of the use of the Web as a research tool is clearly essential.

---

internal examiner and she refused to accept the dissertation despite the fact that the external examiner was satisfied with the work. This dispute dragged out to a quite unsatisfactory conclusion. It is important to be careful when using inexperienced supervisors and examiners.

Because of the rate of change of the many issues concerning supervision, it is important that all supervisors develop their own professional networks, which they can do relatively easily through attending conferences and by publishing collaboratively.

In preparing yourself to supervise do bear in mind that a certain number of masters and doctoral research projects are bound to fail. They will fail because of the student's health, because of the student's financial problems, because students will be made compelling job offers, to mention only three reasons. It is not pleasant for the supervisor when the student terminates but if the supervisor has supported the student well he or she can at least feel that the non-completion was not caused by him or her or was not directly his or her responsibility.

...TO KNOW HOW THE RESEARCH CANDIDATE CAN ACCESS FUNDS...

2.5.3   The requirements of the Ethics Committee

Universities have a specific research Ethics Committee and a number of Ethics Sub-committees and it is important to know what issues this committee considers important. It is necessary to consult the Ethics Committee in advance of commencing the research. It may also be necessary to obtain direction from the ethics committee concerning the type of measuring instrument used or how the findings will be published. Chapter 11 and chapter 20 address these issues in detail.

2.5.4   How to access resources

Resources are required to conduct good research. On a basic level the student will need a desk, a computer, a telephone, a library and photocopying facilities. Many students will have to travel to collect empirical evidence. To establish their own academic network they will have to attend seminars and conferences. All this requires resources and it is important for the supervisor to know how the student can access funds for these purposes.

2.6   Training for the supervisor

Whereas in the past it was assumed that supervision *came naturally* there are now many courses to help new supervisors get started. Some of these are delivered in-house while others are held on a public basis.

There are now training courses available for supervisors both on the process of supervision and the final product (i.e. the dissertation) with an emphasis on delivering high quality education. Video and audiotapes are also available to assist with the supervisor's training. It is the supervisor's responsibility to be aware of what he or she requires and what is available. It is the faculty's or perhaps the university's responsibility to ensure there are adequate funds available to pay for this training either in-house or by sending individuals on publicly available courses.

2.7   The principal or main supervisor

Increasingly more than one supervisor is now being appointed. Where this happens there is usually a requirement that the principal or main supervisor will have worked as a second supervisor at least once before. This is a useful way of having the supervisor introduced to the work involved.

Some universities have decided to use a group of supervisors or a supervisory committee. This is similar to the manner in which supervision works in the USA and it is possible the UK's approach will evolve to this type of group supervision.

2.8   Political issues (politics with a small "p")

Doctoral and masters research is often immersed in Departmental or Faculty political issues. It is sometimes seen as a matter of prestige as to how many and which particular students an academic is responsible for.

In some universities there is open rivalry for doctoral students. This can be highly visible in some institutions. Although it is not really appropriate, senior academics have been known to compete for the better students. New supervisors can find themselves only offered relatively weak students. Research students with highly influential supervisors will have more access to funds than students with less influential supervisors.

There will be topics that are favoured by the institution, and there will be topics that are of little interest. Students need to avoid the less popular topics if they want the full attention of their supervisor or supervisors.

There are also political issues related to the appointment of examiners. A suitable examiner might not be acceptable to the institution or a poor choice of examiner might be made to examine when he or she should not. Care must be taken to ensure that a really suitable examiner is appointed.

A student supervised by an influential member of the faculty may sometimes find that they are provided with a more sympathetic examiner than others.

2.9   The supervisors' first and second dilemmas

There is an inevitable dilemma which many if not most supervisors have to face and that relates to the extent to which they will undertake supervision on a topic which is not directly in their field of expertise. Research topics and research questions do not always arrive neatly delimited within the direct field of expertise of a supervisor. Supervisors may have to stretch their area of interest.

Some universities recognise the problems which this can produce and this is one of the reasons why multiple supervisors are appointed. In some cases one supervisor will be regarded as a subject expert while another will be tasked with ensuring that the methodology pursued is sound.

The supervisors' dilemma refers to how far from his or her specific subject knowledge a supervisor strays. As a supervisor moves away from his or her subject knowledge the less effective the supervisor is likely to be. Also once the supervisor strays away from his or her core competencies there is a tendency for this behaviour to creep in scope[20] and some supervisors take on topics and research questions about which he or she may have little real expertise.

A second dilemma is the extent to which the supervisor should influence the topic the research student undertakes. Inevitably the supervisor will have a considerable amount of influence but this should be used with caution. The difference between influencing and controlling can be on a fine line but the supervisor should ensure that the student chooses a topic which will be of both interest and benefit to him or herself. Supervisors who exert too much influence on a research student are acting

---

[20] The term scope creep is frequently used in project management to denote the situation where a project's requirements increase during the execution of the work. Of course this happens with doctoral dissertations and sometimes a supervisor finds himself or herself taking on something which isn't a perfect match to their competences and during the project the student moves further and further away from their competencies.

unethically. A recent example of this is where the supervisor insisted that the student incorporate issues in the research which were of no interest to the student, but would enhance the research currently being pursued by the supervisor.

2.10 Useful books and/or websites

Dick, B. (1997) *Rigour and relevance in action research*, Available: http://www.scu.edu.au/schools/gcm/ar/arp/rigour.html [09 Aug 2011].

Grover, V. (2001) '10 Mistakes doctoral students make in managing their program', *Decision Line*, May, pp. 11–13.

Jardins, D. M. (1994) *How to be a good graduate student*, Available: http://www.cs.indiana.edu/HTMLit/how.2b/how.2b.html   [09 Aug 2011].

Robey, D. (2001) 'Answers to doctoral students' frequently asked questions (FAQs)', *Decision Line*, March, pp. 10–12.

http://www.timbuktufoundation.org/university.html

Chapter 3

The supervisor and the Dean of Research

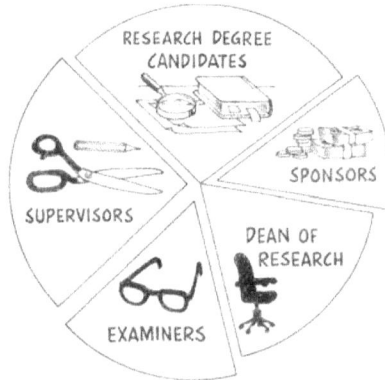

Unlike religion, science did not seek its deepest insights in a kind of transcendental rapture, but like religion it insisted on a kind of monastic purity and discipline as it carries out its researches. Not least, just as religion built its moral strength on the overlapping and consistent testimony of its great figures, so science, too, gained its stature from an immense interconnected testimony that gradually endowed its collective understanding with something of a Church-like infallibility – not in any individual instance, but as a mode of inquiry, a source of understanding.
Heilbroner, R. (1995) *Visions of the Future*, New York: Oxford University Press, p49.

3.1 The stakeholders

There are always multiple stakeholders in every research degree. Besides the student and the supervisor there will be the Director or Dean of Research, the Head of Department, perhaps a sponsor and of course, the examiners. Both the student and the supervisor should keep the Director or Dean of Research, the Head of Department and the sponsors, if any, informed of the progress of the research.

3.2 The role of the Dean of Research

It is especially important for every supervisor to understand the role of the Director or Dean of Research. Director of Studies is the title sometimes given to the university official who is responsible for all research degrees in the institution. The work undertaken by the Director of Studies (Dean of Research) differs from one university to another, but virtually all universities have this officer as a senior member of staff. Sometimes some of the powers and duties of the Director of Studies are delegated to a committee or to the head of each department but even when this happens there will usually still be an individual with this title.

This individual will usually head up a team that will be involved with the admission of the research student, the formal acceptance of the research proposal and in the matching of the research student with a supervisor as well as with the on-going progress of the work. Increasingly, on-going progress reports are required – sometimes every six months. These progress reports are often two-way affairs with the supervisor commenting on the student and the research candidate reporting on the service he or she has received from the supervisor or supervisors. These reports are essential to the proper management of the research degree process. If disputes arise these reports will be the important evidence. It is most important that all the parties concerned are entirely frank and honest in completing these reports. This of course, can be difficult but if issues are fudged, they can come back to haunt the supervisor at a later date.

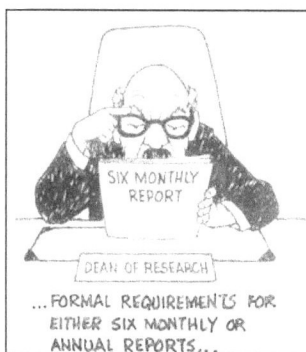

SIX MONTHLY REPORT

DEAN OF RESEARCH

...FORMAL REQUIREMENTS FOR EITHER SIX MONTHLY OR ANNUAL REPORTS...

The Director of Studies will also play a role in the selection of the examiners as well as interpreting the results of the examiners' reports. On the question of examiners, which is addressed more fully later, it is worth noting that the Director of Studies may have specific policies concerning the number of examiners nominated and appointed. For example some universities will require the supervisor to nominate three examiners but will only appoint two, the third potential examiner being kept in reserve in case there is a difference of opinion between the first two.

The Director of Studies will normally be available to discuss with either the supervisor or indeed the student any problems that arise and be prepared to help find solutions. The Director of Studies or Dean of Research will be a first arbitrator if any dispute or disagreement occurs between the supervisor and the student. This individual is an important resource and facilitator in the research degree process.

3.2.1   Responsibilities of the Dean's Office

In the office of the Director of Studies or Dean of Research there is likely to be an individual who knows and understands in detail the university's regulations concerning the awarding of research degrees and it is important for a new supervisor to elicit the help of such a person. These regulations can be complex and it is important that expert help is acquired to help understand them correctly.

The office of the Director of Studies is the focal point for information for students. Details concerning research awards, bursaries and scholarships will be available through this office. The staff should also be well informed about courses available to supervisors (as well as students for specialty subjects and skills) to help hone his or her supervisory skills.

WHEN A SUPERVISOR MOVES TO ANOTHER UNIVERSITY OR BUSINESS SCHOOL...

It is always worthwhile for a new supervisor to get to know the people in the office of the Director of Studies, as there will be many occasions when their advice will be required.

3.3 When there is a need to change supervisor

When a supervisor moves to another university, if the supervisor withdraws, or if the student requests a change of supervisor, the Director of Studies will have to manage this situation. Where the supervisor moves it is usual for the Director of Studies to attempt to find a new supervisor from within the institution. Failing this the Director of Studies can attempt to arrange for the student to be transferred to another institution, and be given full credit for his or her work so far. Where a supervisor withdraws there should be a formal hearing to establish the reason. Supervisors should not be allowed to withdraw frivolously.

Where the relationship between the student and the supervisor has deteriorated, the student may be allowed to change supervisors if an appropriate person can be found. This can be a sensitive matter and needs to be dealt with by the Director of Studies. The more informal and low key this can be, the better it is for all concerned.

There are a number of different ways in which there can be difficulties between the supervisor and the student but from a student's point of view if he or she falls out with the supervisor this can only create problems. Without the full support of the supervisor the examination and the process of having changes submitted and approved can be difficult.

3.4 The awarding of the degrees

It is sometimes the Dean of Research or Director of Studies who finally signs off the authorisation for the award of the degree. If for any reason the student does not agree with the results of the examination then it is to this office that any appeal would effectively be made.

3.5 Graduation

The Dean of Research will also often play a role in the graduation ceremony and whatever other functions are associated with graduation. It is important that the university and its office bearers be seen to be celebrating the success of its research students. It is a considerable achievement to be awarded a research degree and universities and business schools are not always good at making sure this is appreciated.

3.6   Useful books and/or websites

http://www.stir.ac.uk/about/senior-officers-of-the-university/director-of-research-and-enterprise [accessed 10 October 2011]

Chapter 4

Accepting a student

It is an extraordinary era in which we live. It is altogether new. The world has seen nothing like it before. I will not pretend, nobody can pretend, to discern the end. But everyone knows that the age is remarkable for scientific research ... The ancients saw nothing like it. The moderns have seen nothing like it till the present generation.
Daniel Webster, (1847) cited in Davidson, J. and Rees-Mogg, W. (1993) *The Great Reckoning*, London: Sidgwick and Jackson.

The things one feels absolutely certain about are never true.
Wilde O, *The Picture of Dorian Gray*, London: Random House, first published in London 1884

4.1 Selecting research students

There are numerous prospective students interested in undertaking re-search projects, but not all of them are likely to be successful. It is im-portant for the prospective supervisor to be able to make an assessment of a student's potential to successfully undertake the project.

In the first instance it is important that the prospective research degree candidate has the appropriate educational background. A bachelors and a masters degree (for those wanting to undertake doctoral work) in the field of study is a great advantage[21]. However universities will today ad-mit individuals with lesser qualifications provided they believe that the prospective student is capable of achieving the required standard for the research degree.

4.2 Getting to know the prospective student

Before formally agreeing to supervise a prospective student the supervi-sor needs to get to know the individual. It is necessary to establish that the prospective student is properly motivated[22]. For example, they need to know the applicant's strengths and weaknesses; what they have read in their field of study; whether the potential student knows the appro-priate sources of literature; who the main authors in the chosen field are who have influenced their thinking; whether the applicant has the po-tential to work independently; the ability of the applicant to write a pre-

---

[21] It is not uncommon for individuals to wish to undertake research in a field of study quite different to their original studies. For years it has been the practice for engineers wanting to move to a management job to register for MBAs. However even for research degrees subject areas can be switched. For example, individuals with computer science bachelors and Masters degrees sometimes register for information systems manage-ment degrees. Individuals who do this, of course, have a lot of background to catch up on, as they need to know their new field of study and especially their topic area as well as someone who has studied and researched the field before.

[22] Assessing a prospective research degree candidate's motivation is actually quite diffi-cult. As a minimum the would-be supervisor needs to satisfy him or herself that the pro-spective candidate sees the research degree as something of considerable importance. It needs to be clear that there is a real stream of benefits, even if they are intangible benefits such as academic status or general prestige from obtaining the research degree. Of course the problem with motivation is that even when this is initially strong it can decline and one of the tasks of the supervisor is to help the research degree candidate keep their motivation going.

liminary research proposal and whether there is a need for any supplementary courses such as effective writing or statistical interpretation.

An important issue is whether the research question is directly in the field of competence of the supervisor and whether the supervisor is enthusiastic about the topic area. Sometimes this may not be the case and the supervisor needs to be careful not to accept a student whose research interest is too far from his or her own. This is particularly the case when a novice supervisor is involved. An experienced supervisor will be able to accept a broader field of topics and will also be better able to understand where his or her limits are. The supervisor's enthusiasm for the subject area is important as a stimulus to the student and if there is little or no interest or enthusiasm for the topic the prospective supervisor should decline to supervise.

4.3   Accepting only students who can succeed

Having the prospective student make a presentation to the faculty is a useful way for the supervisor getting to know the capabilities of the student. Another way is to have the student critique a piece of work and communicate the assessment in both verbal and written form. If the prospective student performs well at both of these events then there is a good chance that he or she will be able to handle a research degree. Only such students should be accepted on research degree programmes.

4.4   Weak students can be difficult

It is important to note that once a student has been accepted for a research degree it can be really quite difficult or at least unpleasant to insist he or she withdraws. It is therefore essential not to accept anyone too readily until it is clear that they are really motivated and that they have the skill and ability to complete the degree. It is considered a breach of ethical behaviour if the university accepts individuals who are too weak to be able to obtain the degree. Of course a problem arises when a potential student is borderline and he or she might be able to cope. If such an individual is accepted then extra attention should be given to help that person achieve the desired level of competence.

Where a student is not coping the trouble and the effort required to force a de-registration can be enormous. It is always better to try to have the student withdraw themselves from the university rather than to have to force a de-registration. It is worthwhile to ask a prospective student for academic references and where possible to speak to the referees personally.

4.5   The question of chemistry

It is useful if the research degree candidate and the supervisor(s) actually like each other. If there is good chemistry between these individuals then it will make the work easier and more enjoyable. However it is not essential and many research degrees have been obtained even when the student and the supervisor(s) did not like each other much at all.

4.6   Problems between supervisor and student

If problems do arise between students and their supervisor(s) it is important to advise the Dean of Research. These are often relatively simple misunderstandings and can be quickly sorted out. As mentioned before, although it is possible to switch, this should only be done as a last resort. Students should be reminded that *the devil they know might well be better than the devil they don't know!*[23]

4.7   The pastoral/counselling role

Where younger students are involved the supervisor may find him or herself taking on a pastoral and/or counselling role. What this amounts to is that the supervisor makes time to help the student with personal problems that may arise. Of course supervisors are unlikely to be professional counsellors and where substantial problems occur it is essential for them to advise the student to seek assistance from the university services. Older

... MAKE TIME TO HELP THE RESEARCH DEGREE CANDIDATE WITH ANY PERSONAL PROBLEMS...

and more mature students will probably need less help in this respect.

---

[23] At some stage during the course of a research degree, the student is likely to become frustrated with some aspect of the work and this may lead to a feeling that if he or she changes their supervisor the frustrations will go away. This is unlikely to be the case and it is normally better to directly face the matters that are causing the frustration.

4.8   Written language

Universities are becoming increasingly international and there are people from all over the world undertaking advanced studies. One issue experienced supervisors always mention as being a substantial difficulty is when they are asked to supervise students who are not fully competent in English. Even when working with individuals who are fluent in spoken English there can be problems with written English. Writing in a second language, especially at the level required for a research degree, can be challenging. Text written by such students can be unclear to the point of being ambiguous. It is important that the supervisor does not become bogged down as a copy-editor. Some universities specifically prohibit supervisors from editing their students writing[24]. Students whose language is not adequate should themselves arrange for copy-editing. Of course this needs to be done with considerable care as in correcting poor English the original meaning of the text can be changed or even lost. There should not be any suggestion that the copy-editor has changed or influenced the content of the work.

4.9   Student funding

In deciding whether or not to accept a student a supervisor needs to be aware of the type of funding the student is receiving. Funding is sometimes pinned to certain amounts of work or to specific deliverables and this needs to be planned into the work schedule. Also when the research is funded there may be specific consequences of non-completion and the supervisor should know these. The supervisor needs to know that if the student does not complete there may be suggestions of mismanagement of the work on the part of the supervisor. Should there be any doubt in the supervisor's mind that the relationship will not work, he or she should decline to supervise.

Further, continuity of supervision is important, and the supervisor should not undertake to supervise an individual when there is a possibility that he or she will not be with the institution for much longer. Thus academics that are in discussion with other institutions about a new job should not be accepting new students. When the supervisor leaves it is

---

[24] Where this happens it is an attempt by the university executive to direct the research process at a micro-management level which probably is not possible. It is also possibly ethically questionable.

important that he or she makes arrangements for the continuity of the supervision. Universities are usually quite amenable to accepting transfer of registration and recognising the work already done at other institutions.

4.10 Self test for the would be research student

Some of the issues to consider when deciding if a student is suitable are included in the following short test.

Establish for yourself how the prospective student fares on each of these 10 issues. Use Table 4.1 to rate your prospective student on a scale of 1 to 5 on the following personal characteristics, where 1 is low or poor and 5 is high or strong:

Table 4.1: The prospective researcher aptitude self-test

		Low				High
		1	2	3	4	5
1	How much does he/she enjoy reading?					
2	How much does he/she like writing?					
3	Is he/she really a good listener?					
4	How committed is he/she to life long learning?					
5	Does he/she have any research skills?					
6	Is he/she able to be constructively critical of their own work as well as that of others?					
7	How good is his/her verbal communication?					
8	Does he/she have enough money to complete the studies?					
9	How motivated is he/she?					
10	Does he/she have the ability to learn quickly?					
	Total score					

The following is one way of interpreting the results of the above test.

50   This prospective student should be a great catch but make sure that you have been really correct in your answers.

40 to 49   Being a good research student should be well within his or her reach.

30 to 39   The prospective student looks quite reasonable, but he or she will need to 'hone up' some personal characteristics.

29 or less   Think very hard before accepting this person as a research student. You might as his or her supervisor just find the going too tough.

4.11 Summary

Really good students are a great pleasure to work with and it is worth the supervisor's while to take time and to be selective about whom he or she accepts. Remember that taking on weak students will double or triple your work in seeing that person through to his or her degree. On the other hand there is potentially even more satisfaction if a supervisor sees a student through who was not all that strong.

A THOROUGH KNOWLEDGE OF THE USE OF THE WEB AS A RESEARCH TOOL IS CLEARLY ESSENTIAL.

Once a student has been accepted the Department should inform him or her and the formal research work can begin. It should be made clear what resources are to be made available. These may include office space, personal computer, use of the telephone, secretarial support, stationery and postage, conference fees and travel money, printing of business cards, library privileges, and the possibility of tutoring and lecturing for money.

The amount of support varies substantially from institution to institution. What is available should be stated up front.

4.12 Useful books and/or websites

http://www.postgraduatestudentships.co.uk/?gclid=CMPwyYLzxKoCFQc KfAod4QJp7Q [Accessed 10 August 2011]

http://www.ukpass.ac.uk/ [Accessed 10 August 2011]

Part Two
Getting Started with the Research

Chapter 5

The research degree process

I never said a word against eminent men of science. What I complain about is a vague popular philosophy which supposes itself to be scientific when it is really nothing but a sort of new religion and an unquestionably nasty one. When people talked about the fall of man they know they were talking about a mystery, a thing they didn't understand. Now that they talk about the survival of the fittest they think they do understand it, whereas they have not merely no notion, they have an elaborate false notion of what the words mean. The Darwinian movement has made no difference to mankind, except that, instead of talking un-philosophically about philosophy, they now talk unscientifically about science.

Chesterton G.K. (1995) *The Club of Queer Trades*, (first published in 1905), Ware: Wordsworth Classics.

5.1   The research degree process

Research degree processes do vary from university to university and from department to department, but there are definite similarities among them. This section will describe as generically as possible the steps involved in completing a research degree. It is important however to bear in mind that this process is invariably reiterative with a number of steps frequently having to be repeated as the research student's horizons and knowledge of research are broadened.

5.2   Find a suitable university

The first task of a would-be research degree candidate is to find a suitable university. There are a number of criteria that can be used to help make this decision. Most frequently this decision is made on the grounds of availability, cost of fees[25], and closeness to where the applicant lives or works. Language can also be an issue to think about as a number of European Continental universities are accepting students who wish to research and write their dissertation in English.

Of course, the reputation of the university is also important. Sometimes the choice is influenced by the fact that the applicant has a friend or colleague or family member who has already studied at an institution and has recommended it. Some of the famous universities, especially in the USA, can be very expensive and then funding becomes a critical factor in the choice of university.

5.3   Getting on-board

Having identified where to study the applicant needs to apply and be accepted. Sometimes this can be a mere formality, but again it can be a major exercise. Assuming that the applicant has suitable previous degrees and experience he or she will still need to be interviewed by the university and convince them that he or she will be an asset to their research programme. This is a formality that usually involves the applicant completing some forms and being interviewed by the Dean of Research. On other occasions it might be necessary for the applicant to be interviewed by a number of different academics and administrators and also present a seminar to the Department in which he or she wants to re-

---

[25] The differential in fees for EU students researching in the UK can be dramatic ranging from £1,000 to £10,000 or more. Non-EU students pay even more.

search. In addition to this, some universities require a Graduate Management Admission Test (GMAT)[26] to be undertaken and they will use the results of this test as one of the factors to determine whom they accept onto their research programme. There are other tests such the Test of English as a Foreign Language (TOEFL[27]), which is a language proficiency test as well as the Test of Spoken English (TSE), which may be required by some universities.

5.4   Finding out where things are

Once the university has accepted the applicant he or she will be allocated either a mentor or a supervisor or perhaps a provisional supervisor. Whatever this person is called someone will normally be appointed to help the applicant find his or her way into the systems in the institution. This will include finding out where the students work, what computing facilities they have, where the library is located as well as where the canteens are. There is always quite a lot of routine information that any newcomer to the institution needs to know.

5.5   Starting the search for a research question

... MAKE TIME TO HELP THE RESEARCH DEGREE CANDIDATE WITH ANY PERSONAL PROBLEMS...

The first activity the would-be or prospective degree candidate will be expected to undertake is to find a suitable research question. Sometimes this will effectively require little or no work if the individual has already identified one in his or her work environment. On the other hand they may have to scour the academic literature for an appropriate question. Other times the provisional supervisor

---

[26] This is a popular test used by business schools to filter applicants for MBA programmes. It is not frequently used at the doctoral level but it does occasionally raise its head at certain universities. The GMAT is culturally biased and is regarded by many as being essentially an IQ test. A research degree candidate will sometimes resent being asked to undertake a GMAT. There are endless books and many courses available to help degree candidates improve their GMAT scores.

[27] It is surprising how many research degree candidates appear to do well in this test while only having a very rudimentary knowledge of English. Perhaps the acceptance level is too low.

may be able to point the prospective degree candidate towards a research question of interest. As previously mentioned this search activity should not be rushed.

5.6   The research diary

From the outset the research student should be advised to keep a diary in which he or she can record what they have read, what they have discussed and how their thinking is developing. This is invaluable when they need to start writing how they research journey has unfolded. Also this diary may be used as the basis for the regular discussion the student needs to hold with his or her supervisor.

5.7   The research student's glossary

One of the challenges which faces anyone starting a research degree is to learn the language of research. There are a substantial number of new words to learn and until this vocabulary has been mastered the researcher cannot really come to terms with the different approaches, frameworks or strategies available. Having the research student build his or her own vocabulary is an effective way of help him or her develop an understanding of the words required.

5.8   Meeting the other research candidates

Part of the integrating process for any newcomer into a university is to meet other members of the faculty, especially other researchers. This is a question of the socialisation of the degree candidate into the community of scholars.

5.9   Finding a supervisor or supervisors

The applicant should be introduced to a number of prospective supervisors. The task then becomes one of matching the interests of the possible supervisor/s with the needs of the degree candidate. While the degree applicant is finding a supervisor he or she may sometimes be allocated a member of staff who will act as a mentor.

5.10 Research proposal

As will be discussed later in Chapter 7, the writing of the research proposal, which is a substantial piece of work, is a critical part of any research project and should not be rushed. The research proposal is an overview of the research that will be undertaken and can go through a number of iterations before being finalised and may take several months to complete.

It is of particular importance that a research student establishes the department or school requirements for the research proposal. The requirements differ considerably even within one university and much time may be lost if the student does not have the correct guidelines from the beginning.

5.11   Identifying quantitative and/or qualitative skills

Academic research will normally require considerable evidence collection and analytical skills. Some would-be research degree candidates will already be skilled in this respect from having completed a Masters degree by dissertation. However at doctoral level it is usually necessary to have a broader and deeper understanding of these techniques. Some universities in the UK have introduced a Master of Research[28] degree which would-be doctoral candidates are required to complete first.

5.12   The research protocol

As described in Chapter 11, the research protocol is the detailed master plan for the research project that has to be agreed by the supervisor. It can be viewed as a sort of 'loose' contract between the student and the institution. It provides a justification for the research, the intended methods for evidence collection and analysis, as well as a time plan. These jointly provide a structure for the research and help the supervisor assess the capability of the degree candidate to do the research as well as identify areas in need of development for the candidate. Finally the research protocol can play an important role in ensuring an efficient use of research resources.

Like the research proposal the requirements of a research protocol can differ considerably even within one university and much time may be lost if the student does not have the correct guidelines from the very beginning.

---

[28] The Master of Research (MRes) degree can take one or two years and in some cases a full research proposal is part of the deliverable required to be awarded this degree.

5.13 The ethics protocol

There is a separate ethics protocol required at many if not most universities. An application needs to be made by the student for an ethics protocol which outlines in detail how the researcher will behave during and after the research. The ethics protocol should be applied for as soon as the student knows what he or she wants to research and how they intend to obtain the data required (Remenyi at al. 2011). More will be said about this in chapter 11 and chapter 20.

5.14 Additional courses or skills

Increasingly universities are providing comprehensive courses in research philosophy, research design, research methods, research management and more specialised and advanced techniques when required. There is also the question of writing and presentation skills. The supervisor needs to assess which of these the research degree candidate needs to attend. Some of these courses may have to be attended by the student several times. For example both the academic writing and the data analysis courses are difficult to absorb quickly and the ideas need to be reinforced by repetition.

These courses are often intended to encourage students to develop skills which may be used outside of the university environment if he or she chooses such a career.

5.15 Building a personal network

The network required by the research degree candidate needs to be both external as well as internal. The supervisor needs to ensure that the researcher knows about conferences, journals and other ways of establishing themselves in the academic community. Research degree candidates are sometimes hesitant and are thus slow to get out and make research contacts. The supervisor needs to actively help them get over this.

5.16 Scheduling work delivery

During the research project the researcher needs to have his or her ideas subjected to peer review. In the first years of the doctoral degree programme this will usually mean presenting to fellow researchers and to other members of faculty. In addition to oral presentations the supervisor needs to actively assist the research degree candidate in having their work published in a working paper series at the very least.

5.17 Feedback or progress reports

An essential part of the research degree process is feedback on the research candidate's work. The feedback needs to be both verbal and in writing. Both formative and summative feedback is required. Of course this feedback needs to be both critical and constructive. Some universities will have formal requirements for either six monthly or annual reports to the Dean of Research. These sometimes include feedback from the students as to the level of service he or she is receiving from his or her supervisor/s.

5.18 Dissertation submission requirements

Every university will have its own regulatory requirements for dissertation submission and the supervisor needs to help the researcher find out exactly what these are and they need to be closely followed.

5.19 Production of the physical dissertation

Universities in the British Isles normally require four or five copies of the dissertation to be submitted; whereas universities in Sweden can require as many as 200 copies (a copy is sent to each university library in the country[29]). In the UK it is increasingly the case that the dissertation should be submitted unbound until it has been examined. After examination it is re-submitted bound in a hard cover.

Although a number of universities have begun to demand that written work produced by students be delivered electronically as well as on paper this is not yet widely practiced at doctoral level. The reason for requiring an electronic copy of the work is that the university can pass the files through an anti-plagiarism program. Plagiarism has become a big issue at undergraduate level as has the fact that there are now many organisations who will produce essays, assignments and projects for students for a fee. All this type of activity is highly unethical and students who are caught indulging in this sort of behaviour are not treated sympathetically.

---

[29] The recent scandal in Germany where the Defence Minister Herr Guttenberg resigned after he was accused of plagiarism perhaps demonstrates the value of having a dissertation widely distributed as is the practice in a number of continental European countries.

5.20 Submission of the dissertation

The dissertation is normally submitted to the office of the Dean of Research who will then forward it to the examiners. Preliminary checking is sometimes undertaken by this office with regards to the format of the cover and the lead in pages before the work is accepted for examination.

5.21 Appointment of examiners

The Dean in consultation with the supervisor and perhaps also based on suggestions from the candidate will appoint at least two examiners.

5.22 Examination including viva voce

The examination of the research degree is based on the dissertation and in the case of a doctoral degree this is supported by a viva voce during which the research candidate is engaged in debate on the work he or she has done.

5.23 Revision and amendments

Not many dissertations are accepted without some revision or amendments. These can be minor requiring only a few hours' work or they can be major requiring up to one year's additional research. In the case of the latter it is imperative that the supervisor has a clear understanding of exactly what the examiners require.

5.24 Graduation

It is usual for the supervisor to attend the graduation ceremony of his or her students, as the success of the student is also the success of the supervisor and the department.

Although the research process does differ from university to university the above steps are common to most institutions.

5.25 Useful books and/or websites

Information about the GMAT, Available:
    http://www.mba.com/mba/TaketheGMAT [09 Aug 2011].
The GMAT Review, available: http://www.gmat-review.co.uk/ [09 Aug 2011]
English as a Foreign Language, Available: http://www.toefl.org/ [09 Aug 2011].
http://www.prospects.ac.uk/search_funding_bodies.htm [7 Jan 2012]

http://www.columbia.edu/~drd28/Thesis%20Research.pdf [7 Jan 2012]

Chapter 6

Rules of engagement

Each piece, or part, of the whole of nature is always merely an approximation to the complete truth, or the complete truth so far as we know it. In fact, everything we know is only some kind of approximation, because we know that we do not know all the laws as yet. Therefore, things must be learned only to be unlearned again or, more likely, to be corrected.
Feynman, R. (1993) *Six Easy Pieces*, London: Penguin Books, p2.

Our civilization has decided . . . that determining the guilt or innocence of men is a thing too important to be trusted to trained men. . . . When it wants a library catalogued, or the solar system discovered, or any trifle of that kind, it uses up its specialists. But when it wishes anything done which is really serious, it collects twelve of the ordinary men standing round. The same thing was done, if I remember right, by the Founder of Christianity.
Chesterton G K. (1909) Tremendous Trifles, 'The Twelve Men'

6.1 Working with the Research Candidate

The *rules of engagement* mean the agreed manner in which the research degree candidate and the supervisor or supervisors will work together. These rules of engagement need to be spelt out early in the relationship between the parties in order to minimise any misunderstanding. It is not always necessary, but it is generally useful, to put these rules in writing. In fact some universities are insisting on this and see the *statement of agreed working practice* to be a document that is as important as the research proposal. This document can be seen as the commitment that both sides make to each other.

The way that the research degree candidate and the supervisor will work together varies over time. In the first year it might be useful for them to meet every week or every two weeks but by the end of the research the research degree candidate will be largely independent and a meeting once a month should be adequate.

6.2 Two or more supervisors

Increasingly there is more than one supervisor[30] and if two or more supervisors are involved then all parties should agree on the rules of engagement. When there is more than one supervisor, one of the first things to be established is whether the degree candidate will meet his or her supervisors one at a time or whether they will always meet together. For practical purposes it is not usual to insist that they should always meet together. In any event meeting the supervisors one at a time may help the degree candidate build up a better personal relationship with the people concerned.

6.3 The third dilemma facing supervisors

A second supervisor is someone on whom the research degree candidate should be able to look for advice from time to time. Most universities do not intend the second supervisor to fully share the work of the supervision throughout the entire degree process. Thus the dilemma is just how involved should the second supervisor be. In practice it is im-

---

[30] In the UK universities began to use two supervisors for doctoral research in the middle of the 1990s. Some research degree candidates report that they hardly ever see their second supervisor. Sometimes this is the result of the different styles of the people involved.

portant for the student to keep in contact with this person without asking too much from him or her. If this is not done then the second supervisor needs to call for a meeting and to ask for reports. If something is not progressing as it should the second supervisor should know about it and make an effort to move the situation forward.

6.4   Arrangements for meeting and working with your student

On the subject of arrangements for meetings, some supervisors who are supervising several research degree candidates try to minimise their time commitment by holding group meetings. Although group meetings of research degree candidates can be useful, they should not be the basis on which the student has access to his or her supervisor. Group meetings should be an occasional event. Regular meetings between supervisor/s and research degree candidate should be held on a one to one basis without the distraction of having other researchers (or academic staff for that matter) in the same meeting. In simple terms research degree candidates have the right to be given the exclusive attention of their supervisor/s on a regular basis.

The supervisor/s needs to spell out in a reasonable amount of detail how he or she intends to work with the degree candidate. Some supervisors like to have an informal working relationship whereby the student may drop in for a chat whenever they wish[31]. Other supervisors only want to meet their students occasionally and by formal appointment. Both of these arrangements can work perfectly satisfactorily provided both parties concur that this is how they want to work[32]. Do bear in mind that no matter how formally the working relationship is defined at the outset it will evolve over the period of the research and both sides need to be flexible. Some supervisors can have difficulty in realising that the student may be advancing rapidly and will eventually know more about the subject being researched than the supervisor.

---

[31] In some universities there are special open plan working areas or offices for students and some supervisors who like to drop in occasionally and meet with their own and other degree candidates.

[32] A reliable source reported recently that a colleague of his saw her supervisor twice during her three years as a doctoral student. This occurred some years ago. Today, it is unlikely that this would be tolerated in most universities.

A general agreement needs to be reached with regards to the amount of time the student intends to take to complete the research. Masters degrees that stretch over three or four years become less valuable and Doctorates which are allowed to go on for six or seven or even eight years may also go out of date.[33].

As early as possible the supervisor and the student should agree as precisely as possible what work is required, how often they should meet and what written and oral submissions should be made. It is also worth agreeing how many hours a month the supervisor should expect to spend with the student or on the student's work. It is important to establish if minutes of supervisor-student meetings should be kept and if so by whom. Where multiple supervisors are involved procedures concerning who should be at the meetings need to be established. The relationship between the multiple supervisors needs to work well and it is always helpful if everyone has the same understanding as to who will do what and when.

... UNDERSTANDING AS TO WHO WILL DO WHAT AND WHEN.

Arrangements differ and depend on the institution, the individuals involved and the subject being researched. However a typical *statement of agreed working practice* could state that from an agreed date when the degree candidate formally commences his or her research there will be a one-hour weekly or bi-weekly meeting until a research topic is established. Once the research topic has been agreed, they may meet only once a fortnight. After the proposal is accepted and a research protocol

---

[33] The question of full-time and part-time degrees has to be taken into account when discussing the period of time that will be permitted. However there are some research topics which have a clear shelf life. For example, anyone researching the dotcom phenomenon might now find some or all of their work to be of significantly less interest and value than it was only a few years ago- unless the research was a historiography. On the other hand if human resource policies are being studied in the civil service then it is possible that no material changes will take place in either the environment or in the theory of this field over an extended period.

established the degree candidate may only need to see the supervisor/s occasionally. And later on, when the research is being finalised, the degree candidate and the supervisor/s may need to meet more regularly as the final detail of the work is being concluded[34].

Students need ongoing feedback from their supervisor of both a formative[35] and summative[36] nature. Although this feedback will usually be given verbally it is important to have periodic written reports. For a Masters degree this could be once every six months. For a Doctorate a written report is normally needed once a year. As well as the supervisor's comment on the research student's performance, the research student is sometimes required to complete a review of the supervisor and the institution. This is a sort of quality control which many students feel gives them a say about how they are being supervised and allows them to express an opinion about how their research work is progressing. Of course this is to a large extent illusionary as students seldom have the power to influence the direction or the policy of the institution at which they are researching.

It is worth putting on record that if the student is not making adequate progress then there is a procedure for having him or her de-registered. But this can be quite difficult and most universities are reluctant to initiate such a course of action. What is more likely is that students who are not making adequate progress will run out of time and the university's

---

[34] Of course the frequency of meetings will vary enormously according to the individuals involved. Furthermore part-time students will probably have substantially less direct contact with their supervisors than full-time students. Sometimes being more experienced they may require less direct supervision.

[35] The term formative is taken from the word form in the sense of mould. Formative evaluation especially in the context of education is viewed as an iterative evaluation and decision-making process with the overall objective to achieve a more acceptable and beneficial outcome from the project. Formative evaluation is not judgmental but rather focuses on how the current situation can be improved. With regards to research degrees this means regular meetings between the student and the supervisor to discuss progress with the aim of ensuring that the research stays on track and that an acceptable outcome will be achieved.

[36] The term summative is derived from the word sum, and in the context of evaluation or feedback refers to the activity of judging whether a piece of work is adequate. Thus summative evaluation is judgemental and the supervisor will have to make a number of summative evaluations with regards the work of the research student. It is probably useful for the research student to submit his or her work on a chapter basis so that the supervisor may comment on relatively small pieces of work – one at a time.

rules concerning the maximum time a student can be registered will be applied and the student will then be removed from the register.

Not agreeing the rules of engagement with the student may lead to tensions or even arguments and to the supervisor or the student having excessive demands placed on his or her time.

It is worthwhile mentioning that the rules of engagement may change. A degree candidate may find that he or she does not need as much help as was first thought or on the other hand the opposite may also transpire. It is of course worth documenting any changes for future reference.

6.5 Intellectual Property Rights (IPR)

University research occasionally results in a commercially exploitable innovation and when this occurs the question of Intellectual Property Rights arises. Intellectual Property Rights refers to who owns the knowledge produced by the research project and who is actually in a position legally to take commercial advantage of these findings. Who owns the commercial rights to any research findings will depend upon a number of issues.

RESEARCH PROJECT

COPYRIGHT

... IT IS USUAL ...TO REGARD ALL INTELLECTUAL PROPERTY OR COPYRIGHT ARISING... TO REST WITH THE UNIVERSITY...

It needs to be emphasised that in the business and management studies environment this is not a frequent occurrence and although an important issue, it is not one that the supervisor or the institution will frequently have to be concerned with. With younger full-time research degree candidates their research will generally be unlikely to produce much of commercial value. However the issue of Intellectual Property Rights does arise with part-time research degree candidates who may be employed by consulting firms and who are investigating some practical work-related problem. This can especially occur when action research is undertaken. In such circumstances the student might regard his or her research findings to be at least sensitive, if not confidential.

In addition it is usual for the university to regard all intellectual property or copyright arising from a research degree or project conducted at the university to rest with them. This is normally stated in the application

documents that the research degree candidate is asked to sign when registering. This is done primarily so that any controversy that may arise is handled by the institution, which generally has much better access to lawyers than students have. However the need to publish and thus make known the research findings from universities is strong and most universities will be quite accommodating with regards to waiving this right and it is unusual for this to be refused.

The supervisor needs to ensure that the research degree candidate understands these issues and if at any stage during the research it is believed that the results generated may have commercial potential it is important to take advice from the supervisor and/or the Dean of Research. If there is an Intellectual Property Rights issue the research candidate may have to take advice from a specialised lawyer.

Sometimes the supervisor will be asked by the organisation in which the student is researching to sign a confidentiality agreement. This does not often happen but when it does then the supervisor needs to be prepared to comply with this request or the student may have to find another organisation in which to conduct the research.

With regards to the issue of confidentiality it is important that the supervisor should not discuss his or her student's research with anyone else unless asked to by the student. Of course at colloquia and similar meetings it is perfectly correct for the supervisor to engage in debate about the research, but care needs to be taken that the student's results are not revealed before he or she wishes them to be announced.

The most infamous case of a supervisor talking about his student's research might be the Rosalind Franklin case and the discovery of the DNA double helix[37].

6.6   Knowledge in the public domain

In general, universities attempt to place any knowledge that is created by them in the normal course of events in the public domain. This is achieved in a number of ways including the fact that all academics, including research degree candidates are encouraged to publish their research findings in peer-reviewed journals.

---

[37] http://www.chemheritage.org/discover/chemistry-in-history/themes/biomolecules/dna/watson-crick-wilkins-franklin.aspx

When it comes to academic staff this encouragement is so strong that universities frequently underpin offers of tenure and promotion on their faculties' publication record. Of course this is in the best interests of the academics personally and the institution as a whole. Furthermore the funding of universities, with the exception of the small number of private institutions, is primarily paid for by government grants, which ultimately come from the public through taxes. Therefore it is only proper that the findings of the work of these bodies go back to the public.

6.7 Commercially sponsored research

A research degree candidate may occasionally have his or her fees paid by a commercial organisation and in such cases the commercial organisation might feel that it should have primary or even exclusive access to the findings. Universities will have different responses to this situation, but in general the student will be required to place his or her dissertation in the library in order for it to be available for the public. A concession may sometimes be made whereby the university agrees not to make the dissertation available to the general public for a year or two. This is sometimes referred to as placing an embargo on the publishing of the research. In return some universities will withhold the awarding of the degree until the dissertation is placed in the public domain. If a sponsor has supported the research then there may well be special obligations on the researcher and it is important that such an obligation is recognised and complied with.

In summary all research is a potential source of Intellectual Property and the supervisor and researcher should understand the issues underpinning this matter.

6.8 Useful books and/or websites

Copyright information, available: http://sunsite.berkeley.edu/Copyright/ [09 Aug 2011]
Intellectual property rights, available: http://www.w3.org/IPR/ [09 Aug 2011]
Commission on intellectual property rights, available:
    http://www.iprcommission.org/ [09 Aug 2011]
http://www.postgrad_resources.btinternet.co.uk/student-resources01-supervisors.htm [7 Jan 2012]

http://www.jobs.ac.uk/careers-advice/studentships/411/the-relationship-between-phd-supervisor-and-student/ [7 Jan 2012]

http://www.jwelford.demon.co.uk/brainwaremap/super.html [7 Jan 2012]

Part Three
The Research Work

Chapter 7

The research proposal

Considering now the invention, elaboration and the use of theories, which are inconsistent, not just with other theories, but even with experiments, facts, observations, we may start by pointing out that no single theory ever agrees with all the known facts in its domain. And the trouble is not created by rumours, or by the result of sloppy procedure. It is created by experiments and measurements of the highest precision and reliability.
Feyerabend, P. (1993), *Against Method*, 3rd Ed, London: Verso, p39.

7.1   A research proposal

A research proposal is a central part of any research project and a considerable amount of attention needs to be given to this before any student is finally given the go ahead with his or her project. Some universities will not formally register a research degree candidate until a research proposal has been finalised[38]. In these cases a provisional registration is sometimes offered to cover the three to six months a research proposal will typically take to develop.

7.2   The importance of the research proposal

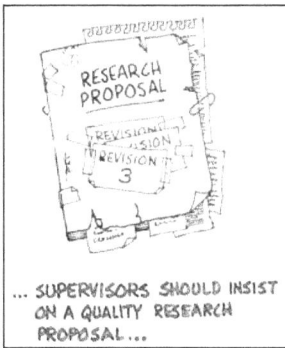

... SUPERVISORS SHOULD INSIST ON A QUALITY RESEARCH PROPOSAL ...

The research proposal has at least two main functions. In the first place it is a statement of what the potential student knows about the topic to be researched. From this point of view the research proposal needs to address both the literature and any other practical experiences that the prospective research degree candidate might have. Furthermore the research proposal also outlines how he or she will go about the research and should illustrate the methodology options that are available. Finally a research proposal should suggest what type of outcome the research project might lead to.

But the proposal is also a provisional agreement between the degree candidate and the institution, including the potential supervisor/s, of what the student will actually do. As mentioned above it is frequently on the basis of the research proposal that the degree candidate is finally accepted and the supervisor becomes fully committed to the project. At the same time research proposals are seldom, if ever, binding contracts between the student and the institution, as it is usually possible and in fact sometimes desirable for the student to make quite extensive

---

[38] In some cases there may be an initial outline research proposal, which will address the general area of research. This would perhaps include a clear statement of the topic to be researched, but it would not normally provide details of the research question. In such cases a second level of research proposal would be required to be produced some time later (perhaps at the end of the first year) in which the research question and other details would be fully set out. Some universities will use the mechanism of registering for a Masters degree instead of this two-staged process.

changes to what was agreed in the research proposal as the project unfolds. The research proposal is probably better understood as both a high-level route map of the research project and also an aide memoir for the parties concerned as to how the project was originally envisaged. It is really quite important for the research degree candidate to be flexible and to be prepared to be opportunistic as to how the research project actually develops.

7.3   Issues addressed by the research proposal

An acceptable research proposal will require the following questions to be specifically addressed:

1. What will the research aim to achieve and exactly what has to be done by the researcher to make this happen? This is the research question and how it will be answered.
2. Why should the research be done? To whom is the research important? This answers the question *so what?* and outlines who the stakeholders might be.
3. What other work has been done in this area and what theories have been applied to it?
4. What is the chosen methodology and why is this methodology considered most appropriate?
5. What are the potential outcomes of the research and in what way will the answering of the research question improve management practice?

Also the research proposal should provide:

1. Some details of the proposed research protocol.
2. A high-level outline of each chapter for the dissertation is helpful. It is not intended that the researcher actually adhere to this, but it is useful to have a rough idea in mind as to the issues which will need to be covered.
3. A suggestion as to how will it be established when enough work has been done.

The exercise of writing a research proposal is useful to both the supervisor and the student. This process makes sure that many, if not all, the research issues that need to be addressed during the research project are well aired at the outset. This minimises any surprises occurring later on during the research project.

7.4   The dimensions of the research proposal

The length of the research proposal is also an important issue. Some universities require relatively short doctoral proposals, which may be as brief as 10 pages long. Other universities ask for much more substantial documents which can be 70 to 100 pages. These longer research proposals are often convertible into the first few chapters of the dissertation. In general shorter research proposals of, say, 20 pages are regarded as preferable, especially if the degree candidate is not to be formally registered until the research proposal has been accepted.

It is also worth noting that sometimes the research proposal is a student filtering mechanism in its own right and would-be students who are not really serious about doing the work required to obtain their degree do not complete the research proposal. It is much better for them to fail at this stage than to spend one or more years trying to do their research and failing then.

Supervisors should insist on a quality research proposal. To reach the required standard the prospective student may have to improve his or her work through a number of revisions. Some institutions may insist that only two or three revisions are allowed. If the student cannot produce a quality proposal then it is unlikely that he or she will be able to do the real thing, i.e. the dissertation later. Of course all the work required for the research proposal should be directly relevant to the dissertation itself.

7.5   Using the research proposal to manage the project

The research proposal is a useful tool with which to manage the research project. It provides a framework to guide the research candidate's efforts. Unfortunately the research proposal is often used as a hurdle the prospective research degree candidate needs to overcome to be fully accepted by the university. If this is the case then once the research proposal has been accepted it is often largely forgotten about. But if the research proposal is referred to from time to time it can provide a reference from which to guide the research degree candidate's efforts.

7.6   Understanding the issues

By the time that the research proposal has been accepted it is essential that the student understands all the requirements, both academic and administrative, for the research degree and has a good appreciation of how he or she will be able to fulfil them. If these issues are not sorted out at this stage, problems will undoubtedly arise later.

An example of a research proposal is provided in Appendix 2. This is not offered as an example of a definitive research proposal, but it is reasonably comprehensive and will give the reader an impression of the level of work required for such a document.

7.7   Mature mid-career candidates

In dealing with mature research degree candidates the research proposal may represent the first piece of formal academic writing they have undertaken in some years. Academic writing does not come naturally to many people and a research degree candidate may have difficulty with this type of writing. The supervisor needs to be prepared to read and critique a number of drafts before the document is ready for presentation.

It is important to leave time for the research proposal processes. It can take months rather than weeks to be delivered in an acceptable form.

7.8   Useful books and/or websites

How to Write a Research Proposal, available:
    http://www.eastchance.com/howto/res_prop.asp [09 Aug 2011].
How To Write A Proposal For The Health Systems Trust, available:
    http://www.hst.org.za/publications/how-write-research-proposal-health-systems-trust [09 Aug 2011].
How To Write A Losing Proposal, available:
    http://people.eku.edu/ritchisong/RITCHISO/losingproposal.htm [09 Aug 2011].
Writing A Research Proposal, available: http://www.warnborough.ie/?learning-resources/writing-a-research-proposal.html [09 Aug 2011].

Chapter 8

Choosing a research question

Managers are not confronted with problems that are independent of each other, but with dynamic situations that consist of changing problems that interact with each other. I call such situations messes ... .managers do not solve problems: they manage messes.

Ackoff, R. (1979) 'The future of operations research is past', *Journal of the Operations Research Society*, 30, p. 93.

We inhabit a world that is always subjective and shaped by our interactions with it. Our world is impossible to pin down, constantly and infinitely, more interesting than we ever imagined.

Wheatley, M. (1992) *Leadership and the New Science*, San Francisco: Berrett-Koeler, p8.

8.1   The challenge of a suitable research question

Having provided an overview of the research proposal in the previous chapter, it is now important to look at the components that make up the proposal. The first step is to find a suitable research question.

The research question is the fulcrum about which the research process revolves. Establishing a suitable research question is one of the most important activities in the whole research degree process. It is surprising just how many doctoral degree candidates have poorly expressed research questions.

Then there is the issue that most academic research questions are at such a high level that they require decomposing into a number of sub-questions. Finding sub-questions is not always an easy matter. Sometimes the proposed sub-questions do not contribute to answering the original primary research question but rather extend the scope of the original research question. This is not satisfactory and the supervisor will have to play an important role in helping the research student find suitable sub-questions.

Once the research question is established the student should be able to state what data will be required to answer the question. Knowing the data requirements should lead to establishing the method of data collection and data analysis.

Some students will have a clearly articulated research question before they attempt to obtain admission to a university or business school. However others will not. Some students will only have a vague idea of what they want to research. Other students may know that they want to develop themselves as a researcher, but have virtually no idea of what topic they should pursue. A supervisor needs to be in a position to help direct students towards a suitable research question and to point out if there are any traps which could occur if they chose a particular research question.

8.2   The research degree candidate's strengths

The first step in directing a student toward a suitable research question is to understand and to develop the research degree candidate's strengths. It is important to be realistic about these strengths and not simply optimistic and encouraging. These strengths can be based on the student's former education or degrees or on his or her working experience. The point here is that although it is perfectly possible for a student to choose to research in a field of study which is new to him or her, the work involved in picking up a completely new subject is really quite substantial. It is far better if the research student can build on previously acquired learning. Traditionally, it was felt that the student should find his or her topic and research question in the established literature and that the primary objective of the early stages of a research project is to get to know as much of the literature as quickly as possible. However, recently it has become more acceptable to identify a topic and research question from the working experiences of the student or perhaps a member of faculty. In fact today it is sometimes thought to be ideal if the topic and research question can be chosen as a result of both the student's former education and also to his or her working experience.

8.3   Brainstorm alternatives

When there is not an immediately obvious topic or research question that the student wants to pursue, the supervisor needs to help the student brainstorm possible alternatives and a variety of techniques may be used in this respect. Most of the brainstorming techniques relevant for finding a suitable research topic will involve some type of scenario analysis. This involves the supervisor and the student answering questions such as:

What are the implications if you research the following topic and answer the following questions?
Why are you interested in the topic?
What literature is available?
Are there likely to be any theoretical justifications for the question?
Will you be able to obtain access to informants to answer your question?
How many informants are you likely to have access to?
How might you be able to collect the evidence?
What sort of evidence will your informants be able and willing to supply?
What sort of analysis will you be able to perform on the evidence?
What are the likely findings going to be?
Who will be interested in your findings?

Hopefully it will be easy enough to decide on the main field of study or discipline the student is interested in. Each field of study or discipline will have major categories or topics and these should be reviewed carefully from the current academic literature. One of these topics will need to be chosen. If the student does not feel that he or she can easily identify with a topic, then he or she can explore several, one at a time, to see what research questions may arise and whether their interest is stimulated. In the case of a doctoral degree it would not be unreasonable for a student to spend up to six months looking at alternative topics and research questions. For a Masters degree the period would need to be quite a lot shorter, say a month or two.

8.4   Several iterations of research question development

Settling on the precise research question will usually require several iterations. A broad question may be a good starting point. However before the main research begins the student will have to ensure that the question has been refined and that there is no ambiguity in this matter. The research question needs to be relevant and answerable within the time and the resources available to the researcher to finish the degree. Furthermore the answer to the question should still be of interest when the research is concluded.

It is important to conclude this part of the research process in a reasonable amount of time. If the student cannot find a research question within a year then perhaps he or she should take a break from the research and come back in a few years.

If the research question has been found by reviewing the literature then the next step is to commence the selection of the research strategy and the research tactics. The literature review will also help with this. The student will be expected to know, from his or her literature review how the research question has been addressed in previous research

... IT IS EXPECTED THAT THE STUDENT SHOULD COMB THE LITERATURE ...

attempts and as a general rule it will be expected that the new researcher will build on the research methodologies that have been applied in the past. However there are plenty of exceptions to this rule and the researcher has to make a case for using a different approach to the research[39]. In this respect, more than anything else, the researcher is

---

[39] Making a case for using a different methodological approach could be based on the fact that a new way of looking at the problem could provide greater insights. It could also be based on a new approach to analysing evidence which has become available.

expected to know how this topic has been researched in the past and to think about the issue of a competent research methodology.

If the research question has been arrived at through the experience of the student or one of his or her colleagues then it is expected that the student should comb the literature in order to ensure that this problem has not already been solved by prior academic or other research. Such a review of the literature should formally contextualise the research question and ensure that its theoretical value is understood. The supervisor should play an active role in this by advising the student which sources of literature would be the most relevant.

8.5   What are the subsidiary research questions?

Finding a suitable research question can be a challenging business and an experienced supervisor can be an enormous help as a sounding board. The supervisor and student can debate issues such as:

What is the main and what are the subsidiary research questions? There are often multiple research questions. How does the research question lend itself to being able to make an interesting contribution to the field of study and in what way? If there is no apparent contribution (and this can be a difficult thing to assess), then the research question may not be adequate. Does the literature confirm that an answer to the proposed research question might be regarded as an adequate contribution? As a first step it is useful to think of an adequate contribution as being a finding of sufficient importance to be welcomed by the academic community. Where a Masters degree is concerned the contribution needs to be only minor, while for a Doctoral degree an adequate contribution has to be more substantial. However it is important not to overstate the substantial nature of an adequate contribution. Doctoral degrees are regularly awarded on really quite modest contributions.

8.6   An example research question

Recently a research student offered the following as a research question.

What Information Systems Strategy facilitates optimisation of management decision making in order to allow sustainable benefits?

Although this is a useful start as it identifies the research area, which is *Information Systems Strategy and it's impact on sustainable benefits through different modes of decision-making*, it does not yet provide sufficient detail to allow the research to be adequately focused.

The research question needs to be more fully explored by considering the detail behind some of these issues. For example *information systems strategy* can mean different things to different people and so the research question needs to explain or define how this term is understood in the context of this question. The term *management decision-making* is at least equally problematical. What level of management is being referred to and what types of decisions are being considered? Then there is the issue of *allowing sustainable benefits*, which presents at least two problems of how to define and measure the notion of benefit and then how to think about the issue of sustainability.

From this example it may be seen that settling on a research question which is not too simple or too difficult and for which it is possible to find an answer is not a trivial matter. The supervisor will often have to work closely with the research student perhaps through several versions of a research question before a really suitable one is found.

A second attempt to produce a usable research question for the above example includes a substantial preamble to explain the context and define some of the variables involved with the question. For instance, this could begin as follows.

> *Achieving sustainable information systems benefits has been a problem that has bothered management, information systems consultants and academic researchers for many years. This is evidenced in both the literature and also from discussions with information systems practitioners. There are problems related to identifying such benefits as well as being able to measure them. There is also the question of whether having achieved information systems benefits it is possible to ensure that they are not transitory. It has been suggested, both in the literature and also in discussions with information systems practitioners that an appropriate Information Systems Strategy can make an important contribution to the potential of an organisation in achieving such sustainable information systems benefits. In this context an Information Systems Strategy is understood to mean the way in which the Information Systems Resources are employed for the benefit of*

the organisation. It is sometimes said that there are a limited number of generic Information Systems Strategies. These have been described by Parsons (1983) as Central Planning, Leading Edge, Free Market, Monopoly, Scarce Resource and Necessary Evil. Each of these generic Information Systems Strategies have specific implications for management decision making specifically with regard to how the technology will be used to directly support the business.

With this preamble in mind the research question could then be re-expressed as follows:

How does the choice of generic Information Systems Strategies such as those outlined by Parson's (1983) directly affect the way managers make decisions as to how to implement information systems to directly support the business? How do these decisions have a direct effect on any benefits identified and to what extent are these benefits sustainable, or are they just transitory?

This research question could then be devolved into several sub-questions of which the following are examples:

1. In what way are the generic Information Systems Strategies described by Parsons (1983) perceived as real alternative choices for organisations?
2. How does the choice of generic Information Systems Strategy actually affect the decision-making involved in deciding how to implement information systems to directly support the business?
3. How are benefits derived from such systems identified?
4. How is the link between these information systems investment decisions and benefits illustrated or explained?
5. How are benefits derived from such systems measured?
6. How are such benefits viewed with regard to their tendency to be sustainable?

The above description is not the only way such a research question could be interpreted. However it does illustrate the work that is needed in moving from a general high-level question down to one that is actually more useable in a research project.

This process can take a number of months and it may be necessary to revise the research question as the research proceeds. However too many revisions of the research question is a sign that the project is not going well and this should trigger a serious review of the students work.

8.7   After the research question

Depending on the type of research, primarily whether it is quantitative or qualitative, the research questions may have to be further narrowed down to what is sometimes called hypotheses, empirical generalisations, or propositions. In a quantitative research project it will be these hypotheses, empirical generalisations, or propositions, which will be tested when a research instrument is created. In a qualitative research project these terms will generally not be used and the focus of the research will not specifically be on testing in the same sort of way.

8.8   The research question as a strategic issue

Before concluding the discussion on establishing a suitable research question it is useful to describe an approach to examining potential research questions from a strategic point of view. By this we mean looking at the research questions in terms of who is really interested in them, who might fund some of the research and what other variables there are in the environment that might impact on the research.

One way of doing this type of analysis is to adopt the approach referred to by Michael Porter (1980) as the five forces model. Porter uses this framework to understand the market or industry pressures which an organisation has to face. However here the question is what opportunities and challenges face the research project based on the selected research question.

Looking at the issue on the right hand side of Figure 8.1 we are invited to think about who will find the answer to the research question important. Hopefully there will be several interested parties for whom the findings of the research will be useful. We could also enquire as to where the findings of the research might ultimately be published. Figure 8.1 is an adaptation of Porter's Five Forces Model.

```
                    ┌─────────────────────┐
                    │  Ease of use by other│
                    │     researchers     │
                    └─────────────────────┘
┌──────────────┐    ┌─────────────────────┐    ┌──────────────┐
│  Suppliers of│    │    Rivalry among    │    │  Consumers of│
│   research   │    │     researchers     │    │   research   │
│   resources  │    │                     │    │   findings   │
└──────────────┘    └─────────────────────┘    └──────────────┘
                    ┌─────────────────────┐
                    │ Different fields of │
                    │  study encroaching  │
                    └─────────────────────┘
```

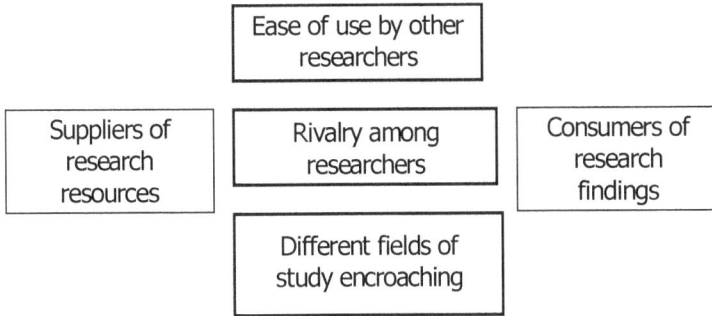

Figure 8.1: Adaptation of Porter's Five Forces Model

Looking at the issue on the left hand side of Figure 8.1 we are invited to think about who might be interested is supporting the research project, either by supplying funds or by other perhaps less tangible means. A question like which organisations might be prepared to give the researcher access could be asked here.

Considering the issue on the topside of Figure 8.1 we need to reflect on how easy it might be for other researchers to directly encroach on this topic. When undertaking a research degree for anything from a year to maybe four or five years it is desirable not to have a large number of what might be regarded as 'competitive' researchers doing the same or similar research.

The box in the lower part of Figure 8.1 refers to whether the suggested research question or a similar type of question is being studied by others in different disciplines. If possible, overlap and duplication should be avoided, but on the other hand it may be worthwhile to collaborate with other researchers who are approaching the same type of issue from a different point of view, and possibly using a different methodology.

Finally the central box in Figure 8.1 suggests that the research degree candidate should reflect on whether the proposed research question will be welcomed by his or her colleagues in his or her Department or Faculty. There could even be rivalry issues in the community as a whole and this could increase the risk profile of the research.

This analysis puts the research question into a useful context for the research degree candidate and helps anticipate any possible problems with any of the constituencies mentioned above.

8.9   The acid test for the research question

Before finally settling on a research question it is really important that the supervisor and the research degree candidate carefully consider the following questions:

1. Is the research degree candidate really interested in the research question?
2. Is the research degree candidate really capable of answering the research question?
3. Is the research suitable for the degree level being undertaken?
4. Is there adequate expertise in the university to help the research degree candidate with the research?
5. Will access to appropriate informants and other sources of data be reasonably easy?
6. Can the research be done in the time required and with the funds available?

If positive answers can be given to these six questions then the research degree candidate has probably chosen a suitable research question. If not, he or she needs to carefully think again.

8.10   Changing the research question

Recently a substantial number of research degree candidates have changed their research question during the course of their doctoral research project. Universities will normally allow this, but in most cases there are formalities involved. Sometimes, when a substantial change is made the research degree candidate may have to submit a revised proposal for approval. In other instances this may not be necessary but it is important that any such changes are recorded in writing and that the rules of the particular institution are observed. The Office of the Dean or Director of Research should be able to inform the student of the requirements.

Research degree candidates are advised not to make major changes if possible and to change as few times as possible. Any change made is likely to result in additional work and corresponding delays.

8.11 Useful books and/or websites

Web research questions, available: http://highered.mcgraw-
hill.com/sites/0070887357/student_view0/chapter1/web_research.html [09 Aug
2011].
The literature review, a few tips on completing it, available:
http://www.utoronto.ca/writing/litrev.html [09 Aug 2011].
How to write a literature review, available:
http://www.unc.edu/depts/wcweb/handouts_pdf/Literature%20Review.pdf
[09 Aug 2011].
http://www.findaphd.com/student/study/study-25.asp [7 Jan 2012]

http://www.apfmj-archive.com/afm2.1/afm_050.pdf [7 Jan 2012]

Chapter 9

Choosing a research strategy

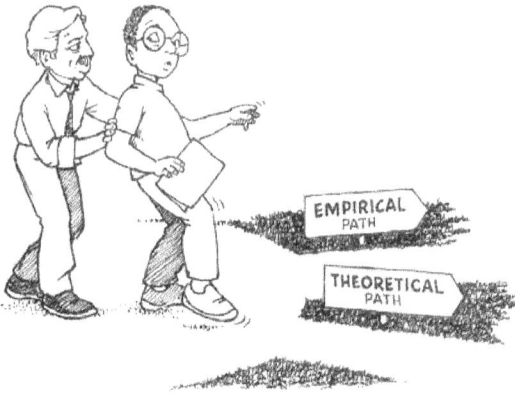

The reasonable man adapts himself to the world; the un-reasonable one persists in trying to adapt the world to himself. Therefore, all progress depends on the unreasonable man.
Shaw, George Bernard, (1903) *Man and Superman*, **"Maxims for Revolutionists: Reason"**

There is no method but to be very intelligent. said of Aristotle, who exemplified not method so much as intelligence itself.
Eliot, T.S, (1920) *The Perfect Critic* **reproduced in Kermode, ed (1975) Selected Prose of T. S. Eliot.**

9.1　Defining a research strategy[40]

Establishing an overall strategy is sometimes said to be the most important step in the initiation of a research degree and the rationale for the choice made should be clearly articulated by both the researcher and his or her supervisor. The primary benefits of clearly articulating the research strategy and design are that it facilitates communication between supervisor and researcher, the Dean of Research and other parties concerned. Furthermore it ensures that an acceptable logical structure is being used for the research. Research degrees often require both empirical observation and logical reasoning. The rules of classification, definition, deduction and sampling, if used, should be articulated in the methodology.

Another reason why the research strategy is so important is that it provides a recognised basis from which the researcher may assert the validity of his or her findings. However, the methodology should not, regardless of all other considerations, dominate the research procedure – 'one must regard all analytical methodologies or structures as mere intellectual frameworks and be cautious about their overuse in detail' (Quinn, 1988). In the final analysis, the researcher's creativity and imagination are of paramount importance and the research strategy is there to support rather than hinder the researcher's creative faculties.

A research strategy may be thought of as providing the overall direction of the research including the high level process by which the research is conducted. At a strategic level the research process is defined in broad terms that take into account the general philosophical approach adopted by the researcher. This includes being aware of the ontological and epistemological assumptions that underpin each different research methodology strategy (Morgan, 1980).

9.2　Research strategies available

Helping a research degree candidate choose an appropriate research strategy is a critical part of the supervisor's function. The term research strategy refers to the high level options for conducting academic research which are available to the researcher and that are outlined in this

---

[40] The term research design is now being used increasingly for what was called research strategy. Research design would also include the issues described in Chapter 10.

chapter. The supervisor needs to be aware of all the main research strategies available to a researcher in the field of study and needs to be able to outline to a complete beginner the pros and the cons of each approach to research. This needs to be done as early as possible so that the research degree candidate may be able to think about the alternatives available and to make a suitable choice that suits his or her topic or research question as well as his or her individual strengths.

A research strategy may be defined as a high level approach to the research that determines much of the detailed work the research degree candidate will subsequently undertake. This high level approach, or research strategy, is often thought to be the researcher's basic philosophical beliefs and understanding of the nature of the research that will be undertaken.

This section discusses the research strategies that are available to the academic researcher when considering his or her research degree. A student should not rush the choice of research strategy but rather go through the options and decision criteria step by step.

It is important that the novice supervisor is aware of the alternatives available and that he or she makes sure that the researcher really understands the implications of choosing one strategy as opposed to another. The available strategies are outlined in Figure 9.1.

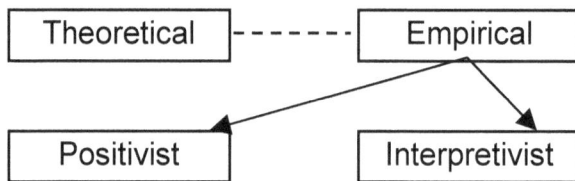

Figure 9.1: Research degree strategies

The two top-level strategic choices are whether the research will be theoretical or empirical.

9.3   Theoretical or empirical

In deciding on a research strategy the student should first decide if the research is to be essentially theoretical or empirical. Theoretical research which relies on secondary data and discourse between knowledgeable informants has been defined as:-

Theoretical research draws on ideas and concepts and through a process of reflection and discourse develops, extends or in some other way qualifies the previous work to create a new explanation, which provides better or fuller explanations of the issues and the relationships involved.

Empirical research relies on primary data and has been defined as:-

Empirical research involves the acquisition of primary data which has been described by researchers as sense perceived data. However not all issues which need to be researched are observable through sense perceived data. Examples of situations which involve non-observable data are particle physics and genetic engineering. Nonetheless research involving situations where there is a clear understanding of how cause and effect directly impacts data is acceptable for the purposes of empirical research. There are other aspects of empirical research where the data is not perceived or experienced directly by the researcher but is obtained by accounts from others. Research which is conducted using interviews or in focus groups is regarded as empirical and it is clear that the researcher has not had a direct experience of the phenomenon. Data collected by questionnaire is in the same category.

In some fields of study deciding which of these two approaches to choose could be a difficult decision. However, in the field of business and management studies the vast majority of research is traditionally empirical in nature and the researcher will find respecting this precedent the easiest way to a successful research project unless there is good reason for doing otherwise. If the researcher undertakes to conduct a piece of theoretical research it should be pointed out that this is likely to mean a considerably greater amount of work in the preparation of a rigorous and well supported argument. The final choice between these two alternatives may well be mostly related to the personal inclination of the researcher.

Theoretical research requires intensive textual investigation and personal discourse while empirical research requires extensive interaction with people and/or with organisations. Within the empirical approach to research there are two major options or research orientations: positivistic or quantitative (an approach essentially derived from the natural sciences) and interpretivist or qualitative (an approach essentially derived from the social sciences).

Appendix 3 provides a fuller description on the role of theory in academic research.

9.4   Theoretical research

Theoretical research draws on ideas and concepts which represents the cumulative body of previous research and through a process of reflection and discourse develops, extends or in some other way qualifies the previous work. This creates a new explanation, which provides a better or fuller insight into the issues and the relationships involved. Theoretical research is perceived to be overwhelmingly cerebral and is epitomised by Agatha Christie's Hercule Poirot[41] when he talks about using his *"little grey cells"*.

In a sense theoretical research is the modern equivalent of Rationalism. Rationalism is a philosophical point of view that asserts that human reason is the main source and test of knowledge. Rationalist are suspicious of empiricism as they argue that human senses can easily be tricked by apparent evidence which in effect has no basis in reality. They claim that reality has an inherently logical structure that can be understood by the human mind. Rational principles from logic and mathematics, in ethics and metaphysics are the keys to understanding the world. This confidence in reason rather than observation is the basis of the Rationalist belief in the superiority of the human mind. Today theoretical researchers would employ a rationalist approach using empirical data.

There are virtually no guidelines for this activity and thus there are no right or wrong ways of conducting theoretical research. This research can be done in the library and in the common room and in the refectory. Ashall (1994) describes Albert Einstein, one of the 20th century's greatest theoretical scientists, as follows:

> *Once, when asked by someone if they could see his laboratory, Einstein took a fountain pen from his pocket and said, 'There it is!' On another occasion he commented that his most important piece of scientific equipment was his wastepaper basket where he threw much of his paper work containing mathematical computations.*

---

[41] In his research methodology seminar Professor Mark Easterby-Smith from Lancaster University used analogies to four different fictional detectives to explain different approaches to research.

As established theories are sometimes incomplete there are opportunities for the researcher to enhance or extend current thinking.

9.5 Empirical research

In contrast, empirical research draws on experience or observation of primary evidence in order to understand a phenomenon being studied. Here the researcher has to go out and meet people or has to collect new evidence in some sort of way. This evidence can be quantitative or qualitative. In this respect questionnaires have been a popular approach to empirical evidence collection. Although some theoretical understanding of the issues and concepts involved is a prerequisite of empirical research, this approach differs significantly from theoretical research and is epitomised by the approach to enquiry used by Sherlock Holmes when he says, "*It is a capital mistake to theorise*[42] *before one has data*" (Doyle 1892). Empirical research requires data or evidence and therefore needs to be actualised through an evidence collection and analysis strategy.

9.5.1 Types of empirical research

The second level choice is whether, when an empirical strategy has been chosen, the researcher approaches the work as a positivist or as an interpretivist. The essence of positivism, also referred to as quantitative research, is that it relies on numbers and on the researcher's skill as mathematical or statistical analyst[43].

In contrast interpretivist or qualitative research looks for different kinds of evidence and is well described by Strauss and Corbin (1998):

> By the term 'qualitative research' we mean any type of research that produces findings not arrived at by statistical procedures or other means of quantification.

---

[42] In academic research the term theorise is normally used in a pejorative way. Theory development is a more acceptable way of referring to this activity.

[43] The terms positivistic research and quantitative research are often used as though these words are synonymous. Similarly interpretivist or qualitative research can mean the same thing, although not always. It is of course rather ironical that the term interpretivist is so highly associated with qualitative research as all research findings need to be interpreted. Even the most numerically based quantitative research will eventually call for interpretative skills.

There is one other approach to research strategy that needs to be considered, which is critical research. This is a relatively new approach, which is not extensively used in the field of business and management studies, and is described later in this chapter.

9.5.2 *The positivistic approach*

The following statements reflect the positivistic or quantitative approach to research:

- A method which resembles that of the natural sciences and thus uses largely, but not exclusively quantitative methods;
- The researcher is objective;
- The objective of the research is to establish general laws underpinned by nomothetic approaches;
- Problems are reducible to smaller or manageable components which may be addressed separately;
- Data and researcher's values are distinct from each other and thus it is possible to conduct research objectively;
- Possible hypotheses are derived by a process of deduction from established scientific theories to be tested empirically;
- Only phenomena which are observable and can be measured or counted deserve to be regarded as data[44,45];
- Testing observations is the final arbiter in theoretical disputes.

When the above characteristics are present in a research project it is sometimes described as complying with the scientific method. However there are scientists who believe that the scientific method is more honoured in its exception than its practice. Rosenthal and Rosnow (1991, p6) state that 'One contemporary philosopher, Abraham Kaplan, when asked to define the scientific method, answered that the 'scientist has no other method than doing his damndest' (Kaplan, 1964, p.27).

---

[44]It is worth noting the comment attributed to Einstein "Not everything that can be counted counts, and not everything that counts can be counted", http://www.marketingprofs.com/3/sterne3.asp

[45] As this is stated here the question of observable data or more correctly sense perceived data is over stated. It is generally accepted that sub-atomic particles are unobservable and still the scientific community perform positivistic research in this field. The same is true for various aspects of microbiology and a number of other fields of study.

The famous Nobel Laureate Professor Sir Peter Medawar made the remark that;- "Boswell-like, I once asked Karl Popper to express in a sentence the quintessence of the teaching of positivism. He at once replied: "The world is all surface.""

An important characteristic of positivism is that the research is normally deductive, which is sometimes described as being "from theory to data", meaning that mostly positivist research tests theory. This type of research is highly structured and the rules for establishing the level of rigour are well agreed.

In general the statements listed above are now recognised as being difficult to maintain to the point where few individuals would argue for their veracity.

See Appendix 4 - A note on positivism and interpretivism.

9.5.3   The interpretivist approach

The following statements reflect an Interpretivist or qualitative approach to research:

- The researcher is not objective and cannot be;
- The aim is to provide an in-depth understanding of the world of the research subjects;
- Generally uses small samples i.e. an idiographic study, that are deliberately selected for their particular criteria i.e. not random;
- Evidence collection methods that typically involve close contact between the researcher and the subjects being studied;
- Evidence which is detailed, information rich and extensive;
- Analysis that is generally open to emergent concepts and ideas;
- Used mostly in inductive research.

An important characteristic of interpretivism is that the research is normally inductive, which is sometimes described as being "from data to theory", meaning that mostly interpretivist research develops theory. This type of research is less structured than positivism and the research method sometimes evolves. The rules for establishing the level of rigour of this type of research are not well agreed and there can be material differences of opinion regarding the meaning of the researching findings.

It is clear that the positivistic or quantitative approach to research and the interpretivist or qualitative approaches are in some respects quite different. In fact according to Checkland (1981):

The investigation of social reality is fundamentally different from the investigation of the natural world.

However there are in fact a number of similarities between these methods and they really should not be seen as being in any form of opposition to one another (Remenyi 2002). The notion that these different approaches have more in common than they have in difference can be traced back to Marx (1844) when he said:

Natural science will in time incorporate into itself the science of man, just as the science of man will incorporate into itself natural science: there will be one science[46].

Both positivist and interpretivist approaches to research challenge the research degree candidate to find evidence to support an understanding of the research question and in so doing leads to a convincing argument claiming that the research has lead to something of value being added to the body of knowledge.

There are different levels at which the term positivist research may be understood and the same is true for interpretivist research. What has been described above is adequate for most purposes. However for those who require a more in-depth discourse on this subject Appendix 4 provides some additional insights[47].

---

[46] Some researchers would say that Marx was wrong but as he did not prescribe a time within which this will happen it would not be entirely sensible to rule out this possibility.

[47] In addition to deduction and induction some research texts refer to abduction which is a term first coined by Charles Saunders Pierce, one of the founding members of the school of research referred to as Pragmatists. Abduction is described by Wadham (2009) as "This is the process before any rational processes begin. It may be a guess or a lateral thought that is then tested. It is often confused with induction itself or the formation of a hypothesis, but these have to begin once the idea is conceived of. It is not a part of induction or deduction but there must be something that causes attention to be focused, hypotheses to be formed or testing to commence".

This is generally not considered to be part of the scientific method but the creative process must begin somewhere. It is probably very close to Einstein's thought experiments that yielded up ideas that he was then able to examine and seek proof for.

9.6 Factors influencing the choice of research strategy

Deciding on the research strategy is the first step in arriving at a comprehensive research methodology. Once a strategy has been decided, consideration can be given to the specific research methods or design that will be used. As a guide to making the strategic decisions the researcher should:

1. Establish a research question or problem;
2. Examine the major constraints imposed by the availability of resources;
3. Decide on a research strategy;
4. Examine the constraints imposed by the research strategy;
5. Choose a research tactic.

The research strategy is determined by four key issues, three of which are to do with resources and one is a direct function of the research question. These key issues are:

1. Research question;
2. Skills and attitude of the researcher;
3. Costs or budget available to the researcher;
4. Time available and target date for completion.

These four factors are shown in Figure 9.2.

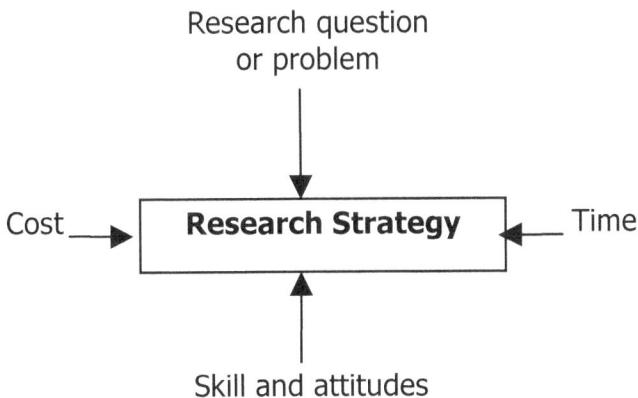

Figure 9.2: The four variables that influence the choice of research strategy.

FACTORS INFLUENCING THE CHOICE
OF RESEARCH STRATEGY

Of these four factors the research question is usually the most important. But the final choice of strategy adopted by the researcher will be
influenced by all four of these factors: the nature of the question, the
costs of carrying out the work, the skills available and the time needed.

9.6.1   *The research problem or question*

The first issue that the researcher needs to consider is the research
problem or question. Some research problems require certain types of
strategies and do not leave much room for flexibility. For example, research into share price performance in relation to risk profiles and return on investment of listed companies on the stock exchange would
generally require a positivistic approach involving the analysis of large
quantities of stock market data. On the other hand research into em-
ployee reactions to random checking in the work place for substance
abuse would probably be more effectively undertaken through the use
of phenomenological work with small groups of informants. Thus, before
thought can be given to a strategy, the research question or problem
needs to be defined.

9.6.2   *Skills and attitude of the researcher*

Hand in hand with the research question there needs to be an understanding of the research skills available and those that are needed. No
matter how appropriate a particular approach may be, if the researcher
does not have the appropriate skills then that particular strategy should
not be pursued. Thus those educated in mathematics or natural and life
sciences should be cautious if they decide to adopt a interpretivist strategy. Phenomenology and positivism are so different that few individuals
can bridge the two research cultures and those who attempt to so do
need to be aware of the potential problems.

9.6.3   Funds available

The amount of money available is another important strategic or design consideration. Research that will be based on questionnaires administered to large samples can be time-consuming and also expensive. If the questionnaires are to be administered by others they will need both training and payment. Thus students often feel that they are better off using small samples requiring a more personal approach. Furthermore the question of money arises in relation to travel expenses. Sometimes researchers try to overcome this obstacle by using fellow students as surrogate informants, but this may introduce biases and is generally considered suspect. In short the financial budget is always an issue as is the ability of researchers to gain access to the type of informants they require.

9.6.4   Time allocated for the degree

Time constraints should also be considered when choosing a strategy. Some Masters degrees, such as the MBA, are designed so that the research element of the degree has to be completed in three to six months if the student is to receive the degree at the following graduation. For this reason it is likely that only a limited number of approaches will be feasible. These days even Masters by dissertation need to be completed well within two years.

9.7   Critical theory research

It is important to mention critical theory research. As said above this approach is relatively new to the business and management studies set of research strategies. There are various different ways of looking at critical research. However one of the more useful is to recognise that critical research questions do not take for granted assumptions underpinning organisational and management practices, but develops knowledge and practical understanding that enables change and points out the possibilities for new ways of thinking and working.

According to Alvesson and Deetz (2000),

> *Critical research generally aims to disrupt ongoing social reality for the sake of providing impulses to the liberation from or resistance to what dominates and leads to constraints in human decision-making.*

And according to Brookfield (1987) there are four components to critical research:

1. Identifying and challenging assumptions behind ordinary ways of perceiving, convincing and acting;
2. Recognising the influence of history, culture, and social positioning on beliefs and actions;
3. Imagining and exploring extraordinary alternatives, ones that may disrupt routines and established orders;
4. Being appropriately sceptical about any knowledge or solution that claims to be the only truth or alternative.

To undertake acceptable critical theory research it is essential to become familiar with the work of the Frankfurt School. The research has to be built on top of the thinking of authors such as Max Horkheimer, Theodor Adorno, Herbert Marcuse, Erich Fromm or currently Jürgen Habermas.

It is important to say that being able to offer a critical analysis of a situation is not enough to be considered a critical theorist although it is a necessity. Powerful critique may be necessary but it is not sufficient.

Critical theory research is by no means universally accepted as satisfactory. In his book *Systems Theory Systems Practice* Checkland (1986) pointed out how obtuse critical theory research can be. In addition there are only a small number of supervisors and researchers who are competent in critical theory research strategy and it is not clear whether this will become a major approach. Certainly, following a critical theory research strategy at this time would be regarded by many as high risk.

9.8   The risk profile of a research degree

From the point of view of a Masters or Doctoral student it is of course important to follow well-established procedures and thus be able to claim that the research has been rigorous. This is because if approaches or strategies are used that are not well established, the risk of an examiner rejecting them is considerable.

It is useful to think of the risk profile of a research degree as having two dimensions. The first dimension is the novelty of the research method and the second dimension is the degree to which the field of study is established. The novelty of the research method will often be to do with introducing a research strategy or technique not normally used in the particular field of study. Thus the introduction of case studies into information systems management research in the 1980s was regarded as being novel. The novelty of the field of study will usually be recognised by the lack of established theory and will be reflected in the difficulty in finding an adequate body of literature. When this is the case the research student may have to undertake a grounded theory approach.

As can be seen from Figure 9.3, if a new methodology is used in a new field of study the risk of the research not being accepted is high. While if an established methodology is applied to a well-researched field of study there is the possibility that the researcher will not be able to argue that he or she has actually added something new to the body of theoretical knowledge.

	New Method	Old Method
New Field of study	High Risk of Failure	Should produce a satisfactory approach
Old Field of study	Should produce a satisfactory approach	Maybe of little value and not worthy of degree

Figure 9.3: The risk profile of a research degree

The safer areas for the research student is when there is either a new methodology in an established field of study or an established methodology in a new field of study.

Settling on a research strategy is an important part of the research degree process and the supervisor needs to take quite a lot of time to explain the decision criteria the research candidate should use. It is possible that this will have to be explained a number of times as it takes time for the full implications of the different strategic choices to really be absorbed.

9.9   Useful books and/or websites

Badke, W. (2000) *Research Strategies*, available
    http://www.acts.twu.ca/lbr/textbook.htm [27 Jan 2004].
Bleicher, J. (1988) Contemporary hermeneutics: Hermeneutics as method, philosophy and critique, London and Boston: Routledge & Kegan Paul.

Blumer, H. (1969) *Symbolic interactionism: Perspective and method*, Englewood Cliffs, NJ: Prentice Hall.

Branham, C. (1997) *A students Guide to Research on the WWW*, St Louis University, available: http://www.slu.edu/departments/english/research/ [27 Jan 2004].

Dyer, W.G. Jr. and Wilkins, A.L. (1991) 'Better Stories, Not Better Constructs, to Generate Better Theory: A Rejoinder to Eisenhardt', *Academy of Management Review* (16:3), pp. 613–619.

Glaser, B. G. and Strauss, A L. (1968) *Discovery of Grounded Theory: Strategies for Qualitative Research*, New York: Aldine de Gruyter.

Habermas, J. (1968) *The Idea of the Theory of Knowledge as Social Theory*, available: http://www.marxists.org/reference/subject/philosophy/works/ge/habermas.htm [09 Aug 2011].

Miles, M.B. and Huberman, A.M. (1994) *Qualitative Data Analysis: A Sourcebook of New Methods*, Newbury Park, CA: Sage Publications.

Morey, N.C. and Luthans, F. 'An Emic Perspective and Ethnoscience Methods for Organisational Research', *Academy of Management Review* (9:1), January, pp. 27–36.

Ragin, C.C. (1987) *The Comparative method: Moving beyond qualitative and quantitative strategies*, Berkeley and London: University of California Press.

Rubin, H. and Rubin, I. (1995) *Qualitative interviewing: the art of hearing data*, San Diego: Sage Publications.

Silverman, D. (1993) *Interpreting qualitative data*, London: Sage Publications.

Strauss, A. (1987) *Qualitative analysis for social scientists*. Cambridge: Cambridge University Press.

Strauss, A. and Corbin, J. (1990) *Basics of Qualitative Research: Grounded Theory Procedures and Techniques*. Newbury Park, CA: Sage Publications.

http://www.groundedtheory.com/ [09 Aug 2011].

Resource papers in action research – grounded theory, available: http://www.scu.edu.au/schools/gcm/ar/arp/grounded.html [09 Aug 2011].

Chapter 10

Developing a research design

Every research tool or procedure is inextricably embedded in commitments to particular versions of the world and to knowing that world. To use an attitude scale, to take the role of a participant observer, to select a random sample ... is to be involved in conceptions of the world which allow these instruments to be used for the purposes conceived. No technique or method of investigation is self-validating ... they operate only within a given set of assumptions about the nature of society, the nature of human beings, the relationship between the two and how they may be known.

Hughes J, (1990) *The Philosophy of Science*, London: Longman.

10.1 The research design

Having decided on the high-level research strategy there is then the issue of the detailed research design[48] that the student will use. A research design involves deciding what data is required, how the data will be compiled and what type of analysis will be performed on the data. It is important that the supervisor provide the student with guidance on this issue.

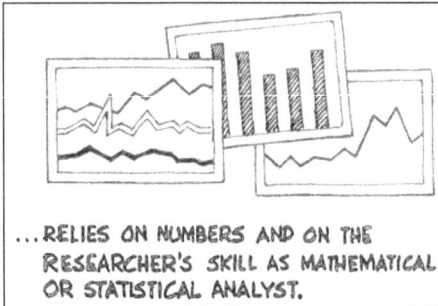

...RELIES ON NUMBERS AND ON THE RESEARCHER'S SKILL AS MATHEMATICAL OR STATISTICAL ANALYST.

There are a large number of research designs that may be used by the research student and the supervisor needs to be aware of these alternatives and the implications of using any one of them[49]. A research tactic may be defined as an evidence collection and analysis approach, which can be used for the purposes of understanding a phenomenon and thus contributing to the body of knowledge. A short list of the better-known research approaches or designs is supplied in alphabetical order below.

- Action research
- Case studies
- Ethnography
- Field experiments
- Focus groups
- Forecasting
- Futures research
- In-depth surveys
- Laboratory experiments
- Large-scale surveys
- Participant–observer

---

[48] The term research design is sometimes interchangeable with the term research tactics or even research methods. However research design is increasingly used and conveys a wider sense than the other words.

[49] The fact that research, or perhaps more correctly science, allows a wide range of methodological approaches is sometimes a problem for students who are more comfortable with a definite formula for research success. Unfortunately for novices this is not the case and researchers have to compile their own individual understanding of what constitutes science or sound research.

- Scenario discussions

It is not suggested that this taxonomy is exhaustive, or that all of these approaches are necessarily suitable for all types of researchers. However, it is a useful list for the purposes of providing a supervisor a basis from which to discuss alternative approaches with a research student.

This list may be considered as a set of well-known and accepted research tactics or tools that are available to the aspirant researcher. It is therefore important for the researcher to be familiar with the characteristics of these tools.

10.2 Action research

Action research (AR) requires a researcher to initiate an intervention in an already established organisation and to manage the intervention towards a pre-agreed objective with the help of individuals who are employed by the organisation concerned. It is a complex approach to research which requires the researcher to have a considerable standing and a degree of authority in the organisation in which the research will be conducted and should not be undertaken lightly. AR requires detailed planning in depth and it is usual for the research to be conducted in one organisation and involving one project only.

AR is one of the fastest growing research tactics or methodologies. It is especially popular with part-time students who are able to solicit the help of their organisations in conducting the research[50]. Action research was developed during the 1960s and has proved particularly useful in the area of managing change. French and Bell (1978) defined AR as:

The process of systematically collecting research data about an ongoing system relative to some objective, goal or need of that system; feeding these data back into the system; taking action by altering selected variables within the system based both on the data and on hypotheses; and evaluating the results of the actions by collecting more data.

---

[50] It is not feasible to conduct action research unless the research candidate has really good access to the organisation. This is usually only available when the student is part-time and is actually working for the organisation concerned.

As a process, action research is dependent upon an external view of the circumstances in which the researcher will work and it essentially involves the following five steps:

1. Taking a picture of the organisational situation,
2. Formulating a hypothesis based on the picture,
3. The manipulation of variables in the control of the researcher,
4. Taking and evaluating a second static picture of the situation,
5. Commenting on what has been achieved and demonstrating that learning has taken place and that this learning may be regarded as having been sufficiently broad and deep to be regarded as having added something of value to the body of knowledge.

The action researcher is involved in an organisational situation where there is not only an expectation that a 'contribution to knowledge' should be made, but also to directly produce usable knowledge that 'can be applied and validated in action' (Gummesson, 1991) within the organisation. In addition Gummesson points out that there is an expectation that the researcher should also develop a sound knowledge of the theoretical categories being used so that they are transcended and transformed into better theory. Figure 10.1 shows the five conceptual stages of AR.

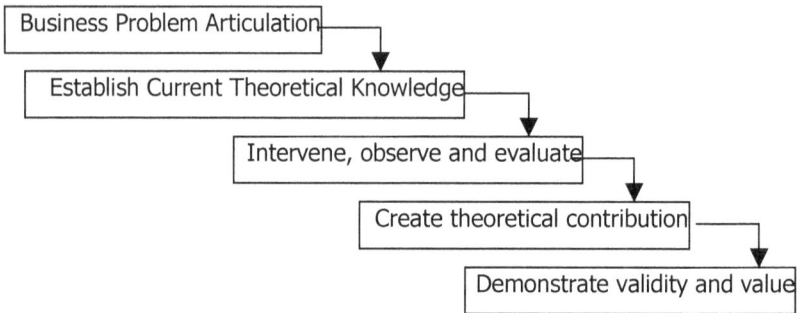

Figure 10.1: The 5 high-level conceptual stages of AR

The above illustrates that action research requires the researcher to have good quality access to data. AR constitutes a potentially demanding process for the collection of data given the location of the researcher within a 'live' situation. The co-operation of staff or company personnel involved is crucial to the success of this research tactic. It is usually thought that the main skill of the AR researcher is to be able to combine the role of a consultant and that of an academic researcher.

Research candidates are well advised not to try to undertake an action research based degree unless they have a sound connection at a high level within the proposed organisation. Without this type of support an AR project is unlikely to succeed.

Concerns are often expressed about the ability of the researcher to be objective about the processes involved and the outcomes achieved during the action research. A way of attempting to strengthen the potential objective is to have all the persons involved in the intervention report on its outcomes.

10.3 Case studies

The case study[51] is a sophisticated research tactic for establishing valid and reliable evidence for the research process as well as presenting findings that result from the research. The case study is a research tactic for the social scientist in the same way as experiments are a research strategy for the natural scientist (Kasanen and Suomi, 1987; Smith, 1990; Jocher, 1928/29). Yin (1989) states that:

> *A case study from a research strategy point of view[52] may be defined as an empirical inquiry that investigates a contemporary phenomenon within its real life context, when the boundaries between phenomenon and the context are not clearly evident, and in which multiple sources of evidence are used. It is particularly valuable in answering **who, why** and **how** questions in management research.*

According to Bell (1993) the case study methodology has also been used as an umbrella term for a family of research methods having in common the decision to focus on an enquiry around a specific instance or event. The philosophy behind the case study is that sometimes only by looking

---

[51] The term case study is used in business and management studies in at least two different ways. It sometimes argued that the term case history would be more descriptive of its function.

[52] Clearly we disagree with Yin's use of the word strategy and prefer the use of the word tactic or design. The word strategy is better reserved for a higher level of decision related to the approach to the research. In the instance of the case study research tactic this approach may be used either positivistically or interpretivistically.

carefully at a practical, real-life instance, can a full picture be obtained of the actual interaction of approaches that can be carried out within a positivistic or an interpretivist research programme.

The case study allows the investigator to concentrate on specific instances in an attempt to identify detailed interactive processes which may be crucial, but which are not transparent to the large-scale survey. Thus it is the aim of the case study to provide a multi-dimensional picture of the situation. It can illustrate relationships; corporate political issues and patterns of influence in particular contexts. Case studies are an important approach and some Masters and much doctoral research work is conducted using this method.

Because of its flexible nature a case study may be an almost entirely positivist or almost entirely interpretivist study or anything between these two extremes, including mixed methods. As the case study is an umbrella term that includes a wide range of evidence capture and analysis procedures, all these different orientations and approaches can fall within its domain.

The following is a checklist of ten characteristics of a case study. A high quality research case should demonstrate many of these characteristics:

1. A case study is a story;
2. A case study draws on multiple sources of evidence;
3. A case study's evidence needs to be based on triangulation of these sources of evidence;
4. A case study seeks to provide meaning in context;
5. A case study shows both an in-depth understanding of the central issue(s) being explored and a broad understanding of related issues and context;
6. A case study has a clear-cut focus on either an organisation, a situation or a context;
7. A case study must be reasonably bounded. It should not stretch over too wide a canvas, either temporal or spatial. However the boundaries of a case study are often broader than other possible research designs/methods.
8. A case study should not require the researcher to become too immersed in the object of the research;
9. A case study may draw on either quantitative or qualitative tools or both for evidence collection and/or analysis but it will not be exclusively quantitative;

10. A case study needs to have a thoroughly articulated protocol.

Supervisors are often asked by their students, How many cases studies should be completed for a piece of research? There is no easy answer to this question, other than it depends on the context in which the research is being conducted. Occasionally one case study may be all that is required. More frequently a small number of case studies is preferred. The small number could be 3 or 4. What can be said with some degree of confidence is that a large number of case studies would not be practical.

10.4 Ethnography

Borrowed from social anthropologists, ethnographic research requires the researcher to become part of the 'tribe' and to fully participate in its society. Ethnographers are said to have acquired knowledge through a lived experience with the group which is being studied. Rosenthal and Rosnow (1991) offer a more formal definition when they say, 'Ethnography is that type of field observation in which a society's culture is studied'. It is usually necessary for the researcher to become involved with the group that is being studied for a substantial period of months or even years. Ethnographic research is very difficult to perform well as the researcher needs to really understand the group. Often researchers in social anthropology lived with their group until they had mastered their language. Famous social anthropologists include Bronisław Malinowski and Margaret Mead. However it appears that in the case of these two researchers the members of the group were lying to them about habits and customs. These examples are interesting in that they clearly demonstrate the importance of triangulation.

In business and management studies it is unusual to find informants lying to the researcher. One of the reasons for this is that the researcher will be triangulating in terms of data and informants and lies will become apparent. But it is also the case that informants will have their own point of view which will result in their putting their own personal spin on the data they supply.

Although this approach has some application in business and management studies it is not used extensively as students seldom get close enough to the research subjects for their work to be considered ethnographic. Also, especially at doctoral level business and management researchers will usually not have the time required for such a protracted study.

Ethnographic research is essentially interpretivist in nature. It is clearly not replicable in the sense that this is understood in quantitative studies, but rather it is comparable whereby similar studies benefit each other, and draw on each other's methods and findings. Any attempt to use ethnographic research as though it is capable of producing positivistic type results would be a gross misunderstanding of its role in business and management research. Ethnography is sometimes said to focus on 'telling' (narrative) rather than 'representative' examples. As a form of longitudinal research it does not normally have much relevance in the research degree arena in business and management studies.

In recent years the term ethnography has splintered and now there is auto-ethnography, critical ethnography, interpretive ethnography, post-colonial ethnography, ethno-drama, and cyber ethnography to mention some of these approaches. By and large these are generally perceived as problematic research methods and should probably be avoided in business and management studies.

A case study and ethnography may have much in common. The difference between the two methods is that an ethnographic study requires the researcher to be intimately familiar with the situation being researched. It has been said that the researcher needs to have a lived experience of the situation before the term ethnography may be used[53]. An ethnography is also longitudinal in the sense that it may take quite some time for the researcher to acquire the appropriate level of familiarity.

10.5 Field experiments

Field experiments are more common and regarded as far more authentic than laboratory experiments in business and management research. The famous Hawthorne studies (Parsons, 1992) that signalled the beginning of formal empirical research in this area were field experiments that provided insight into issues concerning worker productivity.

However there are definite limits to the type of question that can be addressed using field studies. For example, it is not usually possible to

---

[53] Terms like "intimately familiar" and "lived experience" present difficulties to academic researchers as they are indefinable. Who can say how much contact and what sort of contact is required before it is possible to say that the researcher is "intimately familiar" or has had a "lived experience"?

persuade an organisation to deploy substantial resources such as a new computer system for a field experiment so that researchers may study its impact on efficiency or effectiveness. Researchers may have to wait for an auspicious occasion to arise in order to make such studies possible. Similarly, it is seldom the case that an organisation will change its marketing policy in order to understand how this policy change will affect the market. However, a field experiment probably could be conducted around a change of policy or a new investment, and the student would have to obtain the agreement of the organisation to participate in this event as an observer. Field experiments are less positivistic as they clearly do not present the same opportunity for control and replication as the laboratory experiment. Therefore field experiments are approached from a less traditional scientific point of view. The results of a field experiment will often be interpreted in a much more qualitative way.

An action research and a field study can have much in common. The main difference between these two methods is that for a piece of research to be regarded as action research the researcher needs to be responsible for the initiation of the project and to be in charge of its success. In the case of a field study the researcher could be entirely passive and simply observe what is happening. Between these two positions there is the approach which is referred to as participant-observer and which is described later on in this chapter.

10.6 Focus groups

FOCUS GROUPS... THIS IS A RELATIVELY EASY WAY FOR A RESEARCHER TO ACCUMULATE SOME EVIDENCE FROM A NUMBER OF EXPERTS...

This is a research approach for collecting evidence from a highly specialised group of individuals. The evidence collected during a focus group will be largely opinion based as opposed to fact based. It is usually considered necessary to have a group of more than four individuals to constitute a focus group that will debate an issue of interest to the researcher. This is a relatively quick and sometimes easy way for a researcher to accumulate some evidence from a number of experts. But there are problems in finding suitable people to attend the focus group. The management of the event is challenging and an academic researcher will usually need help from an experienced assistant if the quality of the evidence for the focus group is to be assured.

Again, the way in which this evidence is processed is similar to that described below under the heading of in-depth surveys, and the positivistic and interpretivist implications are similar. Focus groups are certainly a useful way of obtaining evidence from experts in an intense or concentrated way (Remenyi 2011).

10.7 Forecasting

Forecasting research tends to be associated with mathematical and statistical techniques of regression and time series analysis (Collopy and Armstrong, 1992; Sutrick, 1993). This type of research may also be regarded as falling under the heading of mathematical simulation. These techniques allow projections to be made on the basis of past or historic evidence. This is usually a highly quantitative approach in which mathematical models are fitted to empirical data or evidence points. This research attempts to establish relationships between different sets of historical evidence and to understand why these relationships exist.

The techniques used in forecasting are essentially positivistic in nature. However, the results of forecasting research can be interpreted in a more qualitative way and thus be integrated into a greater paradigm than simply a mathematical view of the situation.

10.8 Futures research

Although not as mathematical or technical as, but at the same time similar in intent to forecasting research, futures research also provides a way of considering and developing predictions. Like forecasting, futures research has a forward orientation and thus looks ahead, rather than backwards, using techniques such as scenario projections and Delphi studies (McCarthy, 1992; Maital, 1993; Goldfisher, 1992–93). The work involves the summation of opinions of experts as well as attempting to draw divergent expert opinions towards a group consensus. The experts in a Delphi study are normally physically separated and are unknown to one another. The purpose of a Delphi study is to produce a consensus and thus relatively narrow spread of opinions.

10.9 In-depth surveys (interviewing)

This type of survey generally attempts to obtain detailed in-depth evidence from a relatively small number of informants through a series of interviews. In this case a questionnaire is generally not used, but rather the informant is allowed to speak freely on the subject of interest to the researcher.

Sometimes the researcher will have a prepared list of issues and even prompts to use during the interview. Such a list is usually referred to as an interview schedule. Sometimes the researcher will take copious notes during the interview, while on other occasions the interview will be recorded. After the interview it is usual for the researcher to compile a transcript of the responses or discussion that has taken place. At the end of an in-depth survey the researcher will have a series of transcripts and the task is then to analyse these and to produce appropriate findings (Remenyi 2011).

The in-depth survey may be used either in a positivistic or in a qualitative mode. As a positivistic tool the transcript would be subjected to a technique such as content analysis whereby the number of occasions on which an issue is mentioned is counted. These counts are then used to demonstrate the importance of the issue. Correspondance analysis takes similar data to content analysis but provides a much more sophisticated result providing perceptual maps which offer an opportunity for much more analysis and interpretation.

In the hands of an interpretivist, the occurrences of issue or concepts would not be counted, but rather the researcher would postulate the importance of the issues from a more qualitative stance. This type of interpretation would often be referred to as hermeneutics[54]. Hermeneutics provides an approach and a theory of understanding text. It is used extensively in literature and in other studies which rely heavily on texts such as bible studies[55].

10.10 Laboratory experiments

Borrowed from the physical and life sciences laboratory, experiments are sometimes used in business and management research. However,

---

[54] http://plato.stanford.edu/search/searcher.py?query=hermeneutics
[55] http://academicearth.org/lectures/hermeneutic-circle

they are not much used in practice, except in limited or specific circum-stances, because many of the issues that are of most interest to re-searchers cannot easily or convincingly be studied in laboratory settings. Organisations and even individual managers will not usually collaborate in such experiments. Sometimes students are used as surrogates for managers and executives in laboratory settings, but this is not often considered convincing.

Laboratory experiments are nonetheless sometimes employed to an-swer specific questions such as how certain decisions are made concern-ing various aspects of managerial choice. This approach is sometimes also used to explore an idea before embarking on a major survey or case study project. In business and management research for Masters and PhD students, laboratory experiments are used far more frequently in the USA than in other parts of the world (Tung and Heminger, 1993).

10.11 Large-scale surveys

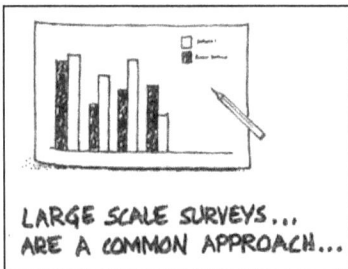

LARGE SCALE SURVEYS...
ARE A COMMON APPROACH...

Surveys are a popular approach to re-search. The term survey is used to refer to both in-depth interviews and data col-lection through large-scale questionnaire use. Surveys, which for the purpose of this chapter are concerned with the ad-ministration of questionnaires, offer an opportunity to collect large quantities of data or evidence (Oppenheim, 1966) in a quick and convenient manner. Questionnaires are often used to collect evidence concerning manage-ment opinions (Remenyi 2011).

Questionnaires allow evidence to be gathered concerning *how much* or *how long* or *when,* but are of less value when the researcher is asking about *how* or *why.* As a general rule the nature of the evidence that may be collected by means of a questionnaire is regarded as relatively super-ficial, especially in comparison to the evidence that it is possible to col-lect from other techniques such as case studies or personal interviews. Surveys are thus more often used as the sole or primary source of evi-dence at the Masters level than at the PhD level[56]. However, some PhD

---

[56] Most research dissertations at both the Masters and PhD levels would require both primary and secondary sources of evidence.

dissertations might include a survey as an attempt to corroborate a theoretical conjecture.

The logic of a traditional survey is strictly positivistic. The evidence is frequently treated as though it were the result of measurements of a machine used in an entirely physical or life science environment. Statistical techniques used for ordinal numbers are increasingly applied with no recognition of the problems of the subjectivity of the opinions[57] (Remenyi *et al* 2011). Although large-scale questionnaire based surveys are still extensively used there is an increasing feeling that they are not suitable for the collection of evidence about top or senior management issues.

10.12 Participant–observer approach

Using the participant–observer tactic the researcher joins a team of individuals who are part of the phenomenon or situation being studied. In some cases there may be only one other person directly involved. The researcher takes part in the phenomenon or project in the same way as the other participant/s, but at the same time focuses on observing the way in which the group operates and the results of their work. This is different to action research in that the participant-observer does not have responsibility for the outcomes of the project taking place. This research technique is essentially qualitative in nature, although some quantitative data may also be involved.

10.13 Scenario research

Similar to game or role playing and focus groups, this research tactic involves collecting evidence from a group of suitably qualified experts who are asked to discuss the implications of a particular hypothetical situation occurring. The group may be asked to comment on the result of a new competitive climate developing in a particular industry, or to consider the results of the deregulation of the telecommunications industry. Using this technique the researcher hopes to elicit useful comments about the opinions of the experts as well as observing how these opinions evolve during their deliberations. This evidence too is collected and processed in much the same way as in in-depth surveys and again the positivistic and interpretivist implications are similar.

---

[57] This is not a problem with the statistics. The issue is the amount of faith the researcher places in the data.

10.14 A list of some research designs

This is not a definitive list of research tactics or designs. Not only are there more options which could be considered, new options are being created all the time. New options arise because a researcher or a group of researchers decide to change some aspect of an established design and when it works they give the new approach a new name. In addition researchers have combined quantitative and qualitative approaches in their design and this has acquired its own nomenclature of mixed methods. Those who wish to embark on a mixed methods design need to look carefully at the pros and cons of this approach as it is not as easy to perform quality mixed methods research as it may sound (Clarke and Creswell 2008).

In the world of business and management studies research there is no compulsion to follow precisely any one prescription on how to design a research project.

10.15 Summary

Research degree candidates often rush to make decisions related to research design. This is usually a mistake as it is important to understand how these tactics and designs will enable different types of investigation and how they can be appropriately matched to different research questions. This is not a trivial matter and most research degree candidates will need help from their supervisor/s in this respect.

In selecting a research design it is important for the supervisor to bear in mind that there are always compromises whereby the rigour of science has to be traded off against the pragmatics of the situation. There always has to be give and take between what might be an ideal research project and what a research degree candidate can actually achieve. Good research will invariably follow the principle of parsimony, also known as Occam's Razor, which states that the simplest solution or explanation is often the best.

10.16 Useful books and/or websites

Eisenhardt, K.M. (1989) 'Building theories from case study research', *Academy of Management Review* (14:4), pp. 532–550.

Rapoport, R.N. (1970) 'Three Dilemmas in Action Research', *Human Relations*, (23:4), pp. 499–513.

Robinson, V.M.J. (1993) 'Current controversies in action research', *Public Administration Quarterly* (17:3), pp. 263–290.

Susman, G.I. (1983) 'Action Research: A Sociotechnical systems perspective', in Morgan, G. (ed.) *Beyond method: Strategies for social science research*, London: Sage Publications.

Susman, G.I. and Evered, R.D. (1978) 'An assessment of the scientific merits of action research', *Administrative Science Quarterly*, (23), pp. 582–603.

Trist, E. (1976) 'Engaging with large-scale systems', in Clark, A. (ed.) *Experimenting with Organisational Life: The Action Research Approach*, New York: Plenum pp. 43–75.

Whyte, W.F. (ed.) (1991) *Participatory Action Research*, New York: Sage Publications.

Chapter 11

The research protocol

It is often said that research cannot be taught.
Ernst Mach, Erkenntnis und Irrtum, Neudruck, *Wissenschaftliche Buchgesellschaft*, Damstadt, p200, 1980, cited by Paul Feyerabend (1993) in *Against Method*, 3rd Edition, Verso London, p 10.

The researches of many commentators have already thrown much darkness on this subject, and it is probable that, if they continue, we shall soon know nothing about it at all.
Mark Twain attributed to, in Battle of Symbols John Fraim p. 106, 2002

11.1 Defining the research protocol

The word protocol is now being used more frequently in academic research than before. It can apply to the setting up of a relatively high level plan such as that described below and it can be used to describe the document or set of documents resulting in ethics approval being granted for the research to proceed. An example of an outline for a combined research proposal and protocol is provided in Appendix 2.

A research protocol is an empirical research issue. It is a plan of what has to be done. As a plan it may sometimes be useful to prepare a protocol of a theoretical research project.

Once the research question has been established and the research strategy and the research design have been settled the research project can really get going. To begin this process it is useful for a research protocol to be developed by the research student and the supervisor should take an active interest by helping in its development. A useful definition of a research protocol is:

> *A document which describes a wide range of aspects of the intended research and which demonstrates that the researcher has thought about all the key issues pertaining to the subject to be researched as well as the processes of the research project and the way the findings of the research will be presented.*

In general a research protocol is a detailed plan of a scientific or medical experiment, treatment, or procedure. In the context of academic research a protocol is an important instrument for ensuring the focus and the subsequent reliability and accessibility of research.

In fact a research protocol has a number of functions, one of the most important being that it is used to demonstrate that the researcher is aware of the magnitude of the task ahead as well as to see if he or she is capable of envisioning the detail of the work required. The protocol can also later be used as evidence that the research was conducted systematically.

At another level the research protocol is a detailed statement or checklist of what the research is trying to achieve, i.e. the focus of the research, as well as a plan that indicates how these research objectives will be met. By understanding the researcher's plan it is possible to see if the product of his or her work is likely to be of sufficient quality to be valid and reliable.

Continuing reference to the protocol needs to be a part of the *modus operandi* of the research degree candidate. A protocol could have the following sections:

- Overview of the research project
- Field procedures
- Evidence collection processes
- Analytical procedures
- Presenting the findings
- Time-based plan and costs
- Ethics

11.2 An overview of the research project

The overview will include a detailed statement of the objectives of the research. In addition it will provide background information to help a reviewer understand the importance of the problem that the researcher is attempting to solve. Thus an important part of the protocol is a list of stakeholders and a statement of why the research is important to them.

The protocol needs to explain how the researcher's ideas relate to existing knowledge that has been generated by others in the field and perhaps by the researcher him or herself. For a large-scale research project, preliminary data, manuscripts, and other material that are relevant to the research might be compiled as a separate appendix to the main document of the protocol.

11.3 Field procedures

Defining field procedures will be necessary for all empirical research projects. The exact form of this section of the protocol will depend upon whether the research is primarily quantitative or qualitative. However the purpose of this section is to think through exactly how evidence will be collected.

The researcher has to work in the real world, and thus cope with real world events during the evidence collection plan. It is seldom easy to collect suitable evidence for research. Numerous problems can occur during this phase of the project and the researcher should consider what might happen and how he or she will cope with these challenges. Some examples of problems include organisations not being prepared to give time to researchers or just being suspicious of them and thus not allowing them access to their staff. When access has been obtained respondents sometimes drop out during the course of the study, corporate documents may not be available etc.

Field procedures need to detail a number of issues including: -

1. Which organisations will be accessed;
2. Definition of who should be interviewed by position and by name;
3. How to access the right people; are there 'gatekeepers' to approach;
4. How to ensure that adequate resources are available especially time – time of informants and time of the researcher;
5. Ensuring the appropriate equipment is available in order to capture the evidence such as lap top computers, cameras, recorders etc.;
6. Developing a procedure for obtaining assistance from informants such as snowballing[58] or assistance from other researchers;
7. A schedule of the required evidence collection activities;
8. Ethical issues which may arise in the evidence collection;
9. Providing for contingencies.

11.4 Evidence collection process

In a research protocol dealing with case study research or research using in-depth interviews it is important to create a set of questions to support the actual evidence collection process[59]. There are two characteristics, which distinguish such a set of questions from those used in a survey.

Firstly, the protocol questions are actually set for the investigator and not for the respondent. The questions are in reality reminders or prompts to the investigator concerning the information which has to be collected.

---

[58] Snowballing is a sampling technique whereby one informant recommends the researcher to another appropriate informant.
[59] These suggested guidelines would actually apply to any form of qualitative evidence gathering approach. Thus it would also be relevant to aspects of action research.

Secondly each question should be accompanied by a list of probable sources of evidence, which cover interviewees' comments, documents, artefacts and observations.

There are at least six possible sources of evidence used in these types of research studies:

1. Direct observations
2. Interviews
3. Documents
4. Archived records
5. Participant-observation
6. Physical artefacts

When collecting evidence a researcher needs to continually think about the audience for which the research is intended. The researcher should not lose sight of the design of the final report. Thus it is helpful even during the evidence collection phase of the research to have an outline of the research report and this should be included in the protocol. This protocol should also indicate to what extent documentary evidence would be used in the final report.

Academic research produces large amounts of documentation. These papers need to be kept for a period of time. It is suggested that all working papers and notes be retained for at least two years after the degree is awarded. Some researchers keep their documentation even longer. In addition these documents may be used to produce an annotated bibliography. These annotations might be helpful to subsequent readers and other research students in suggesting the direction for further research.

The final step in preparing a framework for the evidence or data collection is the conducting of a pilot study, which is sometimes referred to as a field test. This should not be confused with a pre-test which is similar but less formal and normally only involves a few people who are prepared to offer constructive criticism to the student. The pilot study helps the researcher understand if the approach being proposed will be effective and it will also help him or her develop more relevant lines of questions. In some incidences the pilot study may be so important that more resources are utilised at this phase than in the actual collection of the data itself. Thus a pilot study can assume the role of a laboratory for the researcher. At the outset the scope of the pilot can be much broader than the final study. It may be a testing ground for both substantive and methodological issues.

The pilot report should be written so as to highlight the lessons learnt about the research design and the field procedures. In some incidences more than one pilot may be performed.

The location and the informants for a pilot study or studies are often selected primarily or even solely on the grounds of convenience, access and geographic proximity. Therefore the results of the pilot study should not be regarded as an indication of the final outcome of the research.

If a quantitative research approach were to be taken then the evidence collection section of the research protocol would address issues such as the measuring instrument used as well as the sample type and size employed. An important aspect of this is to demonstrate in the protocol why the measuring instrument should be considered capable of producing evidence that could be regarded as valid and reliable. Just creating a list of questions does not per se create a valid and reliable measuring instrument. If this cannot be done there is little use in continuing the research.

All measuring instruments need to be tested via a pilot study.

11.5 Analytical procedures

Having collected an adequate amount of evidence of an appropriate quality the next step in the research project is to either interpret or to analyse the evidence.

A qualitative approach to evidence collection does not presuppose an interpretive approach to the rest of the research. Evidence collected qualitatively may be reduced to numerical values and then analysed using quantitative techniques. A typical example of this is the use of content analysis, which is a quantitative technique. On the other hand a purely qualitative approach such as that used in hermeneutics may also be employed.

Thus if the researcher has employed a qualitative approach the issues to be addressed in the research protocol are to do with:

1. How evidence will be transcribed;
2. How evidence will be coded;
3. How evidence will be processed;
4. Will software be used and if so which products?
5. Will any expert help be required with any of these activities?
6. Are there any ethical issues involved with any of these activities?
7. How the results of the analysis will be presented;
8. How the evidence will be interpreted.

These activities represent a major part of any research project and will consume a material part of the time required for the research degree. Many degree candidates will need help with these procedures and the supervisor needs to ensure that the student has the necessary skills to cope with this part of his or her research.

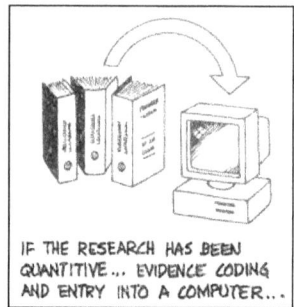

IF THE RESEARCH HAS BEEN QUANTITIVE ... EVIDENCE CODING AND ENTRY INTO A COMPUTER... .

If the research has been quantitative then the issues that need to be addressed in the research protocol are:

1. Evidence coding and entry into a computer;
2. What analytical procedures will be used?
3. What software will be used and what skills are required;
4. Will any expert help be required with any of these activities?
5. Are there any ethical issues involved with any of these activities?
6. How the results of the analysis will be presented;
7. How the evidence will be interpreted;

If a quantitative research approach has been taken then the researcher will possibly be familiar with the work required for evidence coding and entry. Many quantitative researchers will also be familiar with basic statistical techniques to analyse quantitative evidence. However there are a large number of statistical techniques available and the researcher may well need help from the supervisor to find the most appropriate approach for his or her data.

It is important for the supervisor to advise the researcher not to overburden the research with too many quantitative techniques, which can dramatically increase the work required, and provide little extra insight to the research findings.

11.6 Presenting the findings

Research degree findings need to be presented to the academic community and especially to the stakeholders of the research. There are several reasons for this of which the need for confirmation of the value of the research is critical. Remember that, in the words of Wittgenstein (1969):

Knowledge is in the end based on acknowledgment.

In this short expression Wittgenstein captured completely the nature of the academic degree awarding process. To obtain the degree the student's work has to be acknowledged by the supervisor, peers and other members of the academic community but especially by the examiners.

The researcher and the supervisor need to carefully consider how the research findings will be made public so that they may be reviewed and thus be adequately acknowledged. This is a key issue because if the findings are not well presented they could be ignored or even worse rejected. Key issues to consider during the research process are:

1. When to present the findings to the department, school or faculty;
2. Will working or occasional papers be produced along the way and to whom will they be distributed;
3. How can the work be prepared for conference papers and for formal publication opportunities?

When the research is completed the issues are:

1. How the research will be written up;
2. How the dissertation will be laid out;
3. To whom the dissertation will be circulated.

The supervisor needs to make a major contribution in helping the research student think through all these issues.

11.7 A time based plan and costs

As well as identifying key components of the research the protocol may also result in a time based plan showing when the key activities of the research should begin and end. A bar chart or a network plan could be produced. In addition to this the research protocol may also indicate what type of expense is likely to be incurred so that the cost of the research can be highlighted. The supervisor will need to help the student with estimates of all of these issues.

11.8 Ethics

Academe is a field of activity in which there are many ethical concerns. These relate to what is taught, how it is taught, what facilities are offered to students, how academics view their responsibility to students and to other faculty members. There are questions related to matters such as objective and timely feedback to students and more personal matters such as bullying and favouritism, to mention only a few issues. It is said that the Internet has facilitated an increased level of plagiarism which is a major ethical concern. This has resulted in the production of various software packages to detect infringements of this type in academic work. There also appears to be a thriving industry built around the demand from students to have essays, projects and even whole dissertations written for them by ghost writers.

This section of this book is confined to considering issues related to ethics concerning academic research and thus it describes how researchers can handle their application for the approval of an Ethics Protocol.

Conducting academic research to the highest ethical standards is essential for both the researcher personally and the university. If the highest standards are not maintained then the reputation of the researcher and the university could be compromised.

From a high level perspective, ethical concerns in academic research include but are not limited to:-

- The nature of the research question;
- The means by which the research question will be answered;
- The safety and wellbeing of the researcher and all those with whom he or she comes into contact including informants;
- The necessity for the researcher to be open and honest with all those involved with the research.

Research degrees require permission from a Research Ethics Committee before they can formally commence. Some universities are strict and formally state that no retrospective or back dating of ethics permission will be granted while other universities recognise that the starting point of a research project can be open to interpretation.

Research Ethics Committees operate by requiring academic researchers to submit an application for the approval of an Ethics Protocol. In order to consider if a proposed research project will comply with the ethics standards required by the university, the researcher will normally have to complete this detailed form which will explain, inter alia, the nature of the research and how it will be conducted. This form will be accompanied by a Participant's Information Document which will be offered to any informants who may be invited to supply data to the research. An example of such a document is provided in Appendix 5. In addition a copy of any proposed measuring instrument such as a questionnaire or an interview schedule will be required by the Committee. Finally a copy of any correspondence which the researcher proposes to undertake with the informants together with a draft Letter of Informed Consent will be required. An example is shown in Appendix 6. Research Ethics Committees can ask for further information and may also require changes to the documents originally presented so that they comply with the required standard. When the Research Ethics Committee is fully satisfied a letter of approval will be given to the researcher. This letter with copies of the various documents described above is referred to as the Ethics Protocol.

11.9 Bureaucratic interference

Some research degree candidates and their supervisors sometimes see issues like Research Protocols and Ethics Protocols as bureaucratic interference. It is true that they take time and that an application for an Ethics Protocol may be returned by the ethics committee a couple of times before it is finally approved[60]. However these exercises are worthwhile because they make the supervisor and his or her researcher think carefully about the task they have to perform if the researcher is to successfully complete the research degree. Thinking carefully about what is required is one of the best ways of avoiding unpleasant surprises.

---

[60] Sometimes an ethics committee will simply refuse to give its approval and the suggested research project will have to be dropped.

11.10 Useful books and/or websites

Methodological Challenges to Conducting Management Research, available:
  http://www.mdrc.research.med.va.gov/mgt_research/challenges.htm [10 Aug 2011].
Business Etiquette Business Culture – links, available:
  http://www.csulb.edu/library/subj/business/etiquette.html [10 Aug 2011].

Chapter 12

The first steps

Anyone of common mental and physical health can practice scientific research.... Anyone can try by patient experiment what happens if this or that substance be mixed this way or that proportion with some other under this or that condition. Anyone can vary the experiment in any number of ways. He that hits in this fashion on something novel and of use will have fame.... The fame will be the product of luck and industry. It will not be the product of special talent.

Belloc H. (1931) Essays of a Catholic Layman in England, London: Sheed & Ward

The real trouble with this world of ours is not that it is an unreasonable world, nor even that it is a reasonable one. The commonest kind of trouble is that it is nearly reasonable, but not quite. Life is not an illogicality; yet it is a trap for logicians. It looks just a little more mathematical and regular than it is; its exactitude is obvious, but its inexactitude is hidden; its wildness lies in wait.

Chesterton, G.K, (1990) *Orthodoxy – The romance of faith*, New York: Doubleday Dell Publishing Group.

12.1 The first steps

There are many would-be research degree students who would like to have a Masters or a Doctorate and who will register for a degree. However not all of them will complete. In fact some would-be research degree students will register and will never get properly started at all with their degree. Others will work on their degree for a year or two and then drop out. The completion rate at many universities is poor (especially for part-time students, and it is not that good for full-time students either) and this is of a major concern both to the university and the educational authorities, as it constitutes a huge waste of resources.

Fortunately the supervisor can play a major role in increasing the completion rate of research degrees.

In practice students often need help in just getting started with their research and it can be the responsibility of the supervisor to see that the work begins. The reason why the term 'it can be' is used here is because universities differ quite a lot with regards to when the would-be student will become the responsibility of a supervisor. Some universities will match a would-be student with a supervisor almost immediately while others will expect the student to do some totally independent work and to have made some progress towards his or her research proposal before a supervisor is nominated. Universities that delay the formal appointment of a supervisor may have an interim supervisor or have a mentor to look after the student initially. This is a useful compromise as research degree candidates do need some hand holding in the early months of the research.

12.2 Induction programme

In the first days of working towards a research degree it is useful if the student is put through some sort of induction[61] programme where he or she is introduced to the institution and the main individuals that will play a role in helping the researcher. It is also helpful if the researcher is introduced to some of the university rules and procedures. This is all part of the necessary confidence building required before an individual will become a fully-fledged researcher.

---

[61] The induction to the university or business school is not to be confused with induction as an approach to research.

Due to the current emphasis on delivering transferable skills to doctoral research students it is now quite common place for there to be a substantial programme of induction especially where students are taken on in cohorts. The support which students give each other within cohorts is a valuable aspect of the research degree. Of course it is also important to have students meet and engage with other students from earlier cohorts.

Sometimes the new researcher feels that he or she is all alone own and a useful way to counter this and to begin to feel part of a research community is to have the researcher attend a research seminar. Feeling that one is participating in a research community is an important part of getting started. The research community helps in several ways including showing the researcher that others are experiencing the same challenges and thus he or she is not unique in their feeling of insecurity.

12.3 Eating an elephant or climbing Mount Everest

In reality many students need quite a lot of help in getting started. To most students the work involved in getting a research degree, and especially the work required for a Doctorate looks like the effort required to

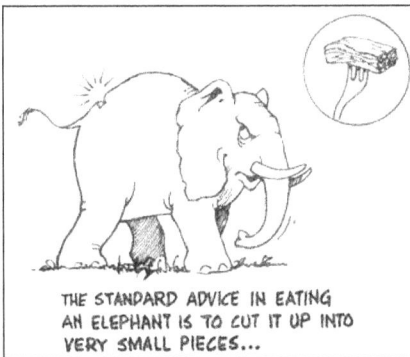

THE STANDARD ADVICE IN EATING AN ELEPHANT IS TO CUT IT UP INTO VERY SMALL PIECES...

climb Mt Everest or as the saying goes to eat an elephant. The standard advice in eating an elephant is to cut it up into small pieces and to eat one at a time over an extended period. The same advice is useful to the research candidate. Thus the first step is to understand the different tasks that need to be undertaken and to schedule them into a research programme. For a mature student this division or disaggregation of the work may be on a high level as such students are often capable of self-motivation and self-management. For less experienced students it may be necessary to spell out the work in some detail.

As mentioned previously the tasks involved are usually to find a problem or a research question. This might be through experience or discussion at work, with peers in groups or individually. It may also be a problem offered to them by the supervisor, or something they have identified for themselves from the literature. The problem needs to be articulated in a structured way so that it is possible to envisage an answer. It will often have to be refined, mostly by reference to the literature.

If the student does not come up with a suitable research problem then the supervisor can play an important role in facilitating a brainstorming session. This could be followed by looking at various scenarios related to how a particular research problem could be developed. It is not good practice for the supervisor to try to impose a research question on a student.

In any event the problem will then have to be supported by a detailed knowledge of the literature so that will be the next step. However it is often too big a task to send a new student off to read 'the literature'. What is often a better approach is to ask the student to read a specific paper and to critique it. Also reading and critiquing other dissertations is a useful way to begin the research process.

In parallel with finding a suitable research problem the student needs to identify an appropriate research strategy and a research tactic. The supervisor can help advise the student in this respect.

The supervisor can also help the student to create his or her own academic network by introducing him or her to other useful individuals. The supervisor may be able to suggest ways of working collaboratively with the student to attend conferences or to publish during the degree. The supervisor may even be able to suggest informants who could become useful sources of evidence to the student and/or to arrange introductions for them to appropriate organisations.

The supervisor or mentor may know the student well enough to be able to recommend courses to augment their research and writing skills. Recall that Appendix 1 provides a list of websites giving advice and assistance on writing skills.

12.4 The research concept note

Getting started with an achievable target is one of the most effective ways to begin. In this case a short *Research Concept Note* (RCN) is written by the student. The purpose of the RCN is to prompt research degree students to think about a number of issues which he or she will have to address when they compile their research proposal. In effect the RCN is a way of encouraging students to start thinking about their prospective research in an academic manner.

A *Research Concept Note* is a short discussion document which is often produced in the form of a table and an example of one is supplied in Appendix 7. There are different ways of using a RCN but whichever approach is used the purpose is the same i.e. to help the student identify issues which need attention.

The RCN may contain up to 1,000 words and could address *up to three* different topics on which the would-be research candidate might like to do research. These can be three different topics, or they can be three slightly different aspects of, or approaches to, a single topic. Each topic as described here only needs a possible suggested title and a brief description.

Before being able to settle on a topic for research the student needs to become acquainted with the literature and the RCN asks the question *Which are the more important journals in the field of study?* This question is answered by an indication of some of the key publications and authors in the field. In addition the student is asked to think about the kind of data that will be gathered, and the type of research methods that might be employed.

An example of a research topic could be:

> **e-Business Risk** - *The risk profile of e-Businesses has not been correctly understood. What is needed is to explore whether there are different and better ways of identifying the entrepreneurs, venture capitalists and other less tangible factors, than have been identified. This is especially pertinent in the Irish economic and investment environment.*

In addition to stating different topics and titles the would-be research candidate should also indicate if he or she has found that topic by reference to the academic literature or by reference to a business or management problem which they have encountered in the work place through consulting or any other means.

An example of publications and authors could be:

> *The key journals in this field are: The Journal of Investment Management, The MIS Quarterly, The Journal of Finance, Electronic Journal of Venture Capital, with accompanying paper titles.*

The key authors in this field are:

> *Bloggs (1993), Smith (2001, 2002), Jones (1980, 1985, 1990).*

Some indication of the type of data or evidence that will be sought during the research process would be useful. An example could be:

> *Data or evidence will include stock market figures, interviews with financial analysts and entrepreneurs in companies/organisations such as: ABC Ltd, ACME Holdings, etc. It will also be important to speak to members of staff.*

The would-be researcher should also indicate what they believe will be their main research method, i.e. whether they will use interviews, questionnaires, action research etc; whether they will be using quantitative or qualitative methods, or a combination of both; and what their level of expertise is in the methods they wish to use.

The RCN has been found to be a good ice breaker and does lead prospective researchers into a research proposal with much less trauma than jumping in the deep end and trying to begin the research by preparing a full proposal.

Students should be told about the RCN in the first weeks of their studies and be made aware that they will have a few months to complete them. This will sensitise the students to the issues and give them a realistic target to meet.

Some supervisors like to work through the RCN with their novice students. Like many other aspects of the written material produced during a research degree the RCN may have to be redrafted a number of times and it is probably useful for the supervisor to closely assist the student during the first draft. By the time the final draft is written the student should be capable of looking after the RCN and the early stages of the research on his or her own.

12.5 Useful books and/or websites

Bezroukov, N. (1999) 'Open Source Software Development as a Special Type of Academic Research (Critique of Vulgar Raymondism)', *First Monday*, volume 4, number 10, October. Available:
http://firstmonday.org/issues/issue4_10/bezroukov/index.html [10 Aug 2011]

Part Four
The Quality of the Research

Chapter 13

Relevance, rigour and originality

It has just been discovered that research causes cancer in rats.

Anonymous

The furore surrounding the publication of The Double Helix did not, however, in the end hinge on hurt feelings or wounded pride. At issue was the account Watson gave of the way scientific discoveries are made. Where conventional twentieth-century accounts made the scientist an omniscient sage, Watson made him more like a carpet-bagging adventurer, driven on by his own competitive spirit and the desire to win at all costs.

Jardine L, (1999) *Ingenious Pursuits*, Little, Brown and Company, P355.

13.1 The relevance and rigour conundrum

There is a considerable amount of confusion about the relevance and rigor issue. For a piece of research to be adequate for a doctoral degree it has to be both relevant and rigorous. Some people have argued that the situation described by Heisenberg's Uncertainty Principle[62] also applies to relevance and rigour. This is not correct. It is perfectly possible to produce research which is both relevant and rigorous. In fact it is essential to so do.

Relevance and rigour are challenging issues that all academic researchers have to face. Some academics consider relevance and rigour to be a controversial set of concerns and there are different opinions, which are often strongly held by different schools of thought. But in fact sound academic research requires both relevance and rigour.

In dealing with the relevance issue the researcher needs to continually ask him or herself *Who cares?* and *So What?* With respect to rigour the question is *How come you can say that?*

It is important that the supervisor discusses this conundrum with the researcher and helps prepare him or her to understand and discuss the research project in these terms.

13.2 The stakeholders and their expectations

Although relevance and rigour are commonly used by academics in the discussion of research degrees, they are seldom carefully defined. This is perhaps not accidental as there are several difficult issues involved in the proper definition of these concepts. One of the main issues with regard to these definitions relates to the question *Who are the main stakeholders or audience for the research?*

As mentioned earlier in this book academic research always has multiple stakeholders, which range from faculty, the student, the supervisor, to other students, to the university authorities, to industrial, commercial and public sector practitioners and eventually the wider community as a whole who pay for universities through their taxes. Thus when the word relevance is used in relation to academic research it is necessary to ask

---

[62] Heisenberg's Uncertainty Principle states that the speed and location of an electron cannot be known at the same time.

the question *relevant to whom?* In other words *which part of the community is this particular piece of academic research aimed at or more correctly intended to assist?* Another way of looking at this is, *Who are expected to be the primary beneficiaries of the findings?* From the diversity of the stakeholders listed above it is easy to see that it is a considerable challenge to produce a piece of research that would satisfy all these different groups. A research project could be said to be relevant if it satisfies the needs of some of the stakeholders. The number of stakeholders whose satisfaction is required is a matter of judgement for the supervisor and the student.

13.3 Defining relevance

One definition of relevance is that research should demonstrate potential meaningful utility regarding its application in the world of business and management. There can be strong relevance and weak relevance. It is also said that there is a continuum between weak and strong rele-

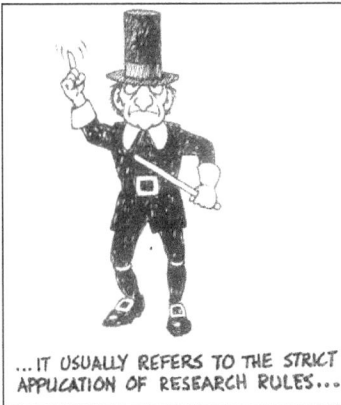

...IT USUALLY REFERS TO THE STRICT APPLICATION OF RESEARCH RULES...

vance. Some researchers would suggest that weak relevance is achieved when the research potentially satisfies the concerns of the community of practitioners (rather than the academic community). It has also been said that a piece of research could only be said to demonstrate strong relevance when in addition to the above it also demonstrates how the finding could be implemented in practice and how its validity is established. If this view were accepted then almost by definition, to achieve strong relevancy, it would be necessary to pursue some sort of action research programme (Zmud 1996). This view is not necessarily shared by all researchers, many of whom would regard this last criterion as too strict or rigid. Furthermore there is still some controversy about the issue of action research itself[63].

However, the issue which is largely agreed upon is that in the world of business and management studies the relevance of research is tightly

---

[63] The relevance and rigour debate has become a major concern in the field of business and management studies and has lead to a new taxonomy, which refers to research being conducted in Mode 1 or Mode 2.

coupled to utility. Business and management researchers generally see their field of study as applied and thus it needs to address an organisational problem and the result of successful research in this field delivers a solution or at least a potential solution to the problem. Of course there can be exceptions to this. For example a doctoral research project could begin by attempting to address a problem which is then discovered to be part of a quite different issue. As a result it is possible that the outcome of the research is the specification of the new problem. Such an outcome could be regarded as relevant and quite acceptable for doctoral research. An example of this occurred when a research student investigated the use of Information and Communications Technology (ICT) in strategy formulation and in so doing found that the main issue was not whether the technology could support strategic initiatives, but rather whether the organisation could demonstrate any Return on Investment (ROI) emanating from the investment at all.

13.4 Defining rigour

Concerning rigour: once again this is a concept more talked about than defined.

Consulting the Oxford Dictionary rigour is defined as:

1. a severity, strictness, harshness. b (in pl.) harsh measures or conditions. c (often in pl.) severity of weather or climate; extremity of cold.
2. logical exactitude.
3. strict enforcement of rules etc. (the utmost rigour of the law).
4. austerity of life; puritanical discipline.

In the academic context when the concept of rigour is discussed it usually refers to the strict application of research rules and logical exactitude. In effect this means that whatever methodology is chosen for the research, its rules have to be scrupulously complied with. For example, when numeric evidence is collected from informants then careful attention will have to be given to the selection of informants and to ensuring that response bias is minimised. Credible sample size will be an issue as well as response rates. Appropriate confidence limits need to have been applied. The tools used for evidence analysis will have to be chosen with care so that the assumptions on which their use is based reflect the research situation under consideration.

In the case of qualitative or interpretive research the rigour issues relate to the manner in which the data was sought, collected and managed. It refers to the way codes were chosen and used in the analysis of the data. It refers to the logic of the arguments used. They relate to the extent that exhaustive alternative explanations were sought. What rigour amounts to is that all the steps in the research need to be carefully applied to ensure their validity. Any misunderstanding or mistakes or deviations made in these research processes could greatly undermine the rigour of the research.

The academic community requires rigour so that sufficient integrity can be assigned to the findings of published research. In the case of qualitative research this may help to allow the findings to be considered replicable (Zmud 1996). Where qualitative research is involved replication is not usually the issue as in general this form of research is so context and time bound to make replication almost impossible. Here rigour is required to make the research credible.

In other words if a rigorous approach is not followed then the research findings will generally not be accepted by the academic community.

In business and management studies it is often said, or at least assumed, that the primary audience is the practicing manager or executive in the industrial, commercial or public sector environment. This would mean that the questions being researched should lead to solutions that would improve organisational systems and management practice. It is also often assumed that in turn this would result in improvements in the return on investment (except for the public sector). This implies that the product of the research should be seen to be of *value-in-use* by the organisational and management community. This is the basis used to support the need for Mode 2 research which was discussed earlier in Chapter 1.

13.5 Value-in-use is not enough

However there is good reason to question whether this assumption about the primary audience is correct. An examination of academic research journals and research dissertations will quickly reveal that much of the research work undertaken by academics and students is aimed at answering rather obscure questions which are probably not of any particular practical use. Much of this research addresses relatively specialised issues, which do not necessarily lend themselves to direct improvements in business systems or management practice. Sometimes it is difficult to see how the findings of academic research can be directly applied at all, never mind how they might be used to improve results, which could lead to better returns on investment in the private sector or for that matter improved organisations in the public sector. Sometimes there appears to be a major mismatch between the academics and practical managers. In fact there is a significant deficit in *value-in-use* for the research findings when it is looked at through the lens of the business and management community. But *value-in-use* is not enough. It is for this reason that no matter how important a piece of market research describing the size or dimensions of a market for a particular product might be, such a study would normally be considered inadequate even for a Masters degree. Being relevant to practitioners alone is not enough for respectable academic research.

However, when we think of the other stakeholders to the research we see that there is another dimension to relevance. The university, the faculty and the students themselves may have an interest in the research being performed or conducted to a high academic standard without it necessarily leading directly to improvements in performance (especially in the short term). Here the proper application of the methodology, the design, the evidence collection approaches and the analyses of the results, to mention only four issues, are seen as the main aspects of research relevance. Of course at the same time these are also some of the elements of rigour.

13.6 The supervisor's fourth dilemma

From the above it is reasonable to think of a doctoral degree as being an event which has multiple benefits to multiple stakeholders.

Supervisors sometimes forget that the most important stakeholder, from the point of view of the student, is the student himself or herself. It is critical that the research delivers benefit to the student as well as the other stakeholders. But the supervisor will generally also wants to further his or her own research interests, which means expanding his or her knowledge in the field and obtaining some peer reviewed papers co-authored with the student.

The main dilemma here is to what extent should the supervisor influence the choice of research question and the choice of methodology.

The question of publishing joint peer reviewed papers with the student is a thorny one. Supervisors should only have their name on a paper provided they have made a substantial contribution to the work involved in preparing the paper. It is now generally agreed that in most cases the supervisor should not be the first author. Some universities insist on this.

13.7 The antithesis of rigour – the *anything goes* principle

But there is yet another side to the relevance and rigour discussion that makes this debate even more complicated. It has been said that in order for a piece of research to be accepted as academically competent it needs to follow the rules of research. It doesn't much matter if the research was theoretical or empirical, positivist or interpretivist – each of these approaches to research has rules and they need to be followed. However Paul Feyerabend (1993) has pointed out in his book *Against Method* that many great knowledge breakthroughs have followed none of these rules.

> *It is clear, then, that the idea of a fixed method, or of a fixed theory of rationality, rests on too naïve a view of man and his social surroundings. To those that look at the rich material provided by history, and are not intent on impoverishing it in order to please their lower instincts, their craving for intellectual security in the form of clarity, precision, 'objectivity', 'truth' it will become clear that there is only one principle that can be defended under all circumstances and in all stages of human development. It is the principle: anything goes.*

This is the simple reality of research. Good research will not be dismissed because the rules of some methodology have not been strictly adhered to. Rigour may well be important but it is not as important as the actual value of the findings. If the researcher presents a convincing argument then irrespective of the method it is probable that the findings will be accepted. This will largely be independent of whether a rigorous adherence to the techniques of research was followed. This is not to say that poor, sloppy or shoddy research is acceptable. For research findings to be taken seriously it is important that they are the result of a rigorous and convincing argument that is grounded in experience and theory.

It should not be expected that a recently enrolled research degree candidate will be capable of quality research that does not closely follow established research rules and the supervisor needs to advise his or her research candidates to be as rigorous as possible in their work.

13.8 Originality

Doctoral degrees require some originality, as do academic papers for peer-reviewed journals. However the issue of originality is quite problematic. It is not easy to either define or describe originality. Dictionaries provide many different meanings for this word. In the research context, being original often amounts to possessing an ability to think creatively and as a result come up with a new way of understanding a phenomenon.

From a supervisor's point of view what needs to be understood is that there are degrees of originality and that from a research degree point of view (even at the doctoral level) only a modest amount of originality is sufficient. Sometimes too big an issue is made of originality and it can cause problems in deciding just how much work needs to be done for a degree or whether a paper is appropriate for publication.

The source of the originality can come from a number of different dimensions of the research. The research question could address a new issue; the research candidate could apply an existing theory or set of theories in a novel way to a different population; a grounded theory approach could be used to create a new theoretical framework; new evidence gathering techniques could be used; a new approach to evidence analysis could be used; established ideas could be revisited and a new meaning derived from them. Some research degree candidates will combine a couple of these new elements in their research in order to establish their claim to originality.

When examiners evaluate a dissertation for the dimension of originality they frequently ask themselves the following question, Does the dissertation tell them something interesting which they didn't know before and which they are now pleased that they are aware of? If an examiner can answer this question in the affirmative then the dissertation has passed the originality test.

Of course prize-winning research will need to break new ground, but this is not usually necessary. Perhaps the requirement for originality in the findings of a Doctorate can be best summarised in the words of Marcel Proust when he said:

The real voyage of discovery consists not in seeking new land-scapes, but in having new eyes.

(http://www.brainyquote.com/quotes/authors/m/marcelprou129874.html)

It is interesting to note the similarity of this to the TS Eliot line "know the place for the first time" which also emphasises that it is our internal per-spective is what really matters.

13.9 Useful books and/or websites

Dick, B. (1997) *Rigour and relevance in action research*, Available:
http://www.scu.edu.au/schools/gcm/ar/arp/rigour.html [10 Aug 2011].

Gibbons, M. Limoges, C. Nowotny, H. Schwartzman, S. Scott, P. Trow, M, (1994) *The New Production of Knowledge, The Dynamics of Science and Research Contemporary in Societies*, London: Sage, p3.

Huff, A. and Huff, J. (2001) 'Re-Focusing the Business School Agenda', *British Journal of Management*, Vol. 12, Special Issue, S49-S54,

Nowotny, H. Scott, P. and Gibbons, M. (2001) *Re-thinking Science Knowledge and the Public in an Age of Uncertainty*, Cambridge: Polity Press.

Rigour and relevance handbook, available:
www.leadered.com/pdf/academic_excellence.pdf [10 Aug 2011].

Chapter 14

When is a dissertation ready?

The whole theory of modern education is radically unsound. Fortunately in England, at any rate, education produces no effect whatsoever. If it did, it would prove a serious danger to the upper classes, and probably lead to acts of violence in Grosvenor Square.
Oscar Wilde spoken by Lady Bracknell, in The Importance of Being Earnest, act 1.1891.

14.1 Defining the standard of a degree

The quality of doctoral degrees not only differs from university to university but they also differ within the same university from faculty to faculty and for that matter department to department and from individual to individual. There are in fact no clear or precise rules and little consensus concerning the required standard of a doctoral degree and this raises the question of how would an external examiner know what standard is being sought[64].

In general terms most academics would agree that a Doctorate is awarded only to those who demonstrate that through their research they have added something of value to the body of knowledge. This demonstration takes both the form of a written submission of a monograph, which is usually about 80,000 words, and an oral examination referred to as a viva voce. A successful viva voce typically lasts two hours. But there are also other options that may be explored. As Williams (2003) says:

...A SENIOR DOCTORATE AWARDED ON THE EVALUATION OF A PORTFOLIO OF PUBLICATIONS PRODUCED AS THE LIFE WORK OF AN INDIVIDUAL.

In some cases a series of perhaps five high quality academic papers may be submitted in lieu of the monograph. The academic papers option is available to many universities, but is not that popular with supervisors or degree candidates. It is usually offered to established academics, who have already been recognised in their field, and have already held reasonably senior positions in universities for some years. It confirms academic status that, in a sense, they already have. It would be unusual for a completely new researcher to be able to apply to undertake a Doctorate through this route[65].

---

[64] The standard of a doctorate for a particular institution may be ascertained by visiting the library and reading doctoral dissertations which have been submitted and for which degrees have been awarded. This is a time consuming business and only the most fastidious examiners have been known to do this.

[65] There used to be a problem with this view of Williams (2003) in that a PhD or for that matter any traditional doctorate should only be awarded for academic work conducted under supervision. What Williams (2003) is describing more closely resembles a senior

By the way, the doctoral degree awarded on the basis of a series of papers written under supervision is not the same as a senior doctorate awarded on the evaluation of a portfolio of publications produced as the life work of an individual. The latter is referred to as a senior Doctorate and not many of these are awarded.

14.2 Examine in two parts

Before the Doctorate is awarded to the degree candidate the dissertation and/or the papers and the viva voce are examined. At least in the UK and in other Commonwealth countries this is usually by one internal examiner and one external examiner (if the degree candidate is a member of the university's staff then it is usual to have two external examiners) and there needs to be consensus from all examiners that the degree candidate has achieved the objective of the degree. As mentioned before the objective of the Doctorate is also sometimes referred to as the contribution made to the body of knowledge, which needs to demonstrate some originality of thought, a theoretical underpinning, relevance to the discipline and rigour in execution. Although it is generally agreed that the contribution required from a doctoral candidate must be evident and clear it can actually be quite modest. Every viva voce candidate must be well prepared to answer this question[66]. Williams (2003) notes:

> *Good research and good doctoral research does not necessarily arrive at the answers to problems. Particularly when research tests theory, it often produces the next layer of good questions rather than good answers. Good questions are an entirely respectable and useful output from a Doctorate [especially if they help extend the current theoretical framework] the bottom line is that the research must engage with current theories.*

---

doctorate rather than a PhD. However today some universities are offering PhDs which combine aspects of William's view with the traditional approach.

[66] As a general rule Commonwealth countries in the southern hemisphere do not hold vivas. Australian, New Zealand and South African universities show a preference for the dissertations of their doctoral candidates to be examined by academics from leading universities in the northern hemisphere and they are unable to fund the travel costs of such examiners. Therefore the dissertation is read by the external examiner or examiners and written reports and queries are submitted to the university. Although this situation is slowly being relaxed and in some cases vivas are being held using local examiners, this is not yet generally the case.

Williams is of course right but research degree candidates do not set out to discover new research questions. If the research degree candidate cannot answer the original research question then the issue of finding new and more pertinent research questions comes into play and a re-search degree may well be awarded for the contribution made in that way.

14.3 Independent research

The primary objective of a doctoral degree is for an individual to be able to demonstrate that he or she can undertake independent academic research. In this respect the doctoral degree process is often compared to an apprenticeship, and the degree candidate to an apprentice in which he or she demonstrates that the skills of research have been learnt by completing a substantive or material research project. In this sense a Doctorate is actually a classical learning-by-doing project. Also at the end of the degree process the newly graduated individual is really only a beginner in the academic research field and will possibly take a few years to hone his or her skills in order to become a fully-fledged academic researcher. The analogy with the apprentice, the journeyman and the master craftsman is often thought as useful in describing the development of an academic researcher[67].

14.4 When has enough work been done?

The question, which continually arises, is how does one know when the student has done enough work of sufficient quality to submit his or her dissertation so that it may be evaluated and found to be worthy of the degree. There is no simple answer to this conundrum. A guideline that we have found useful is to base this decision on an idea in the works of Wittgenstein (1969), which states *"Knowledge is in the end based on ac-knowledgment"*. This thought focuses the student on the fact that he or she is part of a community that will need to regard the research work

---

[67] The term apprenticeship is sometimes thought to suggest a highly controlled or mechanistic approach to doctoral education. However this is not intended. In this con-text the word apprentice is used to suggest that the primary learning comes from the direction given by the supervisor or supervisors. This term apprenticeship is not intended to reflect an emphasis on simple skills training as it would when used in the context of craft and trades. Doctoral education needs to be of the broadest kind as well as being of adequate depth to make a real contribution to the body of knowledge.

and the findings produced as being of sufficient quality to merit the degree.

THE DOCTORAL CANDIDATE NEEDS TO BE QUITE CLEAR ABOUT WHICH COMMUNITY OF PEERS THEY WISH TO BECOME PART OF...

And this happens when that research community recognises the student as being someone who will be able to contribute to the ongoing research 'conversation' in that field. The doctoral research must 'speak to' both a specific research field (or content), and to specific research approaches (or methodologies) shared by a community of researchers in the field. Doctoral research is paradoxically a lonely pursuit but one that initiates the successful candidate into the membership of a community of peers.

14.5 Peer reviewing – the republic of scholars

The student needs to be quite clear about which community of scholars they wish to become part of. 'Peer referencing' is the foundation of all research communities. When you choose a research topic and a research methodology, you are also choosing the particular community of peers that you aspire to join, within the larger research community[68]. It is therefore essential to engage in discussions or 'conversations' with members of that community during your doctoral research; by e-mail, by attending conferences or by publishing papers in journals that they are involved with.

The community which the doctoral degree candidate joins after he or she completes the degree is sometimes called "the republic of scholars" or sometimes "the academy". The term "the republic of scholars" could be interpreted to suggest that all citizens, i.e. scholars, are equal which is not really the case, and secondly that it is independent of other parts of society. Through the claim of academic freedom the universities attempt to distance themselves from other institutions in society. One of

---

[68] The community within which the research is being conducted for a Doctorate is not always easy to define. However it is an important part of the doctoral degree process for the degree candidate, with the assistance of the supervisor or supervisors, to make contact with this community and in so doing to become a part of it.

the ways in which this is apparent is the fact that a doctoral examination cannot be appealed on the grounds of an error in academic judgement. The academic judgement of the examiners is in a way held to be absolute. Reversing an academic judgement is difficult.

14.6 Goodwill of examiners

The student has finished the work and it is of adequate quality and is ready for examination when the supervisor or supervisors say so; when his or her peers think he or she has produced a good piece of work; when he or she has presented at conferences and/or given a number of seminars on the work; and has perhaps had a paper or two published in a journal, and so on. Of course the final say is obviously in the hands of the examiners and it is critical to the whole process of offering and preparing individuals for Doctorates that the university is able to choose *appropriate* examiners who will be 'sympathetic' to the work produced by the degree candidate. In this respect examiners need to have a certain level of goodwill towards both the subject being researched and the research methodology. Checkland (1981) illustrates the subject of 'goodwill' when he described a comment made by Keynes, concerning how Hayek reviewed his book Treaties on Money. Apparently Keynes wrote on his copy of the review, *"Hayek has not read my book with that measure of 'goodwill' which an author is entitled to expect of a reader. Until he does so he will not know what I mean or whether I am right."*

If there is any doubt about the goodwill of the examiner then this matter should be raised as soon as possible. Examiners normally set the pace, the scope and the tone of the examination. It can happen that this will focus on the shortcomings of the dissertation and the knowledge of the degree candidate. If this occurs then it is essential that the degree candidate spells out in detail what he or she claims to be the contribution resulting from the research. Although it would not be correct for there to be an argument during the examination the degree candidate should be sufficiently confident and competent to make his or her point of view clear.

14.7 Degree dissertations need to be targeted at requirements

With regards to depth and scope it always has to be kept in mind that the depth and the scope of the research needs to be appropriate for the three or four years which is the target time in which to complete a Doctorate[69]. Dissertations, which are not of an adequate standard to be awarded a Doctorate, may in some instances be submitted or resubmitted for consideration for a Masters degree[70].

Clearly is it not possible to define the 'products' of doctoral research across the board, or across the spectrum of institutions, but it is quite possible to define the process and criteria by which one can seek to join a particular 'community of peers'. This may be seen as the most obvious outcome of obtaining a doctorate. Thus it is essential that the university be aware of the evolving standards and practices in doctoral education. But at the end of the day the suitability of the dissertation to be awarded a doctorate is always a judgement based on experience and it is essential that this judgement be recognised for what it really is (Feyerabend 1993; Collins 1994).

It is certainly important to remember the words of Checkland (1981), which are just as relevant to the findings of doctoral research as they were to his own subject:

Obviously the work is not finished, and can never be finished. There are no absolute positions to be reached in the attempt by men to understand the world in which they find themselves: new

---

[69] Three to four years is currently the recommended duration of a Doctorate in most subjects. However this situation is relatively new. Previously Doctorates were allowed to take much longer periods of time. Most supervisors or examiners have encountered six or eight or even ten year Doctorates. There have even been examples of Doctorates taking nearly twenty years to complete. It has been said that this long period was due to the doctoral candidate wanting to do his or her best ever piece of work. In fact this is largely an excuse for individuals just not getting on with the research work due to their being distracted with teaching and other responsibilities in the department at the university. The notion of the Doctorate being the lifetime best piece of work was seldom, if ever a reality.

[70] The alternative degree that is sometimes awarded to those who do not quite achieve the doctoral standard is a Master of Philosophy. In general the Master of Philosophy degree may not be as rigorous, not as great in scope and requires a lesser contribution to theory. It is however important not to regard a Master of Philosophy as a failed Doctorate as it does reflect a considerable achievement in its own right. It is sometimes referred to as an exit qualification. In general a Masters degree candidate needs to prove that he or she understands a particular problem in the area in which they have done their research; that he or she is able to analyse the situation and set it out logically; that he or she is able to arrive at logical conclusions or a diagnosis; and that he or she is then able to make proposals for the improvement or the elimination of the problem being studied.

experience may in the future refute present conjectures. So the work itself must be regarded as an on-going system of a particular kind: A learning system which will continue to develop ideas, to test them out in practice, and to learn from the experience gained.

There are certainly dilemmas that research candidates have to face, to do with the balance between scholarship and training and comprehensiveness and adequacy. It is useful to see the work required to produce a competent dissertation as being training in research. However university degrees are not primarily training events, at least not in the narrow sense of the word. University degrees are about scholarship and education and these issues have to be balanced with research training.

The difficulty is that some researchers encounter a problem with regards to the standards they set themselves (or maybe those imposed by an inexperienced supervisor) for their research work. This occurs at both masters and doctoral level but especially with regards to PhD candidates and it arises because the student begins to feel that his or her dissertation needs to be the best single piece of work they will ever do.

They are also likely to feel that the requirement for originality is much greater than it really needs to be. While it is important that the research is well conducted and well written up, it is important to realise that a Masters and even a Doctorate does not have to be at a prize winning standard. What is required is highly competent work, which demonstrates that the researcher, in the case of a Masters degree, has mastered the subject and has demonstrated knowledge of the research techniques used, and at the doctoral degree level has made a modest contribution to the body of knowledge. In the case of doctoral candidates, they will have to demonstrate a thorough understanding of research methodology and research philosophy as well.

14.8 Time is an important issue

As already mentioned it is also increasingly important that research degree candidates complete in time. Masters degrees need to be completed within two years. Doctoral degrees, full-time, should be finalised in about three years[71] and part-time in four to five years. It is sometimes

---

[71] Converting three years' full-time study into a number of hours is a daunting task but the following will give students some idea of the amount of effort required to obtain a doctorate. A week is reckoned to have 40 working hours in a number of countries. There

said that a Doctorate requires about 140 weeks work or approximately 3,000 hours work.

14.9 An entry to more research opportunities

It will most probably be in the research and writing of academic papers that will be undertaken after the Doctorate that most researchers will be able to take on really difficult problems and research questions and thereby demonstrate their real skills.

It is important that when an adequately competent job has been done by the researcher the supervisor encourage the student to conclude the research and submit it for examination.

14.10 Last step in preparing the text of the dissertation

The last step in completing the first draft of the dissertation is to write an Abstract. An abstract is a summary of the research. It is customary to keep the abstract to one page and it should state the research question, the rationale of the research, how the research was conducted, what was found and what its value is to both academe and to practitioners.

14.11 The supervisor's fifth dilemma

Every doctoral degree process has to be terminated. The supervisor has to tell the degree candidate to finish and submit. Both supervisor and student can find this difficult. Through experience the supervisor will become confident as to when this point has been reached.

Students should show their work to anyone who is interested and is competent to comment and seek their advice as well. If others are interested in the work then this is a good sign that the student has achieved something. The formal way of acquiring advice from others is to submit an appropriate part of the dissertation to a conference or to a journal.

---

is on average 4.2 weeks in a month. Some academics would take up to 2 months leave a year. Thus 40 times 4.2 times 10 produces 1680 working hours a year. However research students would not be expected to work 8 hours per day as they would typically have some teaching and maybe even administrative responsibilities. It is probable that the average full-time doctoral candidate would do no more than 1000 to 1250 hours a year. Thus the total amount of work required for a doctorate would be a minimum of 3000 hours and it could be quite a lot more, as many doctorates take 4 or even 5 years to complete.

14.12 Useful books and/or websites

Doctorates, available: http://www.artsandsciences.nl/ [10 Aug 2011].

Graduate Arts & Sciences, Physical Standards for Preparing Theses and Dissertations, available: http://artsandsciences.virginia.edu/grad/phystan.html [10
Aug 2011].

Doctorates and higher doctorates by publication policy, available:
http://www62.gu.edu.au/policylibrary.nsf/alldocscat/fda04639f24890b44a2
56bc20062f724?opendocument [10 Aug 2011].

Abstracts

http://www.lumie.com/help/research-abstracts [7 Jan 2012]

Chapter 15

Helping the student to submit

To write it, it took three months; to conceive it—three minutes; to collect the data in it—all my life.
Scott Fitzgerald, The Author's Apology, a letter to the Booksellers' Convention, April 1920 (published in The Letters of F. Scott Fitzgerald, ed. by Andrew Turnbull, 1963), referring to his novel This Side of Paradise.

15.1 Getting ready to submit

One of the most important things for the supervisor to do is to agree with the student the approximate layout of the dissertation early on in the research process. As a rough guideline a dissertation will need about seven chapters which will include an introduction, a literature review, a description of the research methodology, a description of the research itself, the findings, discussion and interpretation and conclusions, limitations and ideas about future research.

Students need to understand the purpose of each of the chapters and there needs to be regular discussion on these matters with the supervisor.

It is also useful if the supervisor gives the research degree candidate a rough guideline as to how long each chapter should ideally be. This of course will vary enormously depending on the field of study and the topic being researched.

The supervisor needs to discuss the title of the dissertation with the research candidate. The title should be concise – approximately 12 words. Avoid long preambles in the title. Longer titles are sometimes cumbersome to accommodate in the information retrieval system of universities. Of course a subtitle may be used as well. It is frequently the case that the research work drifts away from the original title and that the final title may have to be changed to reflect the actual focus of the work. A series of key words should be carefully selected to reflect the research and the findings, which can be recognised as acceptable terminology in terms of information retrieval systems.

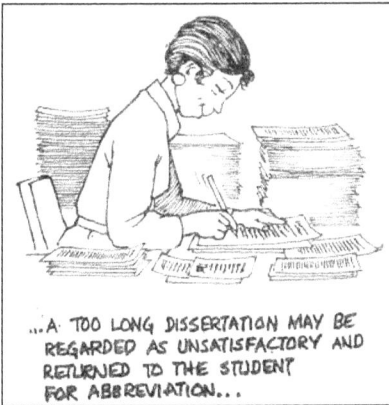

...A TOO LONG DISSERTATION MAY BE REGARDED AS UNSATISFACTORY AND RETURNED TO THE STUDENT FOR ABBREVIATION...

15.2 Writing up

When should a student start writing and what to start with? In the old days it was thought that the student should do the research and when he or she was finished then the research was written up[72]. This is no longer the case. Today research should be written up as it is being conducted. Of course the logical place to start is with the early chapters, but when these are written they should not be regarded as complete. The student may well want to add to even the first chapter right up to the moment of submitting the dissertation.

The length of the overall document will again vary from institution to institution. No credit is given for length. In fact a 'too long' dissertation may be regarded as unsatisfactory and returned to the student for abbreviation. Parsimony is a basic principle of scholarship. However the supervisor needs to emphasise the need for the dissertation to be self-contained, i.e. it needs to tell the whole story. On the other hand the dissertation needs to be concise and relevant. Sometimes the student will try to keep the length of the main body of the dissertation down to an acceptable length by the extensive use of appendices. However these should be used with care.

Within each chapter there should be a consistent structure such as an introduction, a number of sections that develop the argument for that chapter concerned and then a concluding section. Numbering systems used should be simple and consistent. When appropriate the material should be supported by diagrams, figures and tables. These need to be numbered and given appropriate titles. Diagrams, figures and tables need to be placed adjacent to an explanation of their significance in the text of the dissertation.

There is often some degree of freedom as to which referencing system is used, but when chosen the student should be consistent in following the system. The Harvard method is probably most frequently used among academics.

There is no simple rule for knowing exactly when a student has done enough work to qualify for a research degree. The main principle is whether the research question has been answered adequately and that the answer to the research question has been stated in an accessible way. There will always be a judgement to be made here and both the supervisor and the student need to debate this thoroughly. It is also use-

---

[72] Some students still avoid the writing up until the last minute. This is a serious mistake which the supervisor needs to be aware of and discourage.

ful for the other members of the academic community to be consulted. At doctoral level a draft dissertation can be sent to a number of academics and their opinion sought as to whether they consider the work ready for examination. This practice, which makes good sense, is not always admitted to by academics.

15.3 Evidence of scholarship

When the research dissertation is submitted the supervisor and the research student need to be clear that the examination will be looking for evidence of the fact that the research student has developed an appropriate level of scholarship. The dissertation itself will be the primary evidence and thus it needs to reflect a thorough piece of academically rigorous and reflective work. These characteristics are difficult to define, but it is clear that a scholarly piece of work needs to be based on a broad and an in-depth understanding of the accumulated knowledge in the field of study. To be scholarly the ideas have to be expressed in a clear and logical manner and they need to have been 'tested' by systematic reflection on the part of the scholar.

The research student can support his or her dissertation by other publications and by presentations at conferences. Thus right from the start the supervisor should encourage the research student to write up his or her ideas and to have them published or present them at conferences.

It is not necessary that these publications be in the best academic journals[73]. For a research student to be published in a lesser journal or even in an industry or trade journal is a positive sign that he or she is mastering their field of study. The same applies to conferences.

The student needs to make the examiners aware of the conferences at which he or she has spoken on the topic of the research and also the journals or working papers which have been published for him or her on this topic. A list of these relevant achievements should be inserted in the dissertation and this may be referred to as *A List of Other Academic Outputs.*

---

[73] Aiming too high at the league of academic journals is a problem which should be avoided. It can take several months for a paper to be reviewed and during the doctoral degree process there may not be sufficient time for a paper to be re-submitted to another journal after it has been rejected by the first choice of journal.

15.4 Content and structure of the dissertation

Although each university has individual in-house rules that cover the general content and structure of a dissertation the guidelines in Table 15.1 may be helpful for research degree candidates. The supervisor should ensure that all students are aware of these from quite early in the research process.

Table 15.1 Content and structure of a dissertation

Chapter	Contents of chapter	No. of pages
Chapter 0	Acknowledgements, dedication, certificate of 'own work' etc. An attention grabbing Abstract no more than one page long.	Numbers in Romans
Chapter 1	Why is this research important and to whom it is important	10 – 20
Chapter 2	Concepts, theories and frameworks leading to a model and research question - A critical literature review	40 – 60
Chapter 3	Methodology, research design, data/evidence gathering alternatives, possible analytical strategies - Show comprehensive knowledge of a number of alternatives	30 – 50
Chapter 4	The Research Process - The story of the research	30 – 40
Chapter 5	Findings, interpretation, discussion and conclusions - What did we learn from the research and what does it mean including guidelines and frameworks created.	40 – 50
Chapter 6	Limitations and suggestions for future research - How would go about this if you were to start again	30 – 40
Reading list	Approximately 200 contemporary references mainly from refereed journals	
Appendices	Questionnaires + interview summaries + URLs + Glossary etc	50 – 100

Overall a dissertation will normally be in excess of 200 pages, with close on 100 pages additional appendices. Some institutions express this as 80,000 words, while in other institutions 100,000 words is the limit.

15.5 Academic writing

Many doctoral degree candidates have difficulty in expressing themselves to an adequate academic standard. It is really quite surprising just how many people who are in possession of masters degrees cannot develop and sustain a competent level of expression in their native tongue. Furthermore students from abroad whose first language is not English often have even more difficulty with written academic English.

This is a major problem and there is no easy solution. Some universities recognise this and degree candidates are sometimes asked to engage a proof reader to help with this problem. There are two problems with this. First of all it is generally agreed that anyone holding a doctorate degree should be able to write well in the language in which the research was conducted. Being able to write well and thus argue well is a quintessential part of scholarship. Maybe some exceptions could be made for anyone with a disability such as dyslexia. Others have argued that if Einstein had to submit his dissertation in English, perhaps it would not be expressed as well as it should have been. This is not a sensible argument. Outstanding scholars should always write in the language or languages in which they are most comfortable and a university should accommodate this.

The second issue regarding the use of proof readers is that a proof reader could easily, in attempting to improve the English, change in some subtle way the meaning of the work. This could be catastrophic for the research degree candidate. The dissertation presented is the responsibility of the degree candidate and it is not acceptable for him or her to say that he or she did not mean something that is written in his or her presented work.

Research degree candidates who are not competent writers need to spend time working on their ability to write and in cases where their ability is in doubt they need to understand that the obtaining of a research degree is contingent on their ability to express themselves and craft a convincing argument in writing.

15.6 Useful books and/or websites

Visualising the dissertation, available:
   http://www.strath.ac.uk/economics/currentstudents/studyskills/writingadis
   sertation [10 Aug 2011].
Writing an abstract

http://writing.wisc.edu/Handbook/presentations_abstracts.html
[7 Jan 2012]
Writing A *Research Abstract,* available*:*
www.itns.org/pdfs2009/ITNS_Write_Research_Abstract.pdf
Research Abstracts
http://www.lumie.com/help/research-abstracts [7 Jan 2012]

Chapter 16

Evaluating the research

Education is an admirable thing, but it is well to remember from time to time that nothing that is worth knowing can be taught.
Wilde O, spoken by Gilbert, in The Critic as Artist, pt. 1 (published in Intentions, 1891).

16.1 How is the dissertation evaluated?

It has already been pointed out that there are difficult problems in relation to the standard of a doctorate degree and that this is directly reflected in how doctoral dissertations are evaluated. The main problem is that it is difficult to ensure that the university is even-handed and that the same standard is applied to all students who are examined. Different external and internal examiners will have their own views as to what the standard should be and it can be difficult to ensure that they are in harmony. External and internal examiners can disagree and either or both can be less than expert with regards to the internal rules of the university.

In a sense the standard of a university is always on display in the library through reference to the collection of dissertations for which degrees have already been awarded. However some academics would not be anxious to be guided by these dissertations, but would claim that the current dissertation needs to evaluated on its own merits independently of the history of the institution.

In the past it was usual for the supervisor to become one of the examiners of the final outcome of the research (i.e. the dissertation). Although this practice has now been abandoned in many places, it should always be remembered that the supervisor would be by necessity, a sort of examiner. The supervisor needs to advise the student that he or she has finished the research project and that the work is of sufficient quality to be submitted for examination.

This implies several things, the first of which is that the supervisor has really read the student's work carefully and has formed a detailed opinion of it. Obviously if the supervisor is supporting the submission of the work for examination this implies implicitly that he or she regards the work as being of adequate quality to pass the examination.

It is surprising how often the question of how well the supervisor knows the final dissertation arises. During examination supervisors have been known to say that they were unable to read the final document because the student rushed to submit the dissertation in time for an examination date. This should not be allowed to happen[74].

One of the most frequently asked questions by students of research degrees is 'How will my dissertation be evaluated?' and it is essential that a supervisor is able to give a satisfactory answer to this. Of course there is no simple answer to this question, as it will depend to a large extent on the actual degree, the institution, the faculty, the supervisor and the external examiner or examiners concerned. However, there are guidelines that help a student understand how research dissertations are assessed.

16.2 The traditional Masters Degree by dissertation

As mentioned before the traditional Masters degree by dissertation is a direct preparation for a Doctorate. This degree has many of the same attributes as the Doctorate, but the studies are in less depth and with a reduced scope. Thus a Masters degree by dissertation requires the candidate to demonstrate a mastery of the subject area being researched, as well as a comprehensive understanding of the research methodology being used. The work does not, however, have to be original in the way that a Doctorate needs to be. However, there have been occasions when a Cum Laude Masters Degree has been virtually as good as a Doctorate, and perhaps better than some weaker doctorates.

The following is based on an extract from the rules for a Master of Commerce and a Masters of Economic Science degree and it illustrates the typical requirements for much a degree.

The candidate is required to show acquaintance with the methods of research in that he or she:

1. understands the nature and purpose of the investigation;
2. is sufficiently acquainted with the relevant research literature;
3. has mastered the necessary techniques;
4. has an understanding of appropriate scientific methods;
5. is capable of assessing the significance of the findings.

---

[74] One way in which some universities try to make sure that examiners read the student's dissertation is that they ask for a pre-examination report from all the examiners concerned. A meeting of examiners is sometimes held before the examination begins.

The main feature distinguishing a Masters degree from an undergraduate degree is that the candidate is working alone on the dissertation to demonstrate an independent ability to produce high quality work. Of course the candidate will have a supervisor, but the help provided will be in terms of advice concerning the direction of the work. The Masters research project should be such that it can be completed within a year or, at the most, eighteen months of full-time study. However, as with the Doctorate, few candidates complete their Masters degree in minimum time.

16.3 Course work and the Masters Degree

As previously mentioned there is an increasing trend for Masters degrees to be based largely on course work. The rationale for this is that course work Masters degrees are mostly to do with preparing individuals to take on more senior professional work.

Although there is considerable debate as to how rigorous research for this type of degree should be it is generally agreed that it should go some way to meeting the standards laid down for a dissertation required by the more traditional Masters degree. Thus a candidate for this type of degree will still have to be familiar with some of the research methodology issues as well as show a firm grasp of the subject matter being studied.

Of course, the exact research requirements for this type of Masters degree not only vary from university to university, but also from one department, or faculty, to another within the same university. Different supervisors will also have varying views of what is required from the research component of a Masters degree by course work. Thus candidates need to be familiar with precisely what is required of them from their own institution.

16.4 A holistic evaluation approach

Research dissertations are frequently evaluated on a holistic basis, that is to say the examiners decide if the dissertation as a whole meets the objectives laid down by the institution. Here the process of the study may be almost as important as the final output.

One of the holistic criteria is that the document needs to stand alone as an account of the work that has been performed, and should be fully understandable in its own right. The dissertation needs to be well written, well argued and illustrated with appropriate figures and tables in order to prove convincingly the case being presented. The central issue is that the findings and recommendations of the research have been persuasively presented and communicated.

A final holistic issue that examiners consider is the production, presentation and layout of the document or book. In the first place all universities have regulations with regards to the format of the dissertation, and the candidate needs to comply with these strictly. Secondly, the production of the dissertation needs to have been undertaken to a high standard. Thus the candidate needs to ask the question, 'Is the dissertation ready to go on to the university library shelf?'

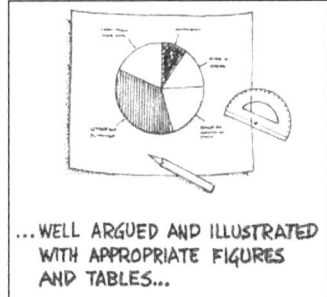

... WELL ARGUED AND ILLUSTRATED WITH APPROPRIATE FIGURES AND TABLES...

16.5 Research report - Course Work Masters Degree

The requirements for the research report at this level vary substantially. Some institutions require a relatively short and simple piece of work, while others ask their candidates to produce a dissertation which is close to that required for a Masters degree by dissertation. The main guideline for this group of degrees is that the dissertation or research report be distinctly different from a business or management report written by a consultant or executive for decision-making purposes. Even this relatively modest piece of academic work needs to show some evidence of acquaintance with some part of the literature and the fact that some thought has been given to the approach or method that has been taken to the research. MBA research reports, in particular, are sometimes criticised for being little more than business or management reports. But such a comment would only apply to poorly prepared research reports. A research report as part of a Masters degree by course work should be academically sound in its own right, that is, it should be correctly documented and should have a modest research question and an attempt to find a sound answer to that question. Although there is substantial variation, these dissertations or research reports tend to be between 40 and 60 pages in length.

16.6 Evaluating a Masters Degree by dissertation

For a Masters degree by dissertation, the dissertation should clearly demonstrate that the candidate is a master of the subject material, that he or she has a comprehensive understanding of the subject which has been addressed, and also that the candidate has understood the methodological issues associated with the approach taken in the research.

It is not usual for the Masters degree candidate to have to demonstrate that something has been added to the body of theoretical knowledge, and thus the work does not have to show the type of originality required for a doctoral degree. Academics often have considerable difficulty in describing the exact difference between the dissertations required for these two degrees. Sometimes it is argued that the Masters dissertation is the result of some 4,000 hours work while the doctorate is the result of about 6,000 hours. However such calculations are quite problematic for several reasons including the fact that quantity is no substitute for quality. There is also the fact that for some Masters and Doctoral degrees the dissertation is only part of the requirement.

A better approach might be to understand that a Masters dissertation is not expected to answer *why* questions to the same extent, but must answer *what questions*, and should say something about *how*. A Masters dissertation can be mostly concerned with *what* questions. A doctorate on the other hand would only deal with questions of *what happened* as *data*, and not as a substantive part of the dissertation. Some of the differences between the requirements for masters and doctoral degrees can be seen in Table 16.1.

A Masters dissertation should clearly demonstrate the candidate's ability to document his or her research to academic standards. The Masters dissertation will follow the same general format as the doctoral dissertation described below but the work will not be as rigorously pursued, as it would be for the higher degree. A Masters dissertation does not have to be a long document. Somewhere between 100 to 130 pages for a Masters degree is normally quite acceptable.

Appendix 8 provides an example of how one university describes the difference between the requirements for a Masters and a Doctoral degree.

Table 16.1: Distinctions between Masters and Doctoral degrees by dissertation

Nature of Enquiry and Results	Masters	Doctorate
Data: What happened?	Can be a substantive part of the dissertation, if coding/categorisation is sophisticated.	Only useful as input.
Relationship between factors/variables: How did it happen?	Often substantive, high value. Required in part at least. Critique not required.	Required. Can be the substantive part of the dissertation. Critique essential.
Underlying theory: Why did it happen?	Not necessary, but would make it exceptional.	Often substantive, high value. Required in part at least.
Prediction and extrapolation: What will happen next?	Not necessary or expected.	Not necessary, but would make it exceptional

16.7 Details that examiners inspect closely

Besides evaluating holistically, as has been discussed above, examiners also look for a considerable amount of detail in each chapter of a dissertation. Although the detail may be regarded in some institutions as less important than the holistic criteria, it is essential if the candidate is to obtain the degree. The following sections look at each chapter of a dissertation separately and highlight the most important issues.

16.7.1 Introduction to the subject

It is important that the introduction captures the imagination of the reader by showing why the subject is important and thus worthy of the award of a degree. Examiners will look for a comprehensive presentation of the background to the problem, which should include a clear and convincing argument that the subject of the research is topical, relevant and important. This implies that the work will lead to the development of guidelines that will be of direct use in business and management situations. The introduction should include key definitions, a brief description of the research tasks, indicating the steps to be followed through the dissertation, and an outline of the main conclusions.

16.7.2 Literature review

The literature review is of considerable importance and needs to be thorough and exhaustive. The references should be taken primarily from the leading academic journals and not from general textbooks. References to relevant textbooks or even to articles in the popular press are acceptable, but these should be kept to a minimum. References should be made to both theoretical and empirical issues pertaining to the research topic. All references cited should be complete and should comply with the convention accepted by the university concerned.

The candidate should not regurgitate the ideas from the literature but rather evaluate and comment on them critically and constructively. There should not be too many direct quotes from referenced works. This is a central requirement, especially for a doctoral degree.

By the end of the literature review the candidate will probably have prepared a conceptual model that describes the key variables relating to the phenomenon being researched and how these variables are linked to one another. This mathematical relationship could be presented as either a narrative or graphical presentation, or both.

16.7.3 Research questions

The research questions need to be directly related to the conceptual model developed from the literature review referred to above. They should be couched in a clear way and be easily operationalised (Miles and Hubermann, 1994). Only a limited number of research questions are required and examiners will usually be critical if too many issues are covered; in some circumstances one research question may be perfectly adequate. Research questions should be focused so they will have to lead to a theoretical conjecture or to hypotheses or empirical generalisations.

16.7.4 Methodology

The question of methodology is complex and there are many different views. The traditional approach to business and management studies was to employ methodologies borrowed from the natural sciences and thus much of the work performed in this field relied on the positivist research paradigm. In recent years however, qualitative research approaches (Patton, 1990) have grown in popularity and today play an important role in research in this field.

It is critical to spell out the philosophical approach being used to underpin the research (Remenyi, 1995). This dictates the research strategy and it is important that it is consistent. The two main philosophical stances used in academic research are positivism and interpretivism and within these there are a number of different research strategies. If an eclectic approach is used this should be carefully justified as many examiners are critical of this as it is difficult to carry out in terms of methodological rigour and clarity, as well as being difficult because it requires a high level of mastery in more than one methodology, which is rarely achieved by researchers (or supervisors or examiners!).

This chapter should include a full description of the process used to gather both primary and secondary evidence, which will normally be both qualitative and quantitative in nature. The methods of evidence collection and proposed analyses should be defined, together with a statement of the limitations of the approach that has been adopted.

16.7.5 Data or evidence collection and analysis

This is one of the most challenging parts of a research degree. The examiners look to see if an appropriate approach has been taken to the actual evidence collection. The questions asked here frequently relate to sampling procedures and instrumentation. Where case studies have been used it is important to state why the particular organisations were chosen (Yin, 1989). Examiners will consider the rigour with which this has

... IF ESTABLISHED PRACTICES HAVE NOT BEEN FOLLOWED THE CANDIDATE NEEDS TO EXPLAIN WHY CONVINCINGLY.

been done. The techniques used to analyse the evidence collected will be closely scrutinised and they need to comply with accepted practice in the discipline being researched. If established practices have not been followed the candidate needs to explain why convincingly.

The results of the interpretation or the analysis need to be presented using traditional presentation techniques, such as tables, graphs etc. The departure point for the analysis is the provision of a profile of the sample that forms the basis for subsequent deeper analysis and generalisations and this needs to be explicitly stated. This aspect of the study is key to assessing the validity of the findings from the research.

Any problems encountered in dealing with the above issues should be stated, together with an explanation as to how they were overcome.

16.7.6 Interpretation of the research findings

This chapter will discuss the findings in a general way as well as focusing on some specific interpretations of the results.

It is essential that the interpretation of the findings are consistent with the analysis. There needs to be a clear logical path from the original conceptual model, to the evidence, to the analysis, and then to the findings. Examiners look to see if the findings constitute a clear addition to the body of knowledge. The question 'Has the work made a clear contribution to the field of study?' will be asked. In establishing this, the examiners will need to decide if the candidate has made a convincing argument (Collins, 1994). In the business and management field one of the most important criteria is whether the results of the research can be put to some practical use. Thus the question, 'Are the findings useful?', is frequently asked. The questions of validity, bias and generalisability have also to be addressed in this chapter irrespective of whether a quantitative or qualitative approach has been taken. It is not essential that the results are generalisable, but this issue needs to be fully discussed.

Sometimes the evidence collected by the research and the analysis thereof does not support the original conceptual model. This does not mean that the candidate's research has been a failure. Failing to confirm a theory or hypothesis can be just as valuable as a positive confirmation, and it could lead to the development of a research theory. Senior degrees may be awarded even where the candidate has not confirmed his or her research hypothesis, provided a contribution has been made to the body of knowledge.

16.7.7 Summary and conclusion of the dissertation

The conclusion provides an opportunity to tie up the loose ends, to state the limitations of the research and to suggest where research in the subject should now proceed. The implications of the research for the management and business community in general should also be stated here.

If any part of the work of the candidate has already been published then this should be pointed out in support of the findings.

The conclusions should finish with a statement of the positive aspects of the research work, even if the research did not fully support the original model or beliefs.

16.7.8 The limitations of the research

Here there is the opportunity to reflect on the research and to discuss its strengths and weaknesses. It is sometimes said that this is the place for reflectivity, meaning that the researcher can reflect on the work in a holistic way and make an evaluation of the dissertation him or herself. This is an important chapter and even a relatively weak dissertation can be substantially strengthened by an insightful account of the research at this stage.

16.8 Management guidelines or recommendations

In this final chapter of a dissertation the findings are restructured in terms of practical guidelines, which can be used by managers in order to improve their performance in working situations.

16.9 The grading of research degrees

Some universities only distinguish between dissertations that have earned a pass grade and those that have not. Thus the candidate can either pass or not pass. In the case of the latter, the candidate is frequently encouraged to do more work. However, some other universities do award Masters and Doctorates *cum laude,* or with distinction. It is difficult to define the requirements for these awards and perhaps all that can be said of a general nature is that outstanding work is required to achieve these accolades.

16.10 A Checklist

The following is a checklist of 22 questions which will be directly useful to doctoral candidates but will also have some relevance to Masters students, especially those hoping to achieve a distinction, and which they should consult before finally submitting their dissertation. The checklist is broken into two parts: general or holistic issues and detailed issues.

General or Holistic Issues

1. Is the identified problem or question clearly specified, structured and articulated?
2. Does the work make a valuable contribution to the body of knowledge and how is this demonstrated?
3. Is the argument in the dissertation convincing?
4. Does the supervisor agree that the work is ready for examination?
5. Is the document about the right length?
6. Is the dissertation ready to be placed in the public domain or library?
7. Are the requirements relating to the certification and the format complied with?

Detailed Issues

1. Is it demonstrated that the subject of the research is important?
2. Is the literature review complete and is it sufficiently critical?
3. Was a new conceptual model developed from the literature review?
4. Is the research question clear and how has it been derived?
5. Does the research question convert to empirical generalisations, propositions or hypotheses?
6. Have the details of the research method been explained?
7. Is there a sound approach to data collection?
8. Have the analytical techniques been fully justified?
9. Is there a clear logical path throughout the dissertation?
10. What is the importance of the findings?
11. Have validity, reliability and bias been adequately addressed?
12. Are the final conclusions sufficiently convincing?
13. Have the limitations of the research been adequately addressed?
14. Have the findings been translated into management guidelines?
15. Does the dissertation suggest further research topics?
16. Does the 'Summary and Conclusions' chapter finish on a positive note?

Only when of these questions have been satisfactorily answered should the candidate present his or her work for examination.

16.11 Some problems encountered by examiners

The supervisor needs to be aware of the major issues which examiners find problematical in doctoral dissertations. The following is a summary from Varadatajan (1996),

1. The justification for the research problem or research question is not strong enough.
2. Theories borrowed or applied inappropriately.
3. The research is not sufficiently focused on the stated objectives.
4. The literature review is inadequately critical and does not directly relate to the research question.
5. Too many new concepts used and/or those used not properly defined.
6. There is an inadequate connection between the underpinning or reference theory and the research.
7. The model used is not convincing and either too complex or lacking in sophisticated.
8. Research questions are inadequate, not grounded in the theory or the proceeding discussion.
9. Measuring instruments and established scales borrowed inappropriately.

If these issues can be avoided then there is likelihood that the dissertation will receive little criticism.

16.12 Additional problems with research dissertations

There are many ways in which a dissertation may be inadequate and a full list would be too difficult to compile here. Here are a few of the more commons issues which arise:-

1. Academic writing is difficult and not all degree candidates will be able to write adequately. Sometimes the suggestion of having the work edited is made. This is a dangerous option as editing can change the meaning of the work. There is also the point that one of the characteristics of scholarship is being able to craft a flawless argument and if the work has to be edited then the student has not made the grade with regards to scholarship.
2. The student may not have complied with the presentation rules of the university i.e. if the Harvard Referencing System was required then it is essential to use it.

3. The university's requirements as regards the descriptive information have to be followed. Recently a dissertation was refused by the Post Graduate Examinations Office because the student number and date of submission were not provided as requested.

4. Dissertations have to be accompanied by various certifications such as the fact that the document contains only the students own work and that this work has not been submitted elsewhere for a degree.

5. Although not common there are sometimes fatal flaws in the work. A fatal flaw occurs when the research is performed so poorly that it cannot be said that the work answers the question or makes a useful contribution to the field of study. Sometimes this happens when inadequate sub-questions are set which do not directly relate to the main research question.

6. Sometimes the data acquired is clearly inadequate. This may be because there isn't enough data collected or it may be because the data has been collected inappropriately.

7. The analytical tools chosen may have been inappropriate.

8. The biases of the research may interfere with any aspect of the work and discredit it.

16.13 If the evaluation of the dissertation is disputed

It is important to note that a student may appeal against a decision regarding the evaluation of his or her dissertation. However the appeal cannot be on the grounds of there having been a poor or unsatisfactory academic judgement[75]. The following statement was extracted from Aston University's website and it is quite representative of the position taken by universities on this subject.

You should note that there is no right of appeal against the academic judgement of examiners. Disagreement with the academic judgement of a Board of Examiners in assessing the merits of an individual piece of work or in reaching a decision on a student's progress or on the final level of an award, based on the marks, grades and other information relating to the student's performance, cannot in itself constitute

---

[75] The grounds for appeal would have to claim that there were errors made in the process surrounding the examination or that the supervisor did not perform his or her function to a satisfactory degree. Because there are always at least two examiners and a chairperson the university takes the position that any academic differences of opinion will be aired and resolved during the examination.

grounds for an appeal. http://www1.aston.ac.uk/registry/for-staff/regsandpolicies/academic-appeals-procedure/grounds-for-appeal/

This claim by universities that "there is no right of appeal against the academic judgement of examiners" has been subject to criticism. Some academics say that this attitude is similar to the head of the Roman Catholic Church i.e. the Pope, claiming to be infallible in matters of dogma. Many people would see this claim to be amusingly self deluding. In the case of academic judgement differences of opinion as to the value of an academic contribution are notorious and yet this claim is made. Perhaps this claim is a legacy from the fact that the original universities evolved from the cathedral schools of the Middle Ages before the Reformation.

In a recent examination in which there were two external examiners as the student was registered for the degree at the university at which he was employed the first external opened the pre-viva discussion with the comment that the dissertation represented a sound piece of work. The second external examiner then proceeded to say that this was one of the weakest dissertations he had the misfortune of examining. The result of this was a long pre-examination discussion before the viva could begin and a difficult experience for the student.

Academic judgement is not only problematic at research degree examinations. Here are two summary statements provided by two referees or reviewers of the same paper submitted to a peer reviewed academic journal.

Referee 1: The paper is timely, terse and rather forcefully presented. I regard it as of far-above-average value to the journal's readers.

Referee 2: A large segment of the paper is historical. The remaining part is speculative, verbose and not well written.

These two examples show how unconvincing the claim is that academic judgement should be unquestioned.

16.14 Summary

This chapter has reviewed some of the research degrees offered by universities. In particular it has considered Masters and Doctoral degrees, including those offered by dissertation only and those obtained through a combination of course work and research. It will be noticed that there is a range of degrees available with a substantial diversity in the amount of research required from a candidate in order to qualify. Thus candidates who have a relatively low inclination to research can select degree options where there is a substantial amount of course work.

The principal issues on which examiners focus for the evaluation of the research work have been outlined, both holistically and in the detail required for typical chapters of a dissertation.

Research degree candidates are offered advice as to what is required in their written output in terms of both academic content and technical presentation. A checklist has been provided which, if used to ensure the dissertation is complete, can assist candidates obtain approval for their work.

Although research is demanding, many graduates report that the research process has been one of the most satisfactory periods of their career and that they have learnt more from this process than they have done during any other part of their education.

16.15 Useful books and/or websites

Mullins, G. and Kiley, M. (2002) 'It's a PhD, not a Nobel Prize: how experienced examiners assess research theses', *Studies in Higher Education*, vol. 27, no. 4, pp 369–386.

Tinkler, P. and Jackson, C. (2000) 'Examining the Doctorate: institutional policy and the PhD examination process in Britain', *Studies in Higher Education*, vol. 25, no. 2, pp 167–180.

Yung, B.H.W. (2001) 'Examiner, Policeman or Students' Companion: teachers' perceptions of their role in an assessment reform', *Educational Review*, vol. 53, no. 3, pp 251–260.

Part Five
The Examination Process

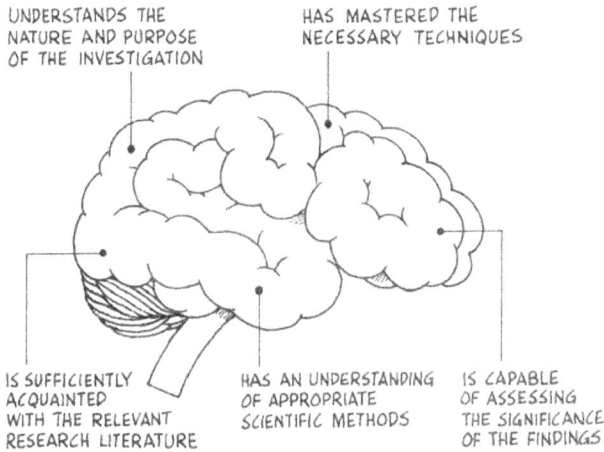

UNDERSTANDS THE
NATURE AND PURPOSE
OF THE INVESTIGATION

HAS MASTERED THE
NECESSARY TECHNIQUES

IS SUFFICIENTLY
ACQUAINTED
WITH THE RELEVANT
RESEARCH LITERATURE

HAS AN UNDERSTANDING
OF APPROPRIATE
SCIENTIFIC METHODS

IS CAPABLE
OF ASSESSING
THE SIGNIFICANCE
OF THE FINDINGS

NECESSARY ATTRIBUTES FOR
A RESEARCH DEGREE CANDIDATE

Chapter 17

The choice of examiner/s

*Learning through doing is a wonderful way of appreciating
knowledge and turning it into useful skills.*
Silverman, D. (1993) Interpreting Qualitative Data, London: Sage Publications p viii.

17.1 The research examination process

Even if a research student is talented and has performed the work to a highly satisfactory level there still may be problems in obtaining the degree. This is due to the peculiar nature of the research degree examination process and it is indeed important that the supervisor plays a full role in this process.

Before describing the examination process it is important to establish that university degrees are normally awarded by the university senate on the recommendation of an examination board. The examination board may operate by delegating to sub-committees or to heads of department or to deans of faculty their powers to recommend the awarding or conferring of degrees. Sometimes there is a sub-committee that deals with first degrees such as Bachelors and a sub-committee that deals with higher degrees such as Masters and Doctorates. It is either a sub-committee or a head of department or a dean who appoints the examiners for a Masters or a Doctoral degree candidate.

17.2 Appointing examiners

The people who appoint the examiner or examiners are usually quite distant to the individual and the subject matter being examined. It is certainly a 'good thing' that they are distant from the individual concerned but it is not necessarily as wise for them to be distant from the subject matter being examined. The main reason for this is that it is necessary to appoint an examiner who is competent and this will mean at doctoral level a world-class or near world-class expert in the field being examined. If this is not hard enough, it is also important that the examiner or examiners appointed be knowledgeable of and 'sympathetic' to the research methodology used by the student. If these two conditions are not correctly met then the research degree examination can go badly astray. The supervisor needs to play an active role in advising the sub-committee or the head of department or the dean as to who would be competent examiners.

As mentioned before, in the past it was usual for the supervisor to become one of the examiners. This was quite widely the practice for Masters dissertations, and continues today in many institutions. But it is now rare, if not unacceptable, for the supervisor to be an examiner at doctoral level. What effectively happened was that the supervisor changed hats when the dissertation was submitted and became an examiner. Although there was much merit in this approach it was generally felt that the supervisor was too close to the student to be an impartial examiner. However even with the current system, it is really important to remember that the supervisor will, by necessity, be an examiner 'by proxy' or at the very least a gatekeeper to the examination process. The research degree is only complete when the supervisor advises the student that he or she has finished. This of course can create a problem as sometimes the student thinks that he or she has finished before the supervisor is ready to accept the work. In the case of a difference of opinion it is advisable for the student to defer to the supervisor. However if there has been a breakdown in the relationship it is usual for the university to allow the student to override the supervisor and insist on examination. Of course this is a high-risk strategy for the student, which has been compared to a turkey voting for an early Christmas.

17.3 The internal examiner

The appointment of the internal examiner is an important matter. On the face of it the internal examiner has equal status to the external examiner and as such is every bit as important. However whereas the external examiner is chosen from a worldwide pool of academics – at least in theory, if the university can afford the travel costs – the internal examiner is chosen from faculty within the university itself. Sometimes it is difficult to find a suitably qualified internal examiner. In some cases a second external examiner has been used.

Although the internal or second examiner has equal say many universities behave as though he or she does not. It is frequently said that the external is the really important person to impress with the quality of the research. Many internal examiners go along with this, but occasionally internals can exert their influence and it has been known that the external wanted to pass a degree and the internal examiner called for it to be failed. When this happens and a discussion under the auspices of the examination chairperson cannot resolve the difference in opinion the usual procedure is for the university to appoint another examiner.

The formal position is that the degree is awarded by a sub-committee of the university senate[76] and that this committee can overturn the decision of an examiner or for that matter both examiners.

17.4 Choosing the examiners

Once the supervisor is confident that the student's work has reached the required standard the dissertation is submitted to the appropriate university official who will normally request the supervisor to advise on potentially suitable examiners. It is common practice for the supervisor to have discussed with the student the names of the individuals who are world-class authorities in the field of study and who are known to be sympathetic to the research methodology used. The supervisor will on the basis of this discussion submit a list of names to the university official in the Dean of Research's office. This list should not include anyone with whom the student has published or with whom the student has closely worked.

17.5 A pre-viva report

The individuals on this list should be known as fair examiners who will do a thorough job in a reasonable period of time. In the past examiners have been known to only superficially read the student's work and thus not be particularly familiar with the dissertation[77], while on other occa-

---

[76] The terminology may differ from university to university but most universities will have a degree awarding body which is normally referred to as the University Senate. This may consist of several hundred professors. The Senate will have a sub-committee which may be called the Higher Degrees Committee or the Post Graduate Degrees Committee. This committee will consider the examiners' reports and make recommendations to the Senate for the awarding of a degree. The Senate would not normally be involved in any one person's degree award. This procedure is different on Continental Europe and differs from country to country.

[77] I was recently told an interesting story about how superficially a dissertation may be read by an external examiner. A doctoral candidate was instructed by his supervisor to reproduce five copies of his dissertation, which was some 600 pages long. This was done and two of the copies were sent to the two external examiners. This doctoral candidate had two examiners because he was on the faculty of the university where he was registered for his Doctorate. While waiting outside the door of the meeting room in which the examination was to take place the doctoral candidate started once again to page through the copy of the dissertation which he had brought with him to the examination. He noticed that in this copy of the dissertation pages 40 to 100 were printed twice and he put this down to an error made by the print-room in his department and did not think much of it. In due course the examination began and it proceeded well and there was a satisfactory outcome with the doctoral candidate only having to make a few minor

sions examiners have been known to delve into excessive details. In the examination process excessive detail is neither necessary nor acceptable.

In more recent times in the United Kingdom both the internal and the external examiner have been required to produce a pre-viva report on the dissertation. The Dean of Research will normally review this report before the viva examination commences. Some universities will allow the research degree candidate to have sight of this pre-viva report several days before the actual examination.

It is not easy to find suitable examiners. Universities generally pay a small honorarium to examiners. It can take five or six hours and 12 to 14 hours to carefully read a masters or doctoral dissertation respectively[78]. The main reward for the examiner is keeping his or herself aware of the type of research that is being conducted. There is also an informal understanding between supervisors that if someone examines for you, in turn you will one day examine for him or her.

Where a viva voce is involved a supervisor may often be permitted to attend. In this respect the supervisor is present as an observer and generally will not participate in the discussion. However, it is useful for the supervisor to be available to the examiners to clarify any points or issues that arise in the discussion concerning, for example, problems that the candidate encountered during the research which necessitated a change in strategy.

---

changes to the dissertation. At the end of the examination one of the external examiners said pointing at the wastepaper basket, "I hate to carry excessive paper, may I now bin this copy of the dissertation". The doctoral candidate said, "Please don't. I would rather put the dissertation through the shredder in my office myself and make sure that there are no copies floating around". On returning to his office the doctoral candidate found that this copy of the dissertation used by the external examiner was rather light and on further inspection it transpired that pages 40 to 100 were missing. The external examiner had clearly not noticed this fact.

[78] A long-standing acquaintance says that a PhD dissertation written at Cambridge University should be kept short. By this he means short enough to be read in less than two hours. The reason for this he asserts is that the average train travel time required for a journey from the major universities in the south of the United Kingdom to Cambridge University is two hours and that is all the time an average external examiner is prepared to devote to reading the documents before the viva voce begins. Clearly this is a rather cynical view of the amount of effort which external examiners are prepared to devote to pre-examination preparation. On the other hand there may be some truth in it.

17.6 Summary

To facilitate the choice of an external examiner/s a short list of examiners should be established in conversation between the supervisor and the student. This short list should be sent to the Dean of Research or the equivalent office bearer as described in chapter 3. The university should ensure that the examiner/s is/are appropriately qualified and that he or she is in sympathy with the research philosophy espoused by the student.

It is important that the examiner does not have a relationship with the degree candidate or have previously worked closely with him or her. It can take two to three months to arrange the examination due to the availability of the examiners.

17.7 Useful books and/or websites

http://ask.metafilter.com/64340/Questions-about-External-PhD-Examiners [7 Jan 2012]

http://www.postgraduateforum.com/threadViewer.aspx?TID=8406 [7 Jan 2012]

http://www.timeshighereducation.co.uk/story.asp?storycode=406493 [7 Jan 2012]

Chapter 18

The viva voce

New knowledge should make a difference in some way, materially, aesthetically, spiritually. A good academic journal should disseminate new information directly to those who can apply it. At minimum, and as a regular matter, a good academic journal should stimulate the research community to improve its performance in creating new and useful knowledge.
King, J.L. (1993) 'Editorial Notes', *Information Systems Research***, 4(4), pp. 291- 298.**

18.1 The viva verses the examination report

The Latin term *viva voce*, or the Defence in North America, refers to an oral examination which is held in many countries but not in all. The viva, as it is usually referred to, stems from the fact that the university wanted to check that it was indeed the author who wrote the dissertation and not a family member or friend. In countries where there was not a large number of suitable qualified individuals to examine doctoral research dissertation a different method of examination was employed. In these countries the dissertation was examined by report and those invited to examine the documents were thought to be world class scholars. The report which is required is often highly structured and thorough and is generally thought to be an adequate approach to examining.

Many academics would argue that the viva voce is an educational experience in itself and as such it is a "good thing". However it can happen that the examiners take a "dislike" to the degree candidate and this can influence the course of the examination and if this happens the viva can become a problem.

18.2 Preparing for the viva

Certain documentation must be made available to the examiners prior to the examination. These include the regulations pertaining to the degree – PhD, DBA, and MPhil etc. – as well as procedures for examining the dissertation, conducting the viva and the nature of the examiners' reports.

Most universities require the examiners to file independent reports prior to the viva-voce examination. These reports form the basis for the pre-viva meeting between the examiners. They also form part of the final submission to the university.

At the pre-viva meeting these reports are used to reach a decision concerning the quality of the work, the issues that need be explored and also to help the examiners decide how the viva will be conducted. It is important that the viva has good structure and is not just a series of random questions.

18.3 The examining committee

Those attending the viva include the degree candidate, the examiners and sometimes the Director or Dean of Research from the university at which the candidate is registered[79]. In most institutions the degree candidate's supervisor can also attend this examination[80]. Normally institutions appoint one internal examiner and one external examiner. The internal examiner will be a knowledgeable individual working at the same university who will frequently be from the same or an adjacent field of study to that of the candidate, but who will not have had any direct involvement in supervising the dissertation. The external examiner will be an expert in the field of study which has been researched and in which the degree candidate is being examined, and will probably hold a senior appointment at a similar university[81].

The viva will normally be conducted between one and three months after the dissertation has been submitted. The actual timing will depend on the availabilities of the examiners, but it is important to hold this event while the material is fresh in the mind of the degree candidate.

While the arrangements described above do vary considerably, in all cases a group of examiners will be assembled for the viva[82]. They will then spend time talking to the candidate and, at the end of this discus-

---

[79] In Continental Europe the Vice-Chancellor may also attend the examination. In this case as soon as the examining committee has declared the result of the viva the degree is awarded and the graduation may take place at the same time. Although this system does allow for the student to fail the viva it very seldom happens. In the USA invited outsiders sometimes become part of the examination committee and are ask to voice an opinion of the research.

[80] Not very long ago it was customary for the supervisor to be one of the examiners. However this has largely been abandoned. In an important sense the supervisor is always a sort of examiner and if a student does not have the full backing of his or her supervisor then the outcome of the examination may not be favourable. At some universities the supervisor may only attend the viva with the express permission of the degree candidate.

[81] The holding of a senior position is sometimes more important than the formal qualifications of the examiners. Where a member of the university faculty is being examined there are sometimes two external examiners and, on occasion, no internal examiner.

[82] Some universities will allow one of the examiners to be absent from the viva and will accept a written report from that examiner. There normally has to be a good reason for this absence. Other universities will allow a viva examination being conducted by video-link. Sometimes a viva may be conducted abroad if the research degree candidate and his or her examiners are all attending, for example, the same conference.

sion, will decide if and under exactly what conditions the degree will be awarded.

18.4 Improper conduct

The student may sometimes be told the name of the examiners in advance. This does not in any way prejudice the examination. However the student should not make any attempt to contact the examiner. Recently a doctoral degree student e-mailed his examiner with what he said was an addendum to the dissertation on the day before the viva. When the examiner enquired of the examinations office if the presentation of an addendum was allowed the administrators dismissed the examiner saying that any contact between the student and the examiner, even the sending of one e-mail, was sufficient to declare the examination process flawed.

18.5 The outcome of a viva

The outcome of a viva can also vary considerably. At the positive end of the spectrum the examiners may decide to award the degree without asking the candidate to undertake any changes or improvements to the dissertation. At the other end, the examiners can, at least in theory, fail the candidate. Although examiners always reserve the right to fail a candidate it is very unusual for this to happen. One of the reasons for this is that an outright failure would reflect badly on both the supervisor and the institution in general. For this reason weak candidates are normally advised not to proceed to examination[83,84].

If the dissertation is not of sufficient quality and the doctoral candidate is seen not to be competent, the usual procedure is for the examiners to request additional work. They can instruct the doctoral candidate to review a body of literature or to repeat or extend an evidence collection exercise that could take at least another year. This outcome would not be regarded as a success.

---

[83] Candidates usually have the right to demand an examination. When a candidate disregards advice not to proceed to examination and forces one, it is often not successful.
[84] It seems that it is acceptable for an examiner to send the manuscript back to the examinations office once saying that the work is not ready for examination. The difficulty arises when the work is resubmitted without any material improvement. At that point the university may feel that it is necessary to examine the student.

An outright failure is unusual and will only occur in extreme circumstances such as when there is clear evidence of complete incompetence or maybe of some form of cheating. The term failure here is being used in the sense that the degree candidate is told that the work is so poor that the university is discontinuing his or her registration and that the work will not be considered for any other degree at that institution. There is another set of circumstances which is sometimes referred to by academics as failure of the Doctorate and this occurs when the degree candidate is told that his or her work is not appropriate for a Doctorate, but that it is adequate for a masters degree such as an MPhil[85].

It is not that uncommon for the examiners, even when the dissertation and the viva are both good, to require some additional work to be done. In fact examiners sometimes, if not often, feel that they need to ask the candidate to add something to the dissertation so that the examiner has made a contribution to or just made their mark on the work. The candidate should not be concerned when this happens.

18.6 The viva process

The oral examination itself has been known to be as short as 60 minutes and as long as all day[86]. It is often the case that the shorter the duration of the examination the more competent the degree candidate. When a viva takes many hours, it can be because the examiners are trying hard to find the positive side of the candidate's research. In most cases two hours is perfectly adequate to determine how much an individual knows about a subject and how well the research has been performed.

Increasingly a viva begins with the degree candidate being asked to give a five minute high level overview presentation of the work. If this is not offered by the chairperson then the student should ask for it. These five

---

[85] With regards to obtaining an MPhil in lieu of a Doctorate the actual mechanism depends on the particular university. In some cases it will be decided that a Masters will be awarded at the end of the unsuccessful viva. In other cases it will be decided that the doctoral degree dissertation will be withdrawn and that the work will be resubmitted for separate reconsideration as a Masters degree. In some cases it may be necessary to allow a period of six months to elapse before the work may be re-submitted for consideration for an MPhil.

[86] There have even been incidents where the viva has run into a second day. However this is very unusual and may be interpreted as the university not being experienced at vivas.

minutes are important and the student should point out three important issues which are:-

1. Where the contribution to the body of theoretical knowledge has been made;
2. How the document can be considered to be adequately scholarly;
3. Papers published and conferences attended during the period of supervised study.

The viva process is, or should be, one of scholarly debate, which is stimulated by the examiners and especially the external examiner. This debate can be challenging, with the candidate being required to face quite penetrating questioning. The examiners will have previously read the dissertation and in some instances will have already shared their personal views by means of a pre-viva report. In the case of strong candidates, the examiners may have decided that, subject to the student not making a fool of him or herself during the viva, the degree is likely to be awarded.

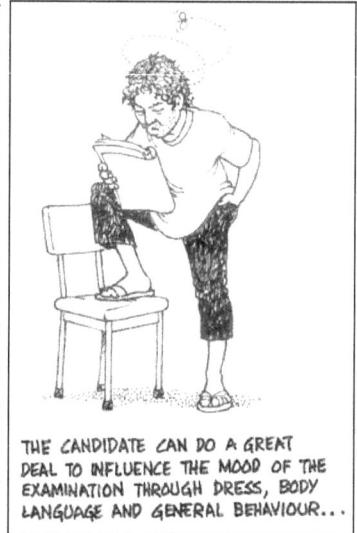

THE CANDIDATE CAN DO A GREAT DEAL TO INFLUENCE THE MOOD OF THE EXAMINATION THROUGH DRESS, BODY LANGUAGE AND GENERAL BEHAVIOUR...

Viva examinations often end with the chairperson asking those present if there are any more questions or final points that they would like to make. The research student should use this opportunity to summarise in two or three minutes – and no longer - the strengths of the dissertation.

18.7 Tone of the viva

The tone of the viva will of course depend upon the individuals taking part and it can vary considerably. The candidate can do a great deal to influence the mood of the examination through dress, body language and general behaviour. It needs to be understood by the candidate that he or she is seeking acceptance by the examiners and thus needs to exude confidence without arrogance. It is extremely important that *egos* do not become involved as this can lead to unpleasantness. The candidate needs to be conscious of the fact that there is a substantial imbalance in power between him or herself and the examiners. The fact that the examiners are friendly does not mean that they agree with what the degree candidate is saying or that they approve of his or her work. On the other hand the examiners need to ensure that the candidate does not feel unduly pressured and that he or she may have a break for refreshments whenever it is required during the examination.

In general terms the viva is not intended to be confrontational or adversarial. The main purpose of the event is to confirm what the student knows about the research and the field of study in order to be confident that the Doctorate has been duly earned. If the degree candidate has obtained an excessive amount of help in producing his or her dissertation, this should become obvious in the debate. Many successful students have reported that the examination was a pleasant experience and that they learnt quite a lot from it. However, it is not guaranteed that this will be the case and from time to time the experience is reported as having been harrowing indeed. The student needs to be prepared for this eventuality.

18.8 Central issues to be raised at the viva

There are seven central issues that should be addressed by the examiners in establishing whether the student has met the requirements. These are high level issues or concerns, which go to the very heart of a doctoral degree.

1. Does the candidate have a thorough understanding of the field in which the dissertation is presented?
2. Is there a clearly articulated research question, which seeks to establish a new theory, refute an old theory or develop an extension of an existing theory?
3. Is the work framed within the body of current theoretical knowledge and has a theory been used as a base for testing new ideas?
4. Has the research been conducted with appropriate procedures, discursive or observational and analytical, quantitative or qualitative?
5. Has the contribution to the body of theoretical knowledge been expressed clearly as a convincing and reflective argument?
6. Has it been demonstrated that the new theoretical knowledge has practical management validity and utility, i.e. potential value in use?
7. Is the work substantively that of the candidate?

If these criteria are met, even if not entirely, then the research should have a sound claim to be regarded as both rigorous and relevant, which is central to the Doctorate.

18.9 A contribution to the body of theoretical knowledge

A contribution to the body of theoretical knowledge is notoriously difficult to define and thus it is useful to think of it in terms of two broad issues.

Firstly it is essential that the student produce some new and interesting ideas as a result of the research. New and interesting ideas can of course have a number of meanings, but certainly the research findings should not smack of recycled motherhoods. There needs to be some angle that the examiners will not have thought of before[87]. Specifically the new angle could be an extension of existing theory, a new application of existing theory or a confirmation or rejection of some aspect of an existing theory[88].

The second issue is that the findings of the research should have in some sense a degree of general applicability. This does not have to be broad, but the research findings should, in the field of business and management studies, be relevant and have real value to a reasonable number of practicing managers.

From the point of view of the viva the examiners will try to probe the student on these issues and concerns using detailed questions in order to evaluate to what extent the candidate has achieved these points.

18.10 When the student has passed

A doctoral examination is normally a two pronged event i.e. dissertation and viva, and the degree candidate has to pass in both of these. A degree candidate who has presented a weak dissertation can to some extent make up for this with a strong showing during a viva. If a weak viva

---

[87] This does not mean that the candidate has to be unknown to the examiner or vice versa. They may well know each other or at least be familiar with each other's work through conferences or journal articles, but the examiners should have encountered the new and interesting ideas in the dissertation through the work of the candidate.

[88] It is possible that a doctoral degree candidate formulates a completely new theory, but this is a rather rare event.

follows a competent dissertation then the examiners will want some explanation for this.

When the dissertation is particularly good a question that sometimes arises is 'When should the student be informed of the examiners' opinion of the dissertation?' There is a fair amount of difference of opinion concerning this. Some examiners prefer to tell the student up front, especially if the work is clearly a pass. It seems that examiners have said, "Well done you have passed provided you don't make a fool of yourself in the next couple of hours". This is intended to minimise the stress level for the student. On the other hand if such a comment is made and the research student performs badly it will be even more embarrassing to inform him or her that their viva performance is inadequate.

Should it be a re-submission or fail it is usually left to the nature of the questioning at the viva that is used to get the student to come to the realisation by him or herself. In general, it seems that the best practice is to delay communicating the opinion of the dissertation until the end of the viva.

At the viva a joint examiners' report is produced on the appropriate university form which can recommend one of the following outcomes: an unconditional pass; pass with some minor revisions; re-submission which involves a major re-write; an MPhil after some re-working; a fail. The examiners normally have to state in writing the reasons for their decision. This joint report together with the pre-viva reports is then submitted to the appropriate university committee for confirmation.

If the decision is to award the degree subject to minor amendments then the examiners should provide the student and the supervisors with details of what is required. Sometimes a list of requirements is drafted with all the parties present immediately after the result of the viva is announced while on other occasions the examiners will offer to produce a written list within a few days. It is always better to finalise the list of changes required there and then when everyone is present and the issues are fresh in the minds of everyone. The time period for completion of minor amendments is normally not more than three months, although this varies from university to university.

Should a re-submission be requested the examiners need to provide a written report setting out what is required including the re-submission deadline, which is normally not more than twelve months from the date of the report. Also, on making the decision the examiners need to indicate whether another viva-voce would be required.

With regards to the academic adequacy of a dissertation supervisors are advised that it is poor practice to inform the degree candidate that he or she should pass. The performance of the student on the day can adversely affect the outcome and it is not possible to anticipate this.

18.11 Dissatisfaction with the result of the examination

Occasionally degree candidates are dissatisfied with the results of the examination process. Universities will generally not hear appeals if the academic judgement of the examiners is being questioned. Therefore the degree candidate may only appeal against the process through which he or she has been put[89].

Universities have their own particular complaints procedures and an unsatisfied student can easily obtain a copy of the rules. An appeal against an examination result usually falls under the complaints process. A form needs to be completed and the doctoral examination review process is set in train. The Faculty or the School will normally consider the application for appeal and they may then pass it on to a higher level in the university. A university officer will seek out evidence pertaining to the situation before the matter is formally considered.

It may take some months for the appeal process to work its way through the university system.

18.12 Summary

It is inevitable that the viva voce is a major challenge. This examination occurs after a long period of study which could be 3 or 5 or 7 years work and if anything goes wrong the loss in time, effort and money can be considerable. For strong doctoral degree candidates the experience of the viva voce can be enjoyable while for weak candidates it can be a disaster.

It needs to be noted that the university wants the degree candidate to succeed, but this cannot ever be assured for two reasons. Firstly there is the performance of the student on the day. Even competent students

---

[89] The process referred to here is both the examination and the whole of the degree preparation.

can have an "off-day" and perform poorly in an examination. Secondly, by definition the external examiner will be at least somewhat unknown to the university. Therefore the viva voce can go wrong.

Care needs to be taken by the Office of the Dean of Research, the supervisor and the research degree candidate when preparing for the viva voce. Slip-ups by anyone in this chain can cause an unsatisfactory outcome.

18.13 Useful books and/or websites

Cryer P, (1996) *The research student's guide to success*, Milton Keynes: Open University Press.

Johnson, B. (1991) Solving Conundrums in Clinical Psychiatry: A Guide to Viva Voce Examinations, Libra Pharmaceuticals Petrochemical Press.

Murray R, (2003) How to Survive Your Viva, London: Sage Publications.

Phillips, E. and Pugh, D. (1987) *How to Get a PhD - A Handbook for Students and their Supervisors*, 3rd edition, Milton Keynes: Open University Press.

Viva voce code of practice, available:
   http://www.lboro.ac.uk/admin/ar/student/exams/cop/viva.htm [10 Aug 2011].

Preparing for the viva voce, available:
   http://as.exeter.ac.uk/support/admin/research/graduation/viva/ [10 Aug 2011].

Chapter 19

Making post-viva changes

The mythology of science asserts that with many different scientists all asking their own questions and evaluating the answers independently, whatever personal bias creeps into their individual answers is cancelled out when the large picture is put together. This might conceivably be so if scientists were women and men from all sorts of different cultural and social backgrounds who came to science with very different ideologies and interests. But since, in fact, they have been predominantly university-trained white males from privileged social backgrounds, the bias has been narrow and the product often reveals more about the investigator than about the subject being researched.
Hubbard Ruth, (1979) 'Have Only Men Evolved?' in
***Women Look at Biology Looking At Women*, ed. Hubbard R., Henifin, M. S. and Fried B.**

19.1 Re-working and/or changes

As a result of the examination process it is frequently the case that the examiners suggest that changes or additions should be made to the dissertation. This re-working may involve what are actually trivial changes which will require a few days or a week of work, or it may be more substantial requiring the student to continue working on the research for even one more year. The additional work required will be spelt out in detail at the end of the viva voce and should be written down by the research degree candidate or his or her supervisor. In fact increasingly universities will issue a formal viva report in which all the required changes are listed.

19.2 Minor and major revisions

As mentioned previously there are usually four outcomes of a viva examination. These are:

1. Pass with no changes;
2. Pass or resubmit with minor amendments/revisions[90];
3. Resubmit with major amendments/revisions[91];
4. Fail.

Only the fourth category described above will mean that the research degree candidate may not obtain the doctoral degree. However it should be pointed out that a *fail* is a very unusual event. Some universities have other outcomes which can include offering the degree candidate a lesser award such as an MPhil. This option is less popular these days as it can be seen as an award for failure which is generally regarded as unacceptable. Some universities will allow a failed doctoral dissertation to be improved and re-submitted for the purposes of consideration for a MPhil degree.

In a similar way *Pass with no changes* is not usual. In the majority of cases the examiners will require some changes, sometimes quite minor ones to be undertaken before the degree is finally awarded.

---

[90] If the outcome is pass with minor changes it is common for the degree candidate to be congratulated by the examiners for having passed.
[91] With this category it may be necessary for the research degree candidate to resubmit to another viva. This is not common but it does from time to time happen.

When changes are called for the type of extra work to be undertaken may be to address additional literature which the research degree candidate has missed in the literature review. This could be a minor revision, and thus a relatively easy matter to which to attend. However any new sources of ideas and concepts will have to be seamlessly integrated into the original dissertation. Sometimes the changes are related to further analysis of the evidence or data collected. This is usually more challenging and may require restructuring the analysis, and probably conducting different types of analysis. This of course will mean changes to the discussion chapter and perhaps the ultimate findings of the research. Sometimes the research degree candidate will be asked to seek additional evidence and this could entail a new measuring instrument, new analysis and new findings. Clearly this constitutes a substantial piece of additional work and would normally be regarded as a major revision.

19.3 Who assesses the changes?

At the examination it will be stated to whose satisfaction this work needs to be completed. This is an important issue because the research degree candidate may have to liaise with the examiners if it is decided that the examiners will finally decide if the improved work is up to standard[92]. Whichever way this decision goes, it is generally the responsibility of the supervisor to oversee this extra work.

If the work is minor this is not a problem but nonetheless it is expected that the supervisor ensure that it is concluded satisfactorily.

If a major revision is required then it may be necessary for the supervisor to re-launch the student in a new research exercise in order to comply with the requirements of the external examiner. In some universities if the revisions are not completed to the satisfaction of the external examiner first time then the student can be failed and receive no award at all – not even a MPhil.

Therefore this assistance is an important part of supervision, which is unfortunately often neglected. The responsibility of the supervisor only

---

[92] Traditionally the internal examiner is asked to verify that the changes required by the examiners are satisfactory. But sometimes both internal and external examiners are involved.

ends when the student graduates or when he or she withdraws or if he or she is failed.

19.4 Summary

Try to establish the changes the examiners require at the end of the examination if possible. If the list is not given at that point it is possible that the examiners will think of additional issues later and include them in the requirements. This is not good practice. It is important for the student to make sure what is actually required as in most cases the outcome of the second submission of the dissertation is either pass or fail.

19.5 Useful books and/or websites

http://www.swan.ac.uk/registry/academicguide/postgraduatetaughtaw ardsregulations/postgraduatetaughtmastersdegrees/18resubmission/ [Jan 07 2012]

Part Six
Ethics

Chapter 20

Ethics of research

If you steal from one author, it's plagiarism; if you steal from many, it's research.
Wilson Mizner, (1953) in: Alva Johnston, The Legendary Mizners, ch. 4.

You may not like this, but you should. If the world ran in strict accordance with Newton's laws, like clockwork, then everything, down to the tiniest particle interaction, would be determined in advance. There would be no scope for free will. It is quantum uncertainty that gives us back the chance to run our own lives and make our own decisions rather than follow a preordained plan.
Gribbin J, ed. (1998) *A Brief History of Science*, London: Weidenfeld & Nicolson, p 77.

20.1 Ethical considerations underpin research

Research ethics affects the supervisor and their students in two ways. The first is that every research student needs to apply for the approval of an Ethics Protocol before the research can begin. This process has been described in Chapters 2 and 5. The second is that the research has to be conducted responsibly and this means complying with a code of good practice.

20.2 Towards a code of good practice

There are numerous issues that arise during a research project which may be regarded as having ethical implications and the supervisor needs to be aware of these and draw the student's attention to them. In addition because of the power imbalance between the supervisor and the degree candidate there is the potential for abuse and problems relating to ownership of the data and ideas (Mauch and Birch 1983).

It is important that the supervisor is able to give the student advice as to how to proceed so that the research work will not be considered to be ethically questionable. Summarised in one expression, these are issues that relate to being scrupulously honest in all matters relating to the research. These include all the usual concerns and may be summarised into three major categories, namely, plagiarism, openness with the informants, and presenting the results fairly.

In addition to these issues there are other ethical considerations that arise directly from the relationship between the supervisor and the student. The first of these and the one that gives the most problems is the question of publishing. It sometimes occurs that the student and the supervisor co-author papers during the student's research. This is in fact to be encouraged. However ethical considerations arise concerning how much work the supervisor needs to do before his or her name may ethically be included as an author on the paper. It has been known for supervisors to take the attitude that all work undertaken by the student during his or her period of supervision should include the name of the supervisor. This is an extreme point of view and would not be acceptable to most academics. The rule normally applied is that before anyone's name should appear on any piece of work, especially published papers, the people concerned need to have made a substantial contribution to the work. The problem that then arises is the definition of 'a substantial contribution'. There is no clear-cut solution to this tricky problem. But supervisors need to be aware of the possibility of criticism arising if their student feels that the supervisor is muzzling in on a publication without having made an appropriate contribution to the work. There is also the ethical issue of whether the paper can subsequently be used by the student as part of his or her dissertation. It is sometimes said by academics that if the supervisor made a contribution to the paper, then to what extent can the student claim that the work is entirely their own?

Another issue relating to the ethics of supervision is the question of the supervisor making time available to the student. Some supervisors are very generous with their time and allow students access whenever they wish. Others can insist on meeting only by appointment. However some supervisors have been known to make appointments with students and not turn up or to be very late or to keep students waiting all day outside their offices until they can fit them in between meetings. This type of behaviour would usually be considered to be unethical. Unfortunately students have little recourse when this happens.

20.3 Research and trust

University researchers, especially those working towards a Masters or Doctorate are in a privileged position. In the case of doctoral candidates, such researchers are working towards the highest degree which a university offers by examination, and this degree will not only give them a qualification but will change their status in society by giving them a title. Further, universities place a high level of trust in the candidates for these degrees. Universities generally assume that Masters and Doctoral candidates will perform their work to the highest ethical standards and thus, except for the advice offered by their supervisors or promoters, researchers in the business and management field are generally left alone to work independently. In this field universities usually require no other verification of the ethical standards used during the research work other than a certificate stating that the research is the personal work of the degree candidate.

In addition to the trust placed in business and management research candidates by the university, business people and others will generally be prepared to discuss their affairs with university degree candidates much more frankly and openly than they would with other people, including non-academic researchers. Therefore, it is considered important that business and management researchers respect the confidentiality of the source of any evidence or information that is supplied to them by informants. This is especially true if there is any question of the evidence having any competitive or commercial sensitivity.

20.4 Handling students who break the code

When some sort of unacceptable behaviour on the part of the researcher breaches trust, universities take the matter seriously. A disciplinary enquiry is normally convened and this body has far reaching powers. However it is probably worth pointing out that in the few cases where a university withdraws a degree from a graduate it is generally because some major ethical irregularity has occurred during the candidate's pursuit of the degree. This of course is an unusual occurrence.

With the availability of so much information on the Web, plagiarism has become a greater concern. Where this is shown to have taken place students have been excluded from the university. However it should be noted that it is sometimes hard to prove plagiarism and before any allegation is made considerable care needs to be taken. Of course there are software products available today which appear to be helpful. Allegations of plagiarism can bounce back at the university and cause unpleasant situations to arise. Let the accusers beware!

20.5 Some central ethical issues

There are a number of key issues that need to be carefully addressed and carefully thought through by the Masters and Doctoral researcher if the integrity of the research is to be ensured. These include, but are not limited to, what should be researched, how the research should be conducted, who is paying for the research and what should happen to the results of the research. Of course, what is considered ethical will vary enormously from individual to individual. However, there is considerable agreement among institutions. This chapter can only suggest some tentative thoughts on important issues. In addition many of the ethical matters concerned do not have clear boundaries and thus there are many grey areas of which the researcher should be aware.

20.6 What should be researched?

What should be researched is an important issue for the Masters and Doctoral student. From a broad societal or macro point of view there are a number of research subjects that may cause ethical concern among certain groups of people. These include genetic engineering, total or whole body transplants, the use of animal organs in human transplant surgery, germ-line gene therapy (Equinox, 1996), strategic defence techniques, such as those that have been labelled 'Star Wars', nuclear weapons, and artificial intelligence (Remenyi and Williams, 1996). However, from a business and management perspective the areas of concern would be related to less lofty issues, such as the implications of employment of new technologies on those employed in the production function in the factory, or for that matter those in the office. There could also be concerns surrounding marketing practices which might infringe on privacy, or which might exert excessive influence or coercion on prospective buyers. Research into ways of controlling and manipulating the workforce could be considered questionable. Information systems that have a built-in bias in favour of financial institutions such as banks or insurance companies, at the expense of their clients, would also be questionable, and research in this field might be considered not quite ethical.

In general there are a large number of business and management research issues that cannot be questioned on the grounds of ethical considerations, and it is probably sensible for research candidates to stay within these parameters. If they do not it is important for the researcher to be aware of the objections that could be raised by those who might query their conduct on ethical grounds.

20.7 How the research should be conducted

In business and management studies *how* the research should be conducted is perhaps of greater ethical concern to the typical Masters or Doctoral candidate than the question of *what* is being researched. There are three aspects of this *how* question. In the first place there is the issue of the collection of evidence, in the second there are the problems associated with processing the evidence, and finally there is the use of the findings.

20.8 Evidence collection

When researching in the business and management field at doctoral level, experiments are unusual, especially in the UK. Rather, research is performed by collecting evidence from informants either through the use of questionnaires or through interviews using an interview schedule, or perhaps through participant observation or action research approaches or methodologies. If video or audio taping is involved it is important to ensure that the informants' permission has been acquired – preferably in writing.

20.9 Openness with the informants

In business and management studies the informants or participants in the study need to know a number of things and be given a series of assurances (Sekaran, 1992). The main issues are as follows:

1. It is imperative that the researcher does not have any hidden agendas.
2. It is essential that the researcher be fully open and honest with the informants and participants. This means that the informants and participants should be made aware of exactly why the evidence is required and exactly what will be done with it once the research has been completed.
3. It is necessary for the researcher to declare if he or she has any connections or relationships with organisations or individuals that could in any way be construed to be competitive to the informant or to his or her organisation. Thus anything that could remotely relate to a conflict of interest needs to be specifically dealt with in advance of any evidence being revealed.
4. Where an informant does not wish to have his or her name associated with the evidence, this request should be respected.
5. The researcher should not obtain evidence from informants under duress. It would not be acceptable for a researcher to have the managing director of an organisation insist that the staff complete a questionnaire if the individuals involved did not wish to so do. The informants should be told that they could withdraw from the interview at any time without any recriminations.

It is usual for the informants or participants to be aware of the final use of the evidence, and if at any stage the researcher wants to change how the evidence will be used, or to use it for additional purposes, it is important that he or she seeks the permission of the informants.

20.10 The integrity of the evidence

The verification of evidence is important. The researcher may feel that the evidence has not been honestly presented by the informant and in such cases an attempt should be made to verify it. To present in an unquestioning way evidence that the researcher feels is suspicious would not be acceptable. Thus the researcher needs to be pro-actively honest rather than passively honest in the presentation of his or her evidence and research findings.

It is also sometimes possible that the researcher has misunderstood the evidence and this should be checked. For example, when using the case study method of evidence collection, the researcher may offer the transcript of the case to one or more of the informants to establish that the situation was correctly understood and properly recounted in the written version.

It is sometimes believed that the original source of the evidence, for example a transcript of an interview, or copies of the original questionnaire, should be kept for a period of time, say somewhere between two and five years, to allow other researchers access to the data[93]. A good example of the need to retain data is in the case of the controversy surrounding the research conducted by Sir Cyril Burt (Medawar, 1986), which led to profound changes in the education system in the UK. Wadeley (1991) suggests that if Sir Cyril Burt had retained his data and made it publicly available, then the issue of whether or not he falsified the data would have been easily resolved.

20.11 Processing the evidence

The researcher needs to give considerable attention to the ethical issues related to processing of the evidence. If the evidence is quantitative then the concerns are to do with numerical and mathematical accuracy, which is relatively easy. Any attempt to window-dress or manipulate and thus distort the evidence is of course unethical, as is any attempt to omit inconvenient evidence. In statistical terms this does not mean that outliers have always to be included in the numbers, but it does mean that the occurrence of such outliers should be reported as part of the findings and a reason supplied for not including them in the statistics. In the case of qualitative evidence, the issues are more complex and sometimes more difficult as the researcher has more subjective evidence to work with. Here the question of giving appropriate importance and thus weight to statements and opinions becomes a central issue and the researcher needs to take great care to balance his or her approach. This is

---

[93] The need for this data would only arise if the findings of the research were in some way challenged.

a difficult line to tread, as it is important that the research should not be overwhelmed with personal biases. It is not a useful or rational strategy to fabricate evidence or deliberately to misinterpret it, as a Masters or Doctoral degree does not rely on the candidate finding or proving a particular result. Even when hypotheses or theoretical conjectures are rejected, the research is perfectly valid and there is no reason why such findings should not lead to the awarding of the degree.

Subconscious bias on the part of the researcher is a problem. Of course triangulation may be used to help in this respect, but in the final analysis an argument based on a judgement is always required (Collins, 1994). This may not be easy to make with personal prejudices playing an overtly influential and important role. The bias problem has been well described by Hubbard (1979) when she said:

> *The mythology of science asserts that with many different scientists all asking their own questions and evaluating the answers independently, whatever personal bias creeps into their individual answers is cancelled out when the large picture is put together. This might conceivably be so if scientists were women and men from all sorts of different cultural and social backgrounds who came to science with very different ideologies and interests. But since, in fact, they have been predominantly university-trained white males from privileged social backgrounds, the bias has been narrow and the product often reveals more about the investigator than about the subject being researched.*

With regards to research findings, it is important that these are honestly presented and not produced in such a way as to support the opinions or prejudices of the researcher. This is indeed hard to accomplish. Ideally the researcher is trying to apply 'disinterested intellectual curiosity' (Trevelyan, 1993), but this is almost impossible as was pointed out by Gould (1980) when he said, 'Science is not an objective, truth-directed machine, but a quintessentially human activity, affected by passion, hopes, and cultural biases. Cultural traditions of thought strongly influence scientific theories.' Sometimes, if not frequently, personal bias is so subtle that the researcher is not even aware of it. In fact, many would argue that a researcher should not attempt to compensate for bias, but should state clearly the possible biases involved and allow the readers to compensate for these themselves.

20.12 Using the findings

Although the researcher will ultimately have little control over this issue, it is important that the intention of the research is that the findings will be used for ethical purposes. Thus research conducted for the purposes of perpetrating a fraud, for example, has no place in a university.

Furthermore the findings of business and management research conducted by Masters and Doctoral students need to be placed in the public domain. This is in keeping with the general spirit of a university, as well as being in recognition of the fact that most universities and most businesses are funded to a large, or at least substantial, extent from public money. Sometimes an informant will give a researcher access to evidence on the grounds that it should not be immediately released into the public domain. This practice is not really in the spirit of academic research. Some universities, although they allow restrictions to be placed on the publishing of evidence of this type, will not allow the degree to be finally awarded, and thus the candidate will not graduate until the research evidence and findings are released into the public domain. Other universities impose a time limit, such as one year, after which the findings are placed in the library.

Of course it is expected that research conducted for a higher degree will only be presented to a single university towards the award of a single degree. It would not be considered acceptable for the findings to be used for a number of different degrees at different institutions.

20.13 Funding the research

The individual candidates themselves often fund doctoral research with, in many, if not most instances, subsidies from the state in one form or another. Only a limited amount of doctoral research is sponsored by private interests, such as commercial organisations. In the case of privately funded academic research it is important that the interests of the sponsor do not influence the research approach or the findings of the work in any way. Thus the central issue here is the possibility of there being a conflict of interest. If doctoral research has been funded then it is essential for the candidate to declare this explicitly to the university and to the supervisor at the outset of the work. All informants who supply evidence for the research should also be aware of this. Of course the external examiner or examiners should also be informed of such arrangements.

20.14 Performance of the work

There are a number of ethical issues relating to the more routine aspects of research work than those mentioned above and these include plagiarism, fudging references, measuring-instrument construction, choosing a sample, assistance from others, misrepresentations of work done, to mention only a few points.

20.14.1   Plagiarism

Occasionally plagiarism is a problem as sometimes candidates may rely too heavily on the work of others, to the extent of copying large tracts of work without acknowledging the source. This is obviously considered unethical and can lead, in extreme cases, to candidates being excluded from the university. As a general rule, although research candidates are required to rely heavily on the ideas of others at the outset of the research, these ideas need to be appropriately referenced. In addition, a dissertation, although it should include some quotations from other works, should not be too reliant on this type of printed evidence. It is sometimes said that a quotation from another piece of work should not be more than 50 to 100 words in length. Of course these are not hard and fast rules, but rather rough guidelines, which if approximately followed, will help avoid arguments.

Recently a new dimension to plagiarism has arisen in the form of self-plagiarism. Self-plagiarism occurs when an author uses too much of his or her text in more than one publication. This most frequently arises in the publication of papers in peer reviewed journals. Some academics claim that if a degree candidate publishes part of his or her research prior to submitting it for examination then they may be guilty of self plagiarism. This view is not held by the majority of academics. Today research degree candidates are encouraged to have their ideas published before examination. Having some part of the research work published in a peer reviewed journal is seen as evidence of it having added value to the academic community.

Sometimes it is argued that there is an element of plagiarism present when a candidate attempts to replicate an experiment that was conducted in another country or was conducted in another set of circumstances. This view is somewhat controversial, and provided there is no outright copying of a previous dissertation we would not accept that replicating an experiment is essentially an act of plagiarism, especially if the original work is correctly referenced. In fact, properly conducted replication of previous work is essential to the process of validation and testing of research. Without it, all sorts of questionable research could gain acceptance.

20.14.2   *The theft of ideas*

A RESEARCHER MAY OVERHEAR OTHERS TALKING ABOUT POSSIBLE AREAS OF RESEARCH OR PRELIMINARY FINDINGS...

Ideas can be stolen. A researcher may overhear others talking about possible areas of research or preliminary findings and pursue these research ideas without reference to their origin. When this happens unpleasant circumstances arise, especially if ideas are stolen from research students or junior members of staff by senior members of staff. This is a particularly difficult area as it is not possible to have much control over ideas and thinking. According to the *Guardian Weekly* – 'Le Monde' section (1988):

Now in the past two decades, the ethics of the scientific profession (at least among mathematicians) have become so degraded that wholesale plundering of ideas (and particularly at the expense of those in no position to defend themselves) has become almost the general rule among scientists. It is at any rate tolerated by all, including the most glaring and ubiquitous of cases.

Ideas can also be stolen by referees who see them in academic papers that they have been asked to review. It is also possible to have an idea stolen by members of funding boards who are given early access to new ideas that require money to proceed.

The only safe position to take to prevent any possible accusation of stealing ideas is for a researcher to acknowledge any and all sources of ideas, be they from journals or books, or from verbal presentations, conversations or discussions. To prevent ideas being stolen, the best course of action is not to discuss interesting thoughts within earshot of colleagues until the ideas are reasonably well developed[94]. This will help

---

[94] Behaving in this way does deprive researchers and especially young researchers of the benefit of dialogue and discourse with colleagues.

reduce such incidents, although clearly it will not eliminate them[95]. It is difficult to protect ideas from unscrupulous referees.

20.14.3   *Fudging references*

Related to plagiarism, but not quite of the same severity, is the issue of quoting an authority without having actually read the original reference, but rather having seen it published in someone else's work. It is considered unacceptable to do this. Any reference made in a dissertation to the work of another should only be made if the research candidate has read the original him or herself. However it is acceptable to use the 'cited by' approach. Thus if the eminent scientist Albert Einstein is quoted in a book by Joe Bloggs, the candidate may use Einstein's words provided he or she states that the quotation was cited by Joe Bloggs in this book and a full reference is given to this work.

20.14.4   *Measuring-instrument construction*

Constructing a measuring instrument can be a critical part of research in the business and management field and there are many ethical issues around how this is handled and how the evidence collected with the measuring instrument is treated.

Increasingly, personal questions are becoming unacceptable. Issues of age, race, sex, religion, educational standard achieved and so on are no longer regarded as issues about which researchers can expect to obtain information without taking extreme care as to the personal ethical and privacy issues. In fact some would argue that it is a good thing that this has become an ethical issue, but that nevertheless this kind of data is essential to many areas of research. Increased care and sensitivity in these matters is in the interests of all concerned.

Researchers are sometimes tempted to state that the questionnaire is anonymous, while at the same time placing some sort of indicator on the document to allow its origin to be determined. The justification that can be given for this is that it enables the researcher to chase up those who have not completed the questionnaire. Such practice is generally

---

[95] Gribbin (2002) points out that colleagues can also be responsible for ideas getting into the hands of others when he discusses how Rosalind Franklin's x-ray photographs were shown to Watson by Wilkins without her knowledge. Gribbin euphemistically refers to this as a serious breach of etiquette.

considered to be unacceptable, and other equally valid (even if more time consuming and complex) ways of tracking data should be used.

Using leading questions that have a high probability of being answered in the manner desired by the researcher is also ethically questionable as well as being bad research design.

20.14.5   *Choosing a sample*

The choice of sample can dramatically affect the results of the research and thus is an important issue. However, it becomes an ethical issue if the sample is manipulated to show a desired result. This may come about in two ways:

1. The researcher may choose only informants whom he or she knows will have opinions to which the researcher espouses.
2. The researcher may discard evidence from informants who do not comply with his or her views.

Samples need to be established honestly, which means they may produce results that will not necessarily support the views and/or prejudices of the researcher. Inconvenient or conflicting evidence should be directly addressed and not hidden or ignored.

20.14.6   *Assistance from others*

The amount of assistance a Masters or Doctoral candidate may obtain from others is a delicate issue. Whatever help is acquired such as proofreading or assistance with diagrams should be listed in the Acknowledgements page.

There have been cases where even minor help has resulted in questions being asked by examiners and this has produced problems that have delayed the awarding of the degree. An example that comes to mind is where a candidate had a science student write a computer program to help with the analysis of some evidence. This caused an examiner's enquiry. However, this particular incident occurred a few years ago and would probably not be treated in the same way today.

A potentially more serious incident took place recently where a Masters student approached a member of staff with a request for help in writing his dissertation. The candidate said that due to pressure of work in his salary-earning job he was unable to complete the dissertation on time and he would pay a large sum of money for help. The implication was that the member of staff would actually write the dissertation for him. Clearly this was totally unacceptable and the offer was declined. From the Masters student point of view he was trying to outsource the writing of his dissertation. Today there are organisations on the web, which will help research degree candidates produce their research[96].

There is much anecdotal evidence of considerable assistance being given to degree candidates. Of course supervisors may extensively assist candidates in a number of ways, but care needs to be taken so that the dissertation does not become predominantly the work of the supervisor rather than that of the student. Research degree candidates and their supervisors sometimes publish joint papers or chapters and this is a perfectly acceptable way in which they may work together and through which the supervisor may give considerable help to the student.

If the candidate seeks help from professionals such as statisticians, then the question of whether a payment is made may become an issue. Many universities would regard paying for help of this kind as being ethically questionable. The key issue is to disclose such assistance, and even better, to discuss it at the research design stage, to clear up such matters before the evidence is gathered[97]. Many universities require the research degree candidate to sign a declaration that the content of the dissertation is his or her own work. Even where this is not a requirement it is taken for granted that the intellectual input to the dissertation is that of the student.

---

[96] The following was recently downloaded from the web. "ARC has been successfully supporting individuals in their research processes since 1980. We consult, advise, tutor, and perform computer analyses for graduate students (doctoral and masters) through their statistics, research, and theses/dissertation processes. Consulting services range from design determination to data analysis and interpretation (both quantitative and qualitative) to defence preparation. Located in San Diego, California we work with individuals both nationally and internationally using mail, phone, fax, and e-mail. Please contact ARC for your free initial consultation and find out how valuable our services can be!"

[97] Most universities will allow research degree candidates to obtain some level of help with a number of issues related to their work provided that it is clear that the student has done the intellectual input to the work. However this is a grey area and care needs to be taken not to rely on too much help from others.

20.14.7   *Misrepresentation of work done*

Because of the high degree of trust placed in researchers it is not diffi-cult for them to exaggerate the amount of work done. Candidates can purport to have conducted 30 interviews when they have only had 20. Interviews and questionnaires can be fabricated.

The amount of work undertaken for the literature review may also be exaggerated. Researchers may say that they consulted texts when they did not. This can lead to misunderstanding of quotations, especially with regards to their context.

Any such misrepresentation is clearly unacceptable and furthermore is highly dangerous. Candidates can be found out and this type of misrep-resentation should lead to the termination of their registration at the university.

20.15 Responsibility to the greater community

So far this chapter has only addressed the researcher's ethical responsi-bility to the integrity of the research itself and to the university at which the researcher is registered. There is however another important dimen-sion to the ethical issue and that is the researcher's responsibility to the greater community or the society of which he or she is part.

20.16 Discovery of unacceptable practices

A serious ethical issue that a researcher may face relates to the discov-ery or uncovering of some misconduct within the organisation being re-searched. This of course is not likely to be revealed through survey re-search, but rather through case study research. There are two levels at which this may occur and these relate to:

1. Unlawful or illegal conduct;
2. Unsatisfactory practices which endanger staff;

20.16.1   *Unlawful or illegal conduct*

It is possible for a research degree candidate, when conducting an in-depth case study, to discover unlawful or even illegal practices. An ex-ample of this would be the discovery that some sort of criminal act was being perpetrated on the firm by the employees, or perhaps by the em-ployees on the firm's customers.

Such a circumstance presents a difficult situation for the researcher. The law requires that the presence of criminal acts or serious fraudulent practices or the laundering of money should be reported to the authorities and it is essential that the researcher comply with the law. This of course may mean the end of the research exercise with the organisation and people involved in this unfortunate situation for the degree candidate. If this happens during an important case study then the researcher's work may be set back by a considerable amount of time. However, this inconvenience, no matter how great, should not lead to the researcher refusing to comply with the law.

20.16.2   *Unsatisfactory practises that endanger staff*

In some respects an even more difficult circumstance may arise where the researcher discovers, for example, that some important business practice essential to worker safety or to customer safety, is not being complied with. What is happening or not happening may not be a criminal act in terms of any legislation, but nonetheless the organisation may be behaving unacceptably. The difficulty here is that although nothing actually illegal is taking place, the situation as discovered by the researcher is highly unsatisfactory.

There are many grey areas in these circumstances and thus it is hard to give any general advice. All that can really be said is that the researcher needs to discuss carefully these situations with his or her supervisor and that an appropriate course of action should be taken. This will usually mean taking the discovery of the questionable situation up with senior officials of the organisation concerned. As already stated, such a course of action may well mean for the degree candidate the end of this part of the research exercise with the organisation and people involved.

20.17 Summary

Academic research is a challenging, but can also be a rewarding activity. Ensuring that research is conducted in an acceptable way and that its findings add something of value to the body of knowledge is extremely demanding. It is not surprising there-

...THERE WILL INEVITABLY BE DISAGREEMENTS AS TO WHAT ACTUALLY CONSTITUTES CHEATING...

RESEARCH FINDINGS

fore that few people succeed as competent academic researchers, especially at the doctoral level. The difficulty of research may have been in the mind of H. G. Wells (1925) when he said, *'Fools make researchers and wise men exploit them.'* Of course those who succeed at research do sometimes achieve fame and fortune, win Nobel prizes, register new inventions or start up biotech companies and make millions of dollars, although it should be admitted that this is a relatively rare occurrence experienced by only the best in the field.

The subject of ethics is one of considerable controversy and different individuals take strongly opposing positions. According to Ewing (1965), *'Ethics, like other branches of Philosophy, is a subject where wide differences of opinion exist between competent authorities.'* In a general sense what is right and wrong is a question that has puzzled humankind and many of our greatest philosophers for millennia (Aristotle, 1976; Kant, 1948; Mill, 1863; Russell, 1946). There are no clear universal answers to the questions of ethics or morals, even within a relatively homogeneous cultural group such as western society (Lacey, 1982). As Wittgenstein (cited in Redpath, 1990:36) pointed out, *'We feel that even if all possible scientific questions can be answered, the problems of life have still not been touched at all'* – and morality is one of the central 'problems of life'. Even within a single institution there may be substantially conflicting views about what is right and wrong. The problem is that although everyone will immediately agree that it is unethical to cheat, there will inevitably be disagreements as to what actually constitutes cheating. Increasingly, though, ethics is a subject which is attracting attention from managers, consultants and academics (Wheatley, 1992) and thus it is likely that this will produce a better and wider understanding of the issues involved.

It is however interesting to note that Bertrand Russell (1976), perhaps in one of his more playful moods, pointed out the highly subjective nature of ethics by saying that, 'Ethics is in origin the art of recommending to others the sacrifices required for cooperation with oneself.'

It is perhaps unfortunate, although in fact realistic, that Russell sees ethics as a sacrifice. As pointed out above, cheating by the individual is not a rational stratagem in research. Either the researcher will be caught and the penalty will be high, or the research itself will sooner or later be discredited. It is interesting that from the point of view of the body of knowledge cheating is irrelevant in the long term, although it can be distracting or even damaging in the short term, as it places the work in the category of poor or wrong findings and at the end of the day no one will care much. This was well expressed by Gould (1988) when he said, *'Fraud [in science] is not historically interesting except as gossip.'* And Oscar Wilde (1891) attempts to dispense with the issue of ethics in a rather cavalier way by saying that, *'No artist has ethical sympathies. An ethical sympathy in an artist is an unpardonable mannerism of style.'*

Irrespective of the plight of the artist, it is crucial to our modern world that there is a high standard of ethics, as without this it would not be possible to operate the highly sophisticated, large-scale, high-technology society which now exists. The operation of railways, airlines, local and international banks, police forces – to mention only a few fundamental institutions – would not be possible without a highly honed sense of morality and ethics and thus a mutually agreed view of what is right and wrong.

Whatever the particular view of an individual with regards to what is right or wrong, many would agree that some notion of ethical behaviour is important in research. The authors believe that this is the case and suggest that one way to ensure a high standard of ethics in research is to focus on the three principles of medical research (Jenkins, 1996), which may be translated in business and management research as follows:

1. Ensure a high degree of respect for the autonomy of the individual i.e. the informant;
2. Work towards the benefit of society as a primary motivation of research;
3. Respect justice or at the very least the law

Research ethics is a challenging subject that the research candidate has to face, and which, if not addressed correctly, may cause the result of the research work to be considered tainted or even invalid. It is therefore necessary for the research candidate clearly to understand the ethical restraints that his or her community places on the way he or she conducts the research work and publishes the results.

20.18 Useful books and/or websites

Lemmens, T. and Freedman, B. (2000) 'Ethics Review for Sale? Conflict of Interest and Commercial Research Review Boards', *The Milbank Quarterly*, Vol. 78, no. 4, pp 547–584.
Plagiarism, available: http://www.plagiarism.org/ [10 Aug 2011].

Plagiarism, available: http://www.web-miner.com/plagiarism [10 Aug 2011].

Avoiding plagiarism, available: http://sja.ucdavis.edu/files/plagiarism.pdf [10 Aug 2011].

Types of academic misconduct, available:
http://www.csu.edu.au/division/studserv/my-life/support/academic-advice/acad-misconduct [10 Aug 2011].

Academic cheating, available:
http://www.tinotopia.com/log/archive/000246.html [10 Aug 2011].

Academic honesty, available:
http://people.ysu.edu/~helorimer/AcademicHonesty.html [10 Aug 2011].

Piltdown Man, available: http://home.tiac.net/~cri_a/piltdown/piltdown.html [10 Aug 2011].

Part Seven
Other Important Issues

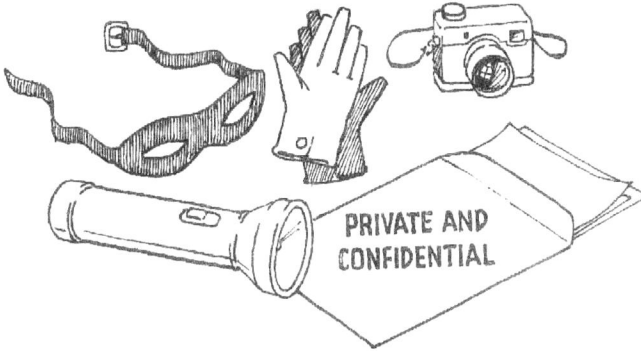

Chapter 21

Helping the student to publish

The process of production and knowledge distribution was never the free, 'objective', and purely intellectual exchange rationalists make it out to be.
Feyerabend, P. (1993), *Against Method***, 3rd Ed, London: Verso, p127.**

In reality, every reader is, while he is reading, the reader of his own self. The writer's work is merely a kind of optical instrument which he offers to the reader to enable him to discern what, without this book, he would perhaps never have experienced in himself. And the recognition by the reader in his own self of what the book says is the proof of its veracity
Proust, M. (1997) cited by De Bottom A, in *How Proust Can Change Your Life***, London: Picador, p25.**

21.1 The pros and cons of student papers

The question of whether a research degree candidate should attempt to have papers published while conducting his or her research is still in some circles controversial. Those who support the writing of scholarly papers while still doing the research for the Masters or Doctorate believe that having such papers published is a major step in asserting that the student has added something of value to the body of knowledge and has made significant progress in becoming a member of the academic community. Examiners do take note of such papers. Papers presented at conferences are also regarded by examiners as a valuable activity for research degree candidates and show evidence of their accomplishments in the field of study.

Those individuals who argue against this sort of work say that the research degree candidate should not be distracted from the main activity of conducting the research work required for the degree itself and that writing academic papers for journals is really quite difficult and that it will slow down the degree process. If the work is planned carefully both objectives can be achieved with little delay. It is correct to say that most universities have a lower publishing output than they would like and many such institutions struggle to motivate even well established academics to write publishable work. Therefore doctoral student publications are generally welcome.

Of course, there is some validity in both of these positions. But on balance most experienced academics would tend to favour research degree candidates, especially doctoral candidates attempting to have at least one paper published during the supervision period. Even if the work required to have a paper published did slow down the completion of the dissertation a little, it may well still be a worthwhile exercise. As mentioned above candidates who have papers published during the research degree process tend to impress examiners.

21.2 The first academic paper

Writing the first academic paper to a standard that it will be accepted for publishing in a refereed journal is no trivial matter. From the research degree candidate's perspective it often looks a truly daunting affair and trying to do this on his or her own is hard both from an intellectual and an emotional point of view. There are several daunting issues that are discussed below. In addition academic reviewers are sometimes quite blunt in their criticism and it is important that a research degree candidate's confidence is not undermined by unkind comments or remarks made by journal reviewers.

As the subject of writing an academic paper is not well addressed in the academic literature it is important for the supervisor to fill this gap. The supervisor needs to put academic paper writing on the agenda at the outset of the degree project. It is important to establish early on the right attitude to writing and to inculcate in the research degree candidate an interest in writing up his or her research right from the very beginning. In some cases it is useful for the supervisor to suggest a framework or set of guidelines for this.

In a number of ways writing academic papers is an extension of the work required for the degree and many of the steps in both these activities are alike. The main difference between writing a dissertation and an academic paper is sometimes thought to be only in the scale of the work. Although it is possible to overstate this similarity there is some truth in the proposition. Whereas the maximum length of an academic paper is likely to be about 25 pages, even short dissertations that accompany Masters degrees by course work are likely to be at least 50 pages long. Masters degrees based on dissertations alone are likely to be more than 100 pages and Doctorates are often between 300 and 400 pages long.

21.3 Why writing publishable papers is a problem

In general there are a number of factors that seem to deter or slow down many academics and research students from publishing. It is important to recognise these problems and find solutions to overcome them. Some of the more common barriers to getting started with an academic publishing career are:

1. Not understanding what is required;
2. Fear of failure;
3. Lack of commitment to the need to publish;
4. Lack of support from the institution or the supervisor;
5. Poor personal motivation.

It is important to emphasise that these factors apply to well-established academics, even some at professorial level, just as much as they affect much less experienced research degree candidates.

21.3.1 *Not understanding what is required*

Many of those who have not yet published a paper in a refereed academic journal believe that the contribution to knowledge that is required to be made in a paper before it is worthy of publishing is much greater than is actually necessary. In discussion with individuals who have felt unable to publish, the comment about their work - 'but that would not be good enough' is frequently repeated. To such individuals the writing of an academic paper appears to be a monumentally difficult task, in some cases it is probably worse than obtaining a research degree. Of course, in reality this is not the case. They often do not understand the criteria which editorial boards impose for a published paper or are not aware of the different types of papers that are acceptable to academic journals. There are many different approaches to writing an academic paper. Such a paper may be theoretical or empirical. It may be based on one case study or a large sample. The variety of research approaches, analysis and synthesis is quite vast (Remenyi et al, 1998). The amount of diversity a new researcher faces is often bewildering and can lead to problems in deciding how and where to start. Once again the real problem is often that of being spoilt for choice and not knowing how to choose from the options available.

21.3.2 *Fear of failure*

The fear of writing a paper and having it rejected is a serious inhibitor to those who have not already established a publishing track record. Indeed, would-be authors really have to be prepared for a considerable amount of rejection. An editor may reject a paper out of hand because it is not on a topic suitable for his or her journal. However, a paper may also be rejected by one or more of the referees for being poorly written, irrelevant, out of date, misinformed, to mention only four possible reasons. Reviewers, especially less experienced ones, can sometimes be hurtful about the work or the ideas of the author or authors, but fortunately most of the criticisms received from editors and referees tend to be constructive. It is, however, by no means uncommon to find quite shallow and unhelpful comments. When this happens the researcher should not take such criticism personally, but should draw on their intellectual and emotional resilience. This should not allow him or her to abandon the project, but rather to take the criticisms as challenges to improve the study or piece of work. Of course, academic reviewers, like theatre or art critics, can sometimes be wrong and authors need to know when reviewers should be challenged. A reviewer may always be challenged by writing to the editor of the journal and putting a counter case to the comments of the reviewer. It is sometimes thought to be surprising just how often this happens. It is well to remember the words of King (1993):-

> *The dissemination of new information is a controversial business, because new information is often surprising. Sometimes it is threatening to existing interests....*

21.3.3 Lack of commitment to the need to publish

From the very beginning of writing an academic paper it is important that there is a strong commitment to the task at hand. If the writer is not fully committed there is a high possibility of abandonment of the project. Typically, working on an academic paper is not perceived as having a high degree of urgency. Although it is no doubt important to publish, it is frequently an eminently postponable event. This is especially true in the case of the first piece of work as this will clearly occur before any research or publishing momentum has been built up. The first research experience, particularly if it is not undertaken as a collaborative effort with an experienced researcher, has nothing to build upon. Thus it will take quite a lot of time.

... THE SUPERVISOR OR EVEN THE DEAN OF RESEARCH CAN BE OPPOSED TO A RESEARCH DEGREE CANDIDATE PUBLISHING UNTIL HE OR SHE HAS OBTAINED THEIR DEGREE.

21.3.4 Lack of support from the institution or supervisor

As mentioned above the supervisor or even the Dean of research can be opposed to a research degree candidate publishing until he or she has obtained their degree. Undertaking research for publication can be demanding (Easterby-Smith *et al.* 1993) and it is easy for the supervisor or Dean of Research to put obstacles in the way.

21.3.5 Poor personal motivation

The expression *'publish or perish'* is well known. The concept behind this slogan is that if university teachers do not publish they will not be confirmed in their posts and they will not be eligible for promotion. Although this may well express the reality which university teachers face, it is totally negative in its attitude. It is a well established fact that threats are not good motivating agents, but often work in the opposite way, i.e. they de-motivate those at whom they are aimed. This is probably especially the case with university teachers who are often strongly independently minded. It would be much more useful if a direct and immediate reward was associated with having academic papers published.

21.4 Factors that contribute to failure to publish

There are a number of factors that may contribute to a paper not being accepted for publication and these include inter alia:

1. Unrealistic expectations, ambitions or targets;
2. Lack of focus;
3. A high risk topic;
4. Lack of theoretical knowledge – failure to build on one's strengths;
5. Lack of methodological skills;
6. Inability to know when to stop;
7. Lack of knowledge of appropriate journals.

Any of the above seven factors can individually or jointly be the cause of the non-completion of an academic paper and ultimately, even if the paper is completed, these issues will probably lead to an inferior piece of work.

21.5 How to produce a publishable academic paper

It is most important for the novice researcher and author to understand that there is a steep learning curve in the production of academic papers. The first paper is a great challenge and may take a long time to complete. However, by the time three or four or five papers have been published the researcher will have learnt how to produce a first class piece of work with only a fraction of the original effort required for the first paper.

A novice will find it helpful to publish jointly with an established author. There are many practical things to learn, and having a coach or collaborator at the outset of a publishing career is helpful indeed. Essentially this is no different to having a supervisor for a research degree. It is sometimes useful to have two or three or even four authors who can bring to the research different disciplinary points of view or even different cultural perspectives. This is sometimes considered an important criterion when the paper is being written with an international journal and an international audience in mind.

21.5.1 Select a suitable topic area

A topic area could be considered suitable if it is of interest to the researcher and if it provides an opportunity to solve a problem which is regarded as being of some importance or relevance to both the academic and the practitioner communities. At the outset of the research the topic area needs to be considered as a provisional area of interest until the literature review has been completed. This area of interest should be related to the researcher's strengths, which are normally associated with some aspect of the research question being studied. However, it is also advisable that the topic area is not too narrowly focused at this stage. It may be interesting to look at other associated disciplines to enquire if there are any interesting inter-linkages.

It is advisable that the researcher does not take on too extensive a project for a publication as this will almost certainly lead to problems that can cause the work to be abandoned. For more than one reason, it is far better for the author to take on several relatively small-scale academic paper projects than one big one. In the first place, the academic community values the number of publications and thus the greater the number the better. Secondly, small-scale projects will usually encounter fewer problems than large scale ones and thus there is a higher probability that they will be completed successfully.

21.5.2 Use the literature

The next step in the preparation of an academic paper is to review the literature in some detail. Depending on the amount of work the student has already done towards the literature review for the degree this might mean reading as much of the academically published material on the subject as possible, or it might require the student to draw on the relevant material for the paper from the literature review already performed. Hamilton and Ives (1983) performed a study to determine which journals are most respected by MIS researchers. The findings of their research suggest that *Management Science, MIS Quarterly, Communications of the ACM, Decision Sciences, Information Management, and Transactions of Database Systems* are the most important journals for information systems academics and professionals. The researcher needs to be cautious of making extensive use of textbooks as even newly published works are inclined to be somewhat out of date due to the length of time publishers require to process a manuscript into a published book. This is especially true with leading edge subjects.

The Web is an especially powerful tool for obtaining access to current issues and ideas. However, as anyone at anytime can place material on the Web considerable caution needs to be exercised when regarding data or information found on the Web as authoritative. In formal academic research references to issues and ideas found on the Web need to be used sparingly and where possible they need to be corroborated with evidence from more traditional sources. Of course, it should be noted that an increasing number of peer reviewed academic journals are now being published online.

Thus, the emphasis of the literature study should be placed on papers published in academically reviewed journals.

By the end of the literature review the student should have a clear view of what he or she wishes to achieve in the proposed paper.

21.5.3 Choose a methodology

Having reviewed the literature the next step in the preparation of an academic paper is to describe the methodology that is used for the research. How a doctoral student handles this issue will again depend, at least to some extent, on how far into the doctoral research process he or she has reached. There are many factors to be considered when choosing an appropriate research methodology. In the first place the literature review should reveal not only a suitable problem to be researched, but also a suitable methodology that has been applied to this type of research question before. This certainly implies that the researcher is familiar with the range of methodologies available, as well as knowing something about their strengths and weaknesses.

The topic to be researched is one of the primary drivers to the choice of methodology. As a general rule precedent should be followed, although this may be abandoned if a suitable case can be made for a new methodological approach. The research culture in the institute is also an important determining factor, as is the skill and interest of the researcher's supervisor. Other stakeholders may also be influential such as the sponsors of the research.

In certain cases researchers may use mixed methodologies. For example having used case studies to establish a grounded theory (Glaser & Strauss 1968), a researcher may use a survey to confirm a theoretical conjecture. Considerable care needs to be taken when multi-methodologies are employed as such an approach may lead to confusing results (Patton 1990).

The choice of methodology can change during the research project. It may be seen as a journey in which the researcher can move from one paradigm to another as his or her understanding of the research problem changes.

21.5.4 Formalise a research question

The literature review should reveal problems or areas of incomplete knowledge in the field of interest. These problems will first manifest themselves as research questions, which need to be reduced to a formal research problem in such a way that it is testable. This means developing a theoretical conjecture and deriving from this a set of either hypotheses or empirical generalisations. For the purposes of a paper, it is possible that one issue arising from the literature will be discussed further.

21.5.5 Collect evidence

A suitable evidence collection strategy is required and the researcher may choose from numerous different combinations such as case studies, action research or surveys to mention only three. In general, business and management researchers ask questions using *how* and *why* evidence collection strategies that focus on these sorts of questions. These tend to be of more value than those which concern themselves with questions of *how much* or *when* and vice versa. Some research questions lend themselves to qualitative data, while others require more quantitative evidence (Remenyi et al, 1998).

21.5.6 Analyse the evidence

Once the evidence has been collected it is necessary to analyse it. The approach to evidence analysis varies enormously. It depends on whether quantitative or qualitative evidence has been acquired. It depends on the mathematical sophistication of the researcher. In general much analysis may be performed with relatively little mathematical or statistical background.

21.5.7 Write the paper

... THE PAPER SHOULD BEGIN WITH A CONVINCING ARGUMENT AS TO WHY THE SUBJECT IS IMPORTANT ...

It is important to catch the reader's attention from the beginning. Both the paper title and the abstract have to be prepared with a focus on attention grabbing. Some authors will spend a considerable amount of time worrying about a paper title for this reason. The abstract should be seen as an appetiser with which to attract potential readers to proceed to read the rest of the paper. Thus the paper should begin with a convincing argument as to why the subject is important and what the paper has to offer. These statements should, where possible, be tied into the literature from which it should be clear that the paper addresses a gap in the published knowledge.

It is then useful to make clear to the reader the research methodological paradigm the author is using in the paper. Thus, for example, there should be a clear statement as to whether or not the paper is theoretical or empirical. There should also be a statement of the practical implications of the work, if any.

In describing the literature review the author should avoid the excessive use of direct quotations from published texts. Such quotations seldom add much value to the argument. It is fundamental to an acceptable literature view, that it should be critical of the established thinking on the subject wherever appropriate. A simple restatement of the thoughts of others also does not add much value. The literature review should not only comment on the state of knowledge of the discipline, but it should also address the research paradigms that have typically been used in previous works.

If the paper being written is based on empirical work it is important to state the assumptions behind how the evidence was collected, as evidence can only be understood in terms of what sample was used and what collection process was adopted. Following on from this it is also important to discuss the types of analytical techniques that were used. Assumptions concerning quantitative and qualitative research paradigms should be clearly articulated. Evidence should not be over-analysed. Often relatively simple statistical techniques will provide sufficient insight to be able to deduce interesting conclusions.

In empirical studies it is most important to ensure that the evidence supports the conclusions drawn. A useful test to apply is to ask if the same evidence could support alternative conclusions. If this is the case then this fact needs to be clearly stated.

The conclusion of an academic paper is sometimes the most creative part of the project. As mentioned above, the evidence must support the conclusions. The conclusions must convince the reader that something of value has been added to the body of knowledge. As Collins (1994) points out, the conclusions deduced from the research need to be carefully argued, in such a way that they will convince the research community.

Generally the conclusions should offer insights into problems or situations and perhaps practical advice. These need to be highlighted as the contribution the author is making to the discipline. It is important that the conclusions should not be *simple motherhoods*, which are completely obvious. On the other hand a research paper, even one published in an international journal, does not have to be capable of winning a Nobel Prize.

21.6 Advice from editors

The following is a summary of advice collected from the editors of three academic journals.

21.6.1 Fundamentals

Novice authors sometimes do not realise that a paper should only be sent to one journal at a time. It is important to comply with this requirement, as there will be substantial embarrassment if the paper is accepted for publication by two journals simultaneously. If a journal refuses to accept a paper for publishing, then the author is free to send it to another journal if he or she so wishes.

Authors need to be realistic about the length of time it can take for a paper to be reviewed. Some journals can obtain comments from referees in a few months (Sloan Management Review, 1995), whereas others can take a couple of years[98].

---

[98] It is quite interesting to note how long it can take some journals to acknowledge receipt of a submission never mind obtain feedback from reviewers. These delays mean

21.6.2 Relevance, rigour and impact

Relevance, rigour and impact are three key issues that are central to an journal editor when considering the publication of an academic paper and are thus issues on which an author needs to focus.

Relevance refers to the requirement that the academic paper addresses issues that are of interest to the target audience of the journal. The issue of rigour concerns the fact that the research reported in the paper has been performed using an appropriate research methodology. The impact issue asks the question as to why top scholars or practitioners would be bothered to read the paper. For this to be the case a high degree of originality is essential.

... ISSUES WHICH ARE OF INTEREST TO THE TARGET AUDIENCE WHICH THE JOURNAL ADDRESSES...

Relevance is always a critical issue but it needs to be matched by an appropriate level of academic rigour. In the words of Galliers (1992):

> *In an applied discipline such as Information Systems, I would argue that it is important that we undertake research that is seen to be relevant by our colleagues in IS Practice, as well as sufficiently scholarly by our colleagues in academia.*

There is little doubt that a similar comment is true for many academic fields of study.

---

that authors who wish to maintain a publishing rate of two to three papers per year need to have six to ten papers submitted to various journals at any one time. This represents a large amount of work in progress.

21.6.3 *Writing style*

Many editors advise contributors to ensure papers are readable, well organised and exhibit good writing style (Management Science, 1995). It is surprising just how many papers are written in a style that makes the ideas expressed in them inaccessible. Reviewers are often critical of papers that are not easy to read, even when the research is sound. Thus papers should be drafted and re-drafted until they read well. Some journals accept the use of graduate level mathematics in the paper with the proviso that it has to be essential for the understanding of the subject. It is sometimes necessary to demonstrate that a paper appeals to professionals as well as academics (Management Science, 1995). Furthermore authors should always ensure that their identity is not revealed anywhere in the body of the manuscript (MIS Quarterly, 1994).

21.6.4 *Choose the prospective journal carefully*

It is important to choose a well-regarded journal, which will draw the academic community's attention to the work. This is essential if the work is to be recognised and if it is to be appreciated by both academics and practitioners. King (1993) expressed this well when he said:

> New knowledge should make a difference in some way, materially, aesthetically, spiritually. A good academic journal should disseminate new information directly to those who can apply it. At minimum, and as a regular matter, a good academic journal should stimulate the research community to improve its performance in creating new and useful knowledge.

The first consideration in the choice of journal is to establish if there exists a match between the prospective journal and the work the researcher is involved in. Thus it would usually be a waste of time to send papers on the future of artificial intelligence or techniques in database design to a journal that publishes in the field of computer security systems.

Papers that add to a continuing debate in a journal usually stand a better chance of being published. Therefore consider whether the proposed paper contributes to an ongoing interest of the journal. If this is the case it is worthwhile ensuring that the paper quotes work already published in the chosen journal.

21.6.5 Instructions to authors

Obtain a copy of the instructions to authors that specify how the paper should be presented to the journal. These should be read carefully and be complied with. They differ from journal to journal and many authors do not notice the difference. It is important to comply with the journal's length requirements. If the paper is too long or too short the journal may reject it.

Papers submitted in the wrong format such as single spaced when double spacing is asked for or using the wrong referencing convention, can create a negative impression from the start. In fact some journals automatically reject all papers that do not fully comply precisely with all the stated instructions to authors.

21.7 Perseverance required

It is not an easy matter to be published in an academic journal and a research degree candidate will usually need quite a lot of help and encouragement from his or her supervisor if this is to be achieved. The key is perseverance as the first attempts may well be rejected. However with the right advice and focused application eventually the work will be published.

21.8 Summary

Having an academic's ideas printed in a peer reviewed academic journal is a positive affirmation that the ideas have value. Thus the supervisor should encourage the doctoral degree candidate to send some of his or her work to a peer reviewed academic journal. However it is important to be realistic. There is a lot of competition to have work published in such journals and many journals have high rates of rejecting papers. This makes being published in such a journal all the better for those who succeed. However rejection can be difficult to take especially as some academics can be impolite in the way they write reviews with the purpose of rejecting a piece of work. It is important for the supervisor to be available to soften such a blow.

21.9 Useful books and/or websites

Hamilton, S. and Ives, B. 1983, *Data Base* 'The journal communication system for MIS research', vol. 14, no. 2, pp. 3-14.

Chapter 22

Other matters

It is good morning exercise for a research scientist to discard a pet hypothesis every day before breakfast. It keeps him young.
Lorenz, K. (1963) *On Aggression*, ch. 2.

One may understand the cosmos, but never the ego; the self is more distant than any star.
Chesterton, G K. (1908) Orthodoxy, 'The Logic of Elfland'

22.1 Integrating students into the academic community

As already mentioned in order to be awarded a degree the student needs to become part of the university community. In general this means understanding the institution and being sympathetic to its objectives and modus operandi.

In reality a research degree is not only a scholarly event but it is rather a combined educational and socialising process. It is far more complex than just writing a dissertation. Of course to be awarded the degree the student needs to show a high level of scholarly or academic achievement, which is reflected in the dissertation or monograph. But this may not be enough. The student will have been a member of an academic community for a number of years and to ensure that the degree is awarded it will be necessary that he or she demonstrates that they can be considered a reliable part of that community.

It is indeed difficult to precisely define what this exactly means and it will of course differ considerably from one institution to another. But suffice to say that the student will need to have a positive attitude toward the institution and be well regarded by many if not most of the people he or she encounters there. In other words intellectual brilliance or creativity alone will not ensure that the degree will be awarded.

It is within the remit of the supervisor to help the research student get to know the university and be known by the key members of the Department and the Faculty and by other members of the University.

22.2 Employment issues

In the past it was not traditional for universities to pay that much attention to the employment potential of their research degree candidates when they have finished their degrees. Business schools tended to invite potential employers to visit and meet their MBA candidates.

It was assumed that research degree candidates would be interested in careers in academe or research institutions and that they would take care of finding such posts for themselves. Furthermore the holding of an advanced degree was seen as the only or at least primary qualification required for an academic post.

Today this is different and many universities attempt to give their students a more rounded education. In fact in the United Kingdom the Economic Social Research Council (ESRC) requires institutions to provide in addition to research training a more general personal development opportunity for students. This extends beyond academic training to encompass wider issues that will be helpful in obtaining employment in business, commerce, industry and government.

22.3 Survival guide for supervisors

There are a number of simple rules supervisors should follow if they are to be successful. These rules may be summarised as follows:

1. Don't rush to take research students, in fact be quite picky.
2. Don't pick up too many half finished dissertations.
3. Make it clear to your research degree candidate what you can do and what you can't/won't do.
4. Make sure that a schedule of work is clearly spelt out and agreed by your student.
5. Have regular review meetings and be as honest as possible – remember that the *law of unintended consequences is always present* and therefore keep clear and unambiguous minutes of these meetings.
6. If the student is not progressing tell the Director or Dean of Research.
7. Don't expect too much from students.
8. If good progress is being made congratulate the candidate and celebrate.
9. Help the student attend conferences and get published.
10. Make sure that the student is well prepared for the viva voce.
11. Set up a dry run at the viva.
12. Attend the real viva so that you know exactly how your student performed and what was actually said.
13. Put time aside to assist the student with post-viva changes.
14. Go to the graduation.

Although research supervision is hard work it can also be good fun. Helping someone obtain a research degree is a great achievement and the supervisor should celebrate this almost as much as the graduate.

Perhaps the most important ongoing issue is that both the supervisor and the student need to be continually aware of how much has been done and how much more work is required. This may be seen as an planning issue where the plans have to be updated on a regular basis. An example of such a plan is provided Appendix 10.

Appendix 1
Additional useful websites

This is a list of useful websites concerning academic literacy or the ability to write in the academic mode.

1. http://www.une.edu.au/tlc/ available: [10 Aug 2011].

A website containing general information on academic writing. Includes interactive exercises for the student and deals with the following topics:

2. http://www.writing.utoronto.ca/advice available: [10 Aug 2011].

A good source of information on many aspects of academic writing. Content is divided between the following subject areas:

General

- Understanding topics, using theses, writing essays etc.
- Reading and using sources
- How to take notes, read critically, analyse content, conduct research etc.
- Specific types of writing
- How to write book reviews, article critiques, bibliographies, proposals, exam essays etc.
- Style and editing
- Advice on how to avoid wordiness, biased language and poor spelling.

Grammar and punctuation

- A list of links to sites dealing with common errors in grammar and punctuation, how to correct them and how to avoid them.
- Some answers for writers of English as a second language
- Some basic grammar rules explained for writing academic papers in English.

3. http://www.ipl.org/div/farq/netciteFARQ.html available: [10 Aug 2011].

This page of the Internet Public Library website deals exclusively with the topic of citing online references. It contains links to websites dealing with the subject of documenting World Wide Web sources in academic writing. It also lists a number of books on the topic of academic referencing.

4. http://libweb.anglia.ac.uk/referencing/harvard.htm available: [10 Aug 2011].

A guide to referencing in the Harvard style.

5. http://owl.english.purdue.edu/handouts/index2.html available: [10 Aug 2011].

An online workshop and handouts on the subject of better academic writing. The following topics are dealt with in detail:

- General writing concerns (planning/writing/revising/genres);
- Research and documenting sources;
- Punctuation;
- Capitalisation and spelling;
- Sentence construction;
- Parts of speech;
- English as a second language;
- Exercises/Answer keys;
- Professional writing.

Each of these sections has many subsections, making the site quite comprehensive.

6. http://www.youtube.com/watch?v=7AxNI3PhvBo

A comprehensive lecture on some of the problems of listening and some recommendations as to how to improve listening through what the presenter calls active listening.

7. http://www.unc.edu/depts/wcweb/handouts/ available: [10 Aug 2011].

An extensive list of printable handouts on the mechanics of writing and writing in specific formats. These handouts are divided into three sections under the following headings:

- Writing the paper;
- Advice on structure, reading, writing, developing arguments etc.
- Writing for specific fields;
- Such as writing speeches, or writing within a particular subject area, like history or philosophy.
- Grammar and mechanics.
- Lists common mistakes and how to avoid making them.

Appendix 2
A research proposal and protocol

The following is an example of a document created by a doctoral student, which is a hybrid of a research proposal and a research protocol. It is presented here as an example of the main issues that need to be addressed. It is not regarded as being an exemplar or a definitive piece of work, but rather an indication of the type of document required.

Title of the Dissertation

A Framework to evaluate e-Commerce adoption by SMEs in the Western Cape of South Africa.

Clarification of Terms and Concepts

e-Commerce - The buying and selling of information, products and services using computers and networks.

e-Business – A collective term where e-commerce, procurement and supply chains operate.

e-Business readiness – Multifaceted components consisting of; well developed infrastructures, ubiquitous access to information and services, supportive government practices and policies and inter-business processes.

Business to business (B2B) - A range of electronic transactions that takes place between businesses.

Information Technology (IT) – The management and processing of Information and equipment.

Information Communication Technology (ICT) – The convergence of the Internet and other telecommunication activities.

Internet - A global network connecting many computers in many countries.

Return On Investment (ROI) - A measure of the net income a firm is able to earn with its total assets.

Small and Medium Enterprise (SME) – The criteria being the number of employees and/or turnover of the business.

World Wide Web (WWW) – A system of Internet servers to facilitate document sharing.

Statement of Research Problem

Thorp (2001) reports that Chief Information Officers (CIOs) are uncertain how to measure the success of e-Commerce adoption in their organisations as well as the IT investment required to sustain these systems in the future. SMEs in the Western Cape need a framework, a theoretical model and a set of guidelines to determine how to measure the success of their e-Commerce initiatives and how to envisage the investment required to sustain this activity. This research will lead to the creation of a theoretical model which may be used to evaluate the success of e-Commerce projects. This model will also allow SMEs to make an assessment of the investment required to sustain the e-Commerce initiative. This will facilitate the development of strategies and guidelines for the efficient and effective use of resources and helping firms in this region to become more competitive.

Background to the Research Problem

Both developed and developing countries have been rushing to participate in the information economy and to build e-business infrastructures (Sarkar and El Sawy, 2003). ICT and IT infrastructure play a fundamental role in providing e-Commerce trading, and leading companies around the world are using the prominent role of IT to implement Strategic Information Systems (Laurindo, Monterio de Carvelho and Shimizu, 2002). e-Commerce enables companies to service their clients and interact with their suppliers in increasingly effective ways as new information technology products, increased bandwidth and faster networks become available. This strengthens the case of Porter (2001), and Evans and Wurster (1999) who state that e-Commerce and e-Business are currently among the top IT applications.

Public discussion on e-Commerce issues often depict the existence and adoption of global e-Commerce as a 'fait accompli', a done deal. *'The world is wired, the globe is booted, and all we need now do is click, sell and shop to our heart's content'* (Dekleva, 2000:3). In fact the reality of e-Commerce adoption is quite different. e-Commerce is not as wide spread as believed and as mentioned above there is much concern about its financial or economic viability. In addition there are questions concerning issues such as legal and political issues, infrastructures, security, trust, fraud and privacy to mention only a few problems.

The challenge of measuring the success of e-Commerce initiatives and how to envisage the investment required is regarded as a central issue in ensuring the large scale acceptance of e-Commerce (Walrand and Moss, 1993; Laurindo *et al.* 2002 and Remenyi, Money and Twite 2000:a; Stansfield and Grant 2003; Benjamin, P. 2002). Some authors such as Mogollon (2004), have suggested the calculation of ROI but for a strategic issue such as e-Commerce this may be too simplistic. What is required is a more holistic view of e-Commerce. Such an approach will help improve corporate effectiveness and may assist in the reduction cost and enhancing customer relationships (Chan and Al- Hawamdeh, 2002).

Literature Review

There is a substantial body of literature on the subject of e-Commerce. This literature review will address some of the key issues in this domain related to e-Commerce success and failure and what can be done to improve the rate of success. This will be done in order to develop an understanding of how e-Commerce success might be measured and how it is possible to envisage the investment required to sustain this activity

This review will then focus on a specific research question and an appropriate methodology to be used in this research study.

Understanding success

Baldwin et al (2001) state that *"to achieve success with e-Commerce, technology needs to become widely available to ordinary people, and SMEs should be prepared to alter their business processes."* Singh (2003) finds personalisation and service orientation to be as important, as well as ease of Website browsing and navigation. Licker (2001) points out that it is important to understand what effect technology has on human affairs and their behaviour.

Lack of Knowledge

One of the obstacles in adopting e-Commerce successfully is the lack of knowledge about the real advantages e-Commerce may offer organisations (Buonanno, et al 1998). The lack of e-Commerce or e-Business[99] knowledge could be the reason why many small businesses either do not get started or fail, and are unable to benefit from online trading opportunities. Castleman (2004) suggests ways and means to encourage and support businesses, for example, the context of small businesses operating in the new economy should first be understood, and then be given appropriate advice and support.

Castleman (2004) highlights the lack of knowledge of Internet, on-line trading and e-Commerce adoption that heightens the fear and anxiety of

---

[99] The term e-Commerce and e-Business are used interchangeably in this document.

loss of control of small business owners. These findings indicate that many small business owners adopting e-Commerce are skilled in IT. For them, adopting e-Commerce does not pose a threat of losing control of their businesses because they maintain an intimate knowledge of them.

Education and training bridges the gap between development and implementation of new e-Commerce initiatives and associated technologies. Singh (2003) maintains that a trained workforce with appropriate knowledge and skills will adopt e-Commerce more readily. He also stresses the importance of considering human factors from the onset of adopting new technology projects, and not after implementation. Adding to the importance of considering human factors, Ratnasingham (2004) states that the lack of Top Management commitment to e-Commerce adoption is an inhibiting factor. In fact in SMEs senior management may not have the strategic vision to initiate e-Commerce investment.

Technical Skills

Chaumont e al (1998) report on the lack of technical skills required by project leaders to manage the implementation of e-Commerce systems. This is often due to SMEs lacking specialised staff. This may be because they are too small or perhaps they do not have the financial resources to retain the appropriate type of staff. Di Romualdo and Gurbaxani (1998), point out that outsourcing is often used in such cases to reduce internal costs and improve business performance.

Understanding how to implement e-Commerce is suggested by Makino (2003) as being a major problem. Makino points out that many organisations do not have an approach or methodology for understanding how to use e-Commerce and states that the lack of technical skills compromises an organisation's ability to take advantage of an e-Commerce business strategy. Similar points are made by Ratnasingham (2004) Chau and Turner (2002).

ICT is enhancing the drive towards globalisation and polarising the business world into companies who are either connected at the core of their business or who are bordering on the digital economy. Moodley (2003) explores why e-Commerce adoption is slow in South Africa and in many parts of the world. Not making a timely transition to e-Business, Third World Countries (TWCs) may be at risk of becoming less competitive in the global market

Relationships

According to Tagliavini *et al.* (2000), e-Commerce adoption results in changes in the organisation experienced mainly by the transformation of relationships, causing important changes in the company's value chain. Suppliers will have to negotiate with retailers where the relationships with customers will become remote and impersonal (Reynolds, 1997).

e-Commerce impacts on SME business patterns and processes whereby supply chains are being reinvented due to rapid increase of the use of the Internet (Ratnasingham, 2004). Just in time (JIT) manufacturing, quick response (QK), vendor-managed inventory (VMI), material resource planning (MRP), efficient consumer response (ECR) and others form a comprehensive supply chain management network (SCMN). Information decisions and processes in SCMN are moving closer to the Internet where global competition, government changing regulations, technology innovation, changing consumer needs and new ways of retailing are all issues SCMN have to incorporate.

Moodley (2003) proposes a virtual corporate value chain where the supply side is linked via Enterprise Resource Planning (ERP) to the demand side, with Intranet workflow being controlled by a corporate portal. This corporate portal in turn interacts with government, suppliers, customers, markets, subcontracting networks and third party agencies. The Internet creates the possibility for organisations to communicate, collaborate and transact at lower cost and enhanced flexibility. The significance of this development is that inter-business e-commerce can now be divided into two categories: Direct trade and open market place based trade between business partners. The former takes place either using the organisation's website with an online purchasing facility that may include EDI, and the latter takes place at various internet-based auctions or exchange sites.

Security, Trust and Fraud

Hossain (2000) reports that the New Zealand Ministry of Consumer Affairs identified an avoidance concept of fraud critical for the success of e-commerce investment. Three steps were taken; early establishment of a certification process for authenticating suppliers, information given to consumers about terms and conditions of payment systems including liabilities, and to undertake International cooperation among businesses, consumers and government agencies. This was in order to create electronic payment frameworks, seal of approval schemes and security services, e.g. public keys.

A key question asked by Filos (2003) about e-commerce is; *"How can you do business with someone you cannot see?"* e-Business relies on technology and infrastructure reducing geographical distances, open communication channels and networks making information systems vulnerable to integrity and security threats. This may undermine the essence of collaboration, nowadays defined as trust. He also sheds some light on research on smart card technology where it is now being extended from the simple 'card swipe' action to devices such as mobile phones, television systems and other web based peripherals. Cognisance of this development must be taken seriously as these methods of transactions would become the norm by the time most SMEs have adopted e-commerce, requiring secure transactions for the simplest of actions or processes.

Perceived barriers and risks of e-Commerce identified by Ratnasingham (2004) rates security, both internally (the firms e-commerce system) and externally (the firms trading partners) which includes government policies, taxes and other audit procedures.

Makino (2003) postulates that virtual enterprises are made up of complex structured companies, thereby making the use of security software complex. The spectrum ranges from Firewall, Encryption, and Virus related to Digital money, Digital certificates, Scam related, Access control and Packet filtering to spoof discovery. This level of sophistication goes beyond the reach of SMEs, expertise and budgets.

Frameworks

From the literature there are reports of many different e-Commerce frameworks. Tagliavini *et al.* (2000) use frameworks for identifying SME profiles by plotting profiles around chosen criteria such as company size, marketing competencies, resistance to change and competitive strategy. They then create tables summarising all the data that can then be used as a look-up table to determine what criteria would need what resource for a particular industry or SME sector. This becomes an *easy to use tool.*

In a study of the e-commerce assurance market, the adoption of Electronic Data Interchange (EDI) was highlighted as the critical element for B2B e-Commerce and a fundamental business tool (Khazanchi and Sutton, 2001). The B2B assurance service was investigated on three dimensions, Application-user level, Business level and Technical level. After the information was collected, analysed, summarised, categorised, etc., a generalised Framework was created - a small sample is shown below.

Generalised Framework for B2B Assurance Service			
EDI Adoption	**Application-User Level**	**Business Level**	**Technical Level**
	*Education and/or training about EDI, standards and EDI transmission options *Understanding potential impediments of EDI adoption *Assessing firm readiness or 'fit' for EDI adoption	*Business process reengineering (aligning business processes for EDI adoption) *Legal and administrative issues of B2B e-commerce *Authentication (e.g. third party confirmation)	*Preparing for EDI implementation *Assessing current IT infrastructure and architecture *Determining transaction formats (ANSI, X12, EDIFAX, or industry specific)
EDI Integration	~	~	~
EDI Outcomes	~	~	~

Source: Khazanchi and Sutton (2001).

The significance of this example is that a similar study could be conducted, but replacing e-Commerce for EDI to design an appropriate e-Commerce framework.

Bui *et al* (2003) conducted quantitative research to find a framework to measure national e-Readiness. The authors used eight factors Knowledgeable Citizens (KC), Macro Economy (ME), Digital Infrastructure (DI) etc. and 52 measures to calculate e-readiness factors. A questionnaire was used to gather information to calculate totals and averages. Benchmarking graphs were drawn and a weighted formula used to determine the e-readiness factors. Two of the fourteen countries and three of the eight factors are shown below with the final calculated country e-readiness factor.

Average factor values and computed e-readiness index by country							
Country	KC	ME	~	DI	~	e-Readiness
China	2.33	1.75	~	2.00	~	2.32
Singapore	4.17	4.58	~	4.00	~	4.21

Source: Bui et al (2003)

The significance of this example is that a similar study could be conducted but to calculate an e-readiness factor for organisations that have adopted or implemented e-Commerce.

The emphasis of Critical Success Factors (CSFs) has been to identify factors that are crucial to a company's success by means of interviewing strategic planning executives (Hossain, 2000). According to the author this has inherent shortcomings by overlooking the management and operational control level aspects of planning, development, implementation and post-implementation phases. In the case of e-Commerce projects, management's concern and support is vital to sustain such projects where risk and investment decisions are key factors to be considered. The eight essential challenges for organisations to consider before adopting e-Commerce, identified by (Viehland and Mitchell, 1997)[1] cited by Hossain (2000), are not sufficient, as additional intra- and extra-organisational relationship factors for successful e-Commerce projects is required in a framework.

Harker and Akkeren (2001) report on research conducted on new (mobile) technologies in organisations where focus groups have the advantage over in-depth interviews. The reason being is that it assists participants to conceptualise the use of the technology. The authors use an eight-minute video clip depicting the use of mobile technologies played to the focus group. An important aspect of this approach is that the features and facilities of the technology can be demonstrated.

Literature Review Summary

From the above literature review it appears that there is no shortage of opinions concerning the value of e-Commerce as well as the challenges facing its implementation. This research will focus on how to develop a framework, a theoretical model and a set of guidelines to determine how to measure the success of e-Commerce initiatives and how to envisage the investment required to sustain this activity. To achieve this the following the research questions will be addressed.

Research Questions

The literature review and discussion point to the fundamental objective of this study which is to establish a framework, a theoretical model and a set of guidelines to determine how to measure the success of e-Commerce initiatives in SMEs in the Western Cape.

The following research questions will be addressed:

1. What success criteria were established for the SMEs at the outset of the e-Commerce initiative and how was it envisaged these would be assessed?
2. What has been learned about the challenges faced by SMEs in implementing an e-Commerce strategy?
3. What tangible and intangible benefits have been derived from the e-Commerce investment?
4. How are the costs of e-Commerce adoption determined?
5. How can SMEs envisage the future investment requirements?

Objectives of the Research

As mentioned above the main objective of this research is to establish a framework, a theoretical model and a set of guidelines to determine how to measure the success of e-Commerce initiatives and how to envisage the investment required to sustain this activity by SMEs in the Western Cape.

The framework developed by this research will be based on the experiences of organisations which may be regarded as providing the best practice established by SMEs in the Western Cape.

This will allow a theory and a model to be produced which may be used by other SMEs to evaluate e-Commerce policy and to establish an appropriate framework and guidelines.

Research Design and Methodology

A number of different research designs have been considered.

Grounded Theory approach

In order to develop the framework, the theoretical model and the guidelines a grounded theory approach will be taken. A grounded theory approach is required because there is not at present any other established theory as to how SMEs in the Western Cape may establish their success. According to Glaser and Strauss (1967) grounded theory emerges through the process of concepts discovery to move data to abstract concepts and stages and this will be required to develop the framework and theoretical model and the guidelines.

In collecting the evidence in order to ground the theory a case study approach will be used.

Qualitative research

From the literature review it is clear that the primary approach to this type of research is qualitative in nature and this is supported by use of case studies. According to Mouton (2001); Remenyi, Williams, Money and Swartz (2000:b) and Tellis (1997), case study research is one of the most effective ways of studying contemporary problems in complex settings.

Case Study approach

A case study approach is particularly valuable when *who, why* and *how* questions have to be dealt with in management studies, and Yin (1994) states that a case study may be defined as an empirical inquiry that investigates a contemporary phenomenon within a real life context. Lubbe (1996) states that case studies are regularly used by organisations to handle business related issues.

The case study approach to research is a tried and tested and well established. Case study methodology provides a way of establishing valid and reliable evidence in business and management studies and will provide a solid foundation for this research.

Bias in Case Study Research

Stake (1994) points out that case study research is not free from bias due to the fact that an interviewer and interviewee may not remain objective during the interview process, resulting in evidence not being totally bias-free.

At least three problem areas are identified that could contribute to the evidence not being bias-free:

1. Difficulty by individuals (interviewees) to remember and give accurate information
2. Disclosure of information by individuals
3. The consequences of trust and confidentiality when revealing information

However these problems will be minimised by adopting triangulation (Remenyi, *et al.* 2000:b,p142), which means obtaining evidence from multiple sources to ensure that a view is not obtained from only one informant.

According to Mouton (2001) the strength of the case study methodology is the in-depth insight obtained, and establishing rapport with the research subjects. Researchers must be aware of these facts and should aim to use multiple sources to improve the reliability of information obtained. Tellis (1997) states that case studies are multi-perspectival analysis, where the researcher is able to consider the relevant groups of participants and the interaction between them.

Case Study Protocol

The protocol of the case study consists of the instrument (interview schedule or question sheet) as well as the procedures and rules to follow when conducting the research.

Interview Structure

Section A

- Demographic Information about the Interviewee

Section B

- Demographic Information about the organisation

Section C

- Questions will be developed to typically cover some of the following areas:
  - o The use of e-Commerce in the organisation
  - o Perceived Benefits of e-Commerce
  - o Implementation problems

- System justification
- Procedures used
- IT investment aspects (budgets)
- Human resources

Field Protocol

The field protocol of a case study is an important document describing the activities, before and during the interviews to gather research evidence. The following list is proposed:

- At least 3 Interviewees will be used for each case study. This is for data triangulation and validation (Remenyi, *et al.* 2000:b,p142).
- At least two of the interviewees should be senior managers, reporting to a board member or equivalent.
- Contact with interviewees will be made through a trusted intermediary (i.e. gatekeeper) wherever possible.
- Initial contact with interviewees arranged at the highest level possible in the organisation.
- Get to know a gatekeeper or guide as soon as possible.
- Record all interviews.
- Support verbal information with documentary evidence wherever possible.
- Plan visits effectively by arranging multiple interviews so as not to waste valuable time.
- Attempt to conduct interviews in the interviewees' offices or natural environment – considering the bias-effect discussed above.
- Engage as many staff members as possible, from secretaries and support staff to the higher echelons in the organisation in order to learn as much about the organisation as possible.
- It is envisaged that letters of confidentiality will have to be signed before information will be revealed in the interviews.

Case Study Reports

To comply with basic scientific methods of classifying, observation of relationships, descriptions of sequences and consequences, reports should be designed to continuously document the research process. The main sections of the case study report will correspond to the research questions.

Data Analysis

Although the main method to gather data will be by conducting in-depth interviews, both quantitative and qualitative data will be used in the analysis and reporting phases of the research. This is to facilitate easier interpretation of some results, e.g. graphs and tables as well as trends and line graphs.

Therefore, the approach to data analysis, will draw on content analysis, concept analysis, hermeneutics (Remenyi *et al.* 2000:b), and diagram-matic illustrations as suggested by Miles & Hubermann (1994).

Hermeneutics: "Study of the methodological principles of interpretation and explanation of written text." (Remenyi et al,. 2000:b:283)

McGowan *et al* (2001) report that the authentication and approaches outlined by Miles and Hubermann (1994) were used successfully to ana-lyse their in-depth interviews with small firm entrepreneurs in a re-search study with reference to using the Web in their businesses.

Delineation of Study

This research will focus on SMEs in the Western Cape Province of South Africa. The SMEs used in the case study will be randomly selected and not from a specific industry.

The SMEs selected will not be restricted to trading in the Western Cape, but globally.

e-Commerce projects may be run/managed internally or may use an outsourced model.

Significance of Research

According to Sarkar (2003), countries recognising the importance of e-Business readiness should develop specialised e-Business strategies to exploit their unique capabilities, resources and geographic positions. This research study concentrates on SMEs in the Western Cape of South Africa, in-line with the above findings.

Although the Web and related technologies are available and used by individuals and organisations, the literature indicates that no significant adoption of e-Commerce has taken place by SMEs in the Western Cape.

When e-Commerce is adopted, it is only used to a limited extent such as electronic mail and Internet Banking (Williams and Warden, 2003).

Expected Outcomes, Results and Contributions of the research

To create a framework and a set of guidelines for e-Commerce adoption evaluation that will be available to IT managers, CIOs, Executives, Financiers and Entrepreneurs when considering implementing e-Commerce. New factors may be identified, not considered before, when adopting e-Commerce, e.g. the impact of e-Commerce on IT investment.

The contribution to the body of knowledge is important, as there is little evidence of the existence of e-Commerce measurement frameworks available to ensure successful implementation of e-Commerce.

Summary

This research will use a case study approach to formalise an evaluation framework and a set of guidelines for e-Commerce adoption. This will assist industry and funders when considering to embark on e-Commerce projects. New factors may be identified when adopting e-Commerce, e.g. the impact of e-Commerce on IT investment.

Proposed Work Plan and Time Parameters

TASK#	ACTIVITY	START	END
1	Literature review	Apr 'XX	On going
2	Industry contacts	Jun 'XX	On going
3	Formulate research methodology	Oct 'XX	Nov 'XX
4	Development of questionnaire	Nov 'XX	Dec 'XX
5	Collection of data	Jan 'YY	May 'YY
6	Data analysis	Jun 'YY	Aug' YY
7	Writing thesis	Sept 'YY	On going
8	Completion	Dec 'YY	May 'ZZ

Appendix 3
A note on some aspects of theory

Theory is the intellectualisation or abstraction of explanations of the world about us. A statement of theory includes the variables involved, processes which occur and outcomes that are observed or achieved or expected.

The importance of theory is often underestimated by managers and business people and by those who are commencing an academic research degree. Theory is sometimes thought of as being only relevant to highly intellectual "boffins" who are in some way distant from the "real" world. There is hardly anything further from the truth. Theory is ubiquitous in all aspects of our beliefs and behaviour. It informs the way we see and understand the world around us and as such it is a fundamental part of our personal, professional, and academic lives. Christensen and Raynor (2003) pointed out:-

> *Every action that managers take and every plan they formulate is based on some theory in the back of their minds that makes them expect that the actions they contemplate will lead to the results they envision.*

When it comes to academic research theory plays a major role especially at the doctoral level. It informs both research questions at the outset of the research and theory is again required to be an integral part of the outcome of academic research.

One of the principle objectives of academic research is to add something of value to our theoretical understanding in the field of study. However not everyone has a clear view of what theory is and how it should be used. In fact the word theory is problematic as it is used in a variety of different ways and can offer a range of different meanings including: speculation, supposition, guess, conjecture, proposition, hypothesis, conception, explanation, and model.

The most frequently used meanings of the word are:-

- **A theory is a speculation** – my theory is that the first horse to lead the pack in the race is unlikely to finish first.

- **A theory is a belief** – my theory is that if you spare the rod you will spoil the child.
- **A theory is a guess** - my theory is that he will come later this afternoon.
- **A theory is abstract reasoning** – my theory demonstrates how value is associated with the perception of utility.
- **A theory is a series of inter-related concepts** – the concept of a black hole brings together a number of different astronomical issues and relationships.
- **A theory is an explanation** – Newton's Third Law of Action and Reaction explains why motor vehicles are wrecked when they collide at speed.
- **A theory is an aid to comprehension** – Einstein's Theory of Relativity allows us to better understand how time and space are interconnected.
- **A theory is a component of a body of knowledge** - Modern Architectural Theory rejects the linear structures fashionable in the 1960s.

In academic research theory may be defined as an explanation bringing together ideas and concepts which point out how and/or why a particular situation occurs. It may also indicate how that situation will develop or progress.

Sutton and Staw (1995) suggest that,

> *Theory is about the connections among phenomena, a story why acts, events, structure, and thoughts occur. Theory emphasises the nature of causal relationships, identifying what comes first as well as the timing of such events.*

Interestingly Sutton and Staw use the word story when it is more common to describe theory as an explanation. Explanations come with various levels of completeness and to be recognised as a theory the amount of explanation may not be great. For example, Newton's theory of gravity explained why objects fall to the ground, but it was not able to offer any understanding as to why gravity exists. Einstein advanced this argument but even he did not offer an explanation as to why time-space warps in the way it does when it does. The use of the word *why* in the Sutton and Staw definition is challenging and it is not always easy to understand or express.

A more complete definition begins by understanding that human kind seems disposed to find patterns and generalise from them. This is quintessentially a cognitive process which requires the intellectualisation or abstraction of explanations[100]. A theory will typically consider the variables involved, processes which occur and outcomes that are observed or achieved. A high level example is the Theory of Supply and Demand. In this theory price changes are the input variables, the response of the buyers and sellers represents the processes taking place and the changes in the quantity of goods supplied and sold are the outcomes.

Theory development is sometimes described as one of the highest levels of scholarly enquiry in that it requires a high degree of intellectual abstraction. Theory may also be seen as the use of a vocabulary which will introduce newcomers to the concepts involved in the field of study. Sound theory development is not easy, in fact it is difficult and academics will argue that it is one of the main benefits which they provide to society. However it is generally thought that in business and management studies there is not an adequate theoretical base and that much of the theory which is available is not strong or complete (Weick 1995).

When a theory is developed by a researcher and before it is commonly accepted by the research community in which the researcher is working it is sometimes referred to as a theoretical conjecture. The term theoretical conjecture should not be confused with the word theorising which is often used in a pejorative sense. Theorising can be simply unstructured speculation which is presented without adequate rigour and reflection. Theory building or development on the other hand requires a methodology such as that described by Carlile and Christensen (2005).

Theory is often supported by primary data but this is not always the case. Before Darwin postulated his Theory of Evolution of the Species he had accumulated data for many years and spent considerable time reflecting on this data. On the other hand Einstein appears to have developed the Special Theory of Relativity with no empirical data by imagining what it felt like to sit on and travel with a beam of light. Of course, Einstein's theory was not achieved without any data, but rather by the support of secondary data that represented the findings and thinking of

---

[100] Humanity's need to find patterns can sometimes lead to mistakes. There are many examples of researchers attributing cause and effect to associated variables which only appear to be connected in some way, but are not actually.

others. The approach taken by Einstein is sometimes referred to as a Thought Experiment. In a thought experiment someone or a group of people speculate about a set of circumstances and try to consider all the possible consequences of their speculation. For a thought experiment there does not need to be any intention to physically conduct an experiment. Thought experiments can appear to be nothing more than a conversation, but if used correctly they can be powerful tools to advance scientific thought[101].

In business and management studies theoretical findings are normally based on empirical research requiring the collection of a substantial body of primary data. However theoretical research including thought experiments also have a role to play.

Some of the more important words associated with theory are:-

A Model

The word model is itself used in several ways but its essential meaning is that it is a representation of something. Models are often used for the purposes of demonstration, building and testing of a theory.

A model of a new building is someone's, probably the architect's, view of what the proposed new building will look like and to some extent its functionality. It offers an opportunity to view the proportions of the building and sometimes this type of model is portrayed with pre-existing buildings around it allowing the relative size and location to be studied. In this case the testing aspect of the model relates to both the aesthetic appeal and the apparent functionality of the building.

A less tangible and more intellectual model would be a set of financial statements or projections showing what the organisation believes the state of the financial affairs will look like at a particular time in the future. Such models are normally computer based allowing the planners in the organisation to perform what-if analysis on the model.

A model will be based on a theory and as such it may be seen as a representation of the theory. A model will often be used to attempt to test

---

[101] It is possible to see a thought experiment as a form of dialectic in the sense that a carefully conducted thought experiment will involve a number of different explanations which will compete with one another as occurs in the thesis, antithesis, synthesis process of the dialectic.

the theory on which it is based. Routinely aeronautical engineers build model aircraft and test their designs in wind tunnels. Automobile manufacturers do the same with steering and brakes. In many cases data representing a variety of different conditions under which the artefact which has been modelled will have to operate is used to test the engineering proposed.

Some researchers suggest that modelling and model testing are more appropriate in quantitative research than in qualitative research as they imply the use of numbers (Silverman 2000). This is a rather narrow view of modelling as non-numeric models based of flow charts and other graphical representations can be of critical value to understanding relationships and processes.

In recent years the word model has sometimes taken on a different meaning as it has been used in a more colloquial sense. Organisations and people now talk about what is actually a financial model in a different way. The question is asked, *What is your business model?* This is another way of putting the question *How do you intend making money out of your proposed product or service?* This question could be restated as *What theory of business are you proposing to use or What theory of business does your plan, if you have one, suggest?*

A Paradigm

The word paradigm is often used in a similar way to theory but may refer to a situation where the scope is broader than is usual for a theory. The word paradigm refers to a world view or shared beliefs (Tashakkori and Teddlie 1998) and thus it may be applied to epistemological concerns (Morgan 2007). The contemporary meaning of the word may be traced back to Thomas Kuhn (1962) who described how scientific theories change. Kuhn was arguing against Karl Popper's (1959) view that once a theory is shown not to work by the process of falsification, the theory is then abandoned or dropped by the scientist. Kuhn's argument is that scientists encounter a large number of anomalies in working with theory and that one or even a small number of anomalies are not sufficient for a theory to be abandoned. However according to Kuhn a series of anomalies have an accumulative effect and eventually the theory will collapse and a new paradigm will come into being.

A Theorem

A theorem is a statement which can be derived and proven (at least if it is mathematical) from a theory. The word theorem is used extensively in mathematics, especially in geometry. Theorems can be proved in terms of the axiom agreed by mathematicians whereas theories cannot be proved, at least in the same sort of way. Theorems are sometimes written in a symbolic form. They are usually accompanied by a corollary, which is a statement that directly follows as a result of a theorem.

A Framework

In the context of academic research a framework is an intellectual structure or scheme which may be used for understanding ideas or concepts, how they function and how they relate to one another. Thus a framework may be thought of as consisting of rules to provide a structure to a discussion or an enquiry. It may also be seen as a map and as such it is sometimes reduced to a diagram.

In academic research the terms conceptual framework, theoretical framework and thematic framework (Ritchie and Lewis 2003) are typically used. Each of these has a slightly different meaning, but they all refer to a way of understanding the issues involved in the research processes.

A framework can be as simple as a taxonomy[102], but it can also take some of the characteristics of a theory. An example of a simple taxonomy is the arranging of education into groups which are labelled as primary, secondary and tertiary. Another commonly used taxonomy is to see organisations as being either private sector or public sector. In information systems research the strategic grid[103] is an example of a framework for understanding the management of different types of systems.

But the word taxonomy may also be used to describe the study of the general principles of scientific classification. This is also referred to as a classification scheme.

---

[102] Taxonomy and typology are sometimes thought to be similar. Taxonomy is the science and practice of classification while typology is the study of types.
[103] The strategic grid is sometimes referred to as the McFarlan Grid as it was developed by Warren McFarlan at Harvard University.

A Hypothesis

A hypothesis is a claim supported by theory or experience which the researcher wishes to test. It is also sometimes referred to as a proposition[104]. There may be many hypotheses derived from one theory and a research project may test one or many of these. Colloquially the word hypothesis is sometimes used as a synonym for a guess, but this is not acceptable in academic research where there should be a clear justification for a hypothesis. But a hypothesis does have a degree of uncertainty associated with it. Medawar (1986) cites Kant as saying:-

Hypotheses always remain hypotheses, that is, suppositions to the complete certainty of which we can never attain.

A similar point has been made by Jung (1995) who took the idea of the contingent nature of scientific knowledge in general and expressed this by reference to the evolving nature of scientific understanding as follows:-

As I saw it, a scientific truth was a hypothesis[105] which might be adequate for the moment but was not to be preserved as an article of faith for all time.

In business and management studies research the word hypothesis is sometimes used as a provisional claim and the term working hypothesis is then relevant. In research, hypotheses are not said to be proved. When an hypothesis is tested and when there is insufficient evidence to support it, the hypothesis is rejected. If there is not sufficient evidence to reject it, the hypothesis stands pro tem.

A law

A law may be seen as a summary of a theory. If we talk about the Law of Supply and Demand[106] we are using a type of shorthand. *The Law of Supply states that when the price of a commodity increases the supply of*

---

[104] The term proposition is normally used in qualitative research while the term hypothesis is used in quantitative research. Some researchers will use the word proposition to suggest a higher level of abstraction than hypothesis and thus claim that a proposition may contain or refer to several hypotheses.

[105] Jung is using the word here as we would use the word theory.

[106] The Law of Supply and Demand is attributed to Alfred Marshall from Cambridge who was in the late 19th century, the leading economist in the UK.

that commodity increases. What this means is that producers have a cost structure which plays an important part in what they can achieve in the market place. Their activities in the market place including the amount they can produce and what they hope to sell is directly affected by the price the product commands. We could drill down further and examine their costs in more detail or we could look more closely at their revenues to see how the Law of Supply works in practice. The summary statement made above, which we referred to as the Law of Supply, is sufficient for most purposes.

Although Economics has many laws, business and management studies, which is regarded by some to be in some sense Applied Economics, has very few. As the term law implies a higher degree of confidence in the matter under consideration than many business and management re-searchers would believe they had.

A Principle

A principle, such as Archimedes's Principle[107] is another way of talking about a law which is described above. Another is the Peter Principle. The term Principle is not in common use today.

A selection of commonly used theories

There are numerous theories in every academic field of study. Theories from the physical sciences include Plate Tectonics Theory, Gravity Theory, Quantum Theory, the Theory of Relativity. From the life sciences we have Cell Theory, the Theory of Evolution, the Germ Theory of Disease. From the Social Sciences we have the Diffusion of Innovation Theory, the Theory of Homo-Economicus, the Efficient Markets Theory, Theory X and Theory Y (human resource management). It is highly unlikely that anyone could provide an estimate of the numbers of theories which are in our intellectual inventory but there are likely to be thousands if not tens of thousands.

---

[107] Archimedes Principle states that if a body is wholly or partially immersed in a fluid it apparently loses weight and the weight it loses is proportional to the amount of the fluid it displaces.

To whom does the theory apply?

Theories can sometimes be applied to the whole of society. The Law of Diminishing Marginal Utility is believed to be one such theory. Whereas other theories may apply only to specialised circumstances.

Glaser and Strauss (1968) describe substantive theory and formal theory. Substantive theory is highly focused and may only apply in special circumstances similar to situations in the development of the theory. Thus the fact that the theory would not apply to everyone does not invalidate its ability to be referred to as a theory. This is one of the main distinctions between theory in social science and theory in the physical and life sciences.

It is worth mentioning that in the life sciences when drugs are being tested it is common for there to be side effects which will not cause any great deal of discomfort or harm to everyone, but which are sufficiently important for there to be warnings on the drug when sold to the public[108].

Where it is possible to so do, formal theory, which can be more easily generalised will deliver greater understandings to a greater number of people. The grounded theory method of Glaser and Strauss opened up theory building to anyone who was prepared to read their method and to accept their approach. Whether the grounded theory method led to substantive theory or formal theory depended upon the topic being researched and the ability of the researcher to obtain suitable access to appropriate informants[109] as well as their skills as researchers.

---

[108] The question of side effects is an interesting one. There are drugs which will have some side effect for many people but there may also be a small number of people for whom the drug will cause severe problems. The Pharmaceutical Industry copes with this by inserting into every packet of pills sold a document warning against all known side effects.

[109] Grounded theory method is regarded by many to be one of the more important developments in social science research in the 20th century. It supplied a method which allowed an unexceptional researcher, such as a doctoral degree candidate, to claim that they could make a respectable theoretic contribution to their field of study. Prior to the Grounded Theory Method it was generally thought only the most exceptional researchers, such as Webber, Durkheim, Keynes, Maslow etc, could claim to have developed a theory.

But it has to be understood that even formal theory should not be seen as a final explanation of a phenomenon. Giddens (1990) pointed out how fragile our understanding can be when he said:-

> *In science, nothing is certain, and nothing can be proven, even if scientific endeavour provides us with the most dependable information about the world to which we can aspire. In the heart of the world of hard science, modernity floats free.*

The value of a theory

The word theory is sometimes used in a pejorative way. "It is only a theory" implies that what is being said may not be valuable. Another version of this same sentiment is, "That's alright in theory but what about in practice?" However these types of statements are usually made by individuals who do not really understand the nature of a theory or how it underpins human activity as described by Christensen and Raynor (2003) above.

From an informed point of view Lewin (1952) says:-

> *There's nothing more practical than a good theory.*

Lewin's comment does beg the question of what might constitute "a good theory" and this is discussed below.

The importance of theory in business and management studies has been highlighted by Keynes (1936) when he said:-

The ideas of economists and political philosophers, both when they are right and when they are wrong, are more powerful than is commonly understood. Indeed the world is ruled by little else. Practical men, who believe themselves to be quite exempt from any intellectual influence, are usually the slaves of some defunct economist.

The words of both Lewin and Keynes suggest that not all theory is "good" theory and this issue was also taken up by Ghoshal (2006) who is highly critical of much of the theory produced by business schools. Ghoshal coins the expression "the pretence of knowledge" and attributes this to some of the current woes in our society.

His argument concerning the pretence of knowledge points out how in business and management studies there is a direct connection between what is proclaimed to be a theory by high visibility academics and the behaviour which these proclamations inevitably encourage. Thus Michael Porter's Generic Strategy Model or Theory caused many organisations to think of their activities in these terms for the first time.

Good and bad theory

The history of knowledge indicates that there have been many bad theories. In the context of this note the term bad theory means a theory that did not work, or a better explanation displaced the bad theory. Such bad theories include: the view that our planet was flat, that the Earth was at the centre of the solar system (if not the universe), spontaneous generation, phlogiston theory, cholera was a air based disease, Martian canals, phrenology , physiognomy, the universe can be understood using a cosmological constant, HIV/AIDS is caused by poverty, if we travelled at more than 50 miles per hour human internal organs would explode, the age of the Earth by James Usher, women are not adequately responsible to have the vote, black people are intrinsically less intelligent than white people, to mention only a few examples. Bad theories persist until a better theory is developed which more successfully describes the issues involved.

On the other hand good theories are those which provide a sustained usefulness to society. Good theories resonate with experience. Good theories explain and in some cases may even help to predict. Good theories tend to last for quite some time but it is important to be cautious about this. Claudius Ptolemy's theory of the solar system persisted for about 1600 years despite the fact that it was wrong.

Ethics and theory

In general theory is ethically neutral. When the Theory of Demand and Supply explains how a free market works it does not imply that this is how society should work. The Theory of Demand and Supply is entirely agnostic as to whether price rises are helpful or hinder our social or political or moral objectives. Keynes' (1936) book The General Theory of Employment, Interest and Money was read by German politicians before it was read in England and the application of his thinking led to the recovery of the German economy and can be seen as a contributor to the causes of the Second World War.

What is the use of theory in academic research?

A question which is sometimes asked is, what is the use of theory in academic research? As mentioned before academics regard theoretical developments to be one of their primary objectives and one of the main benefits they deliver to society. Leaders in many fields of study who have produced new theoretical insights about our world and how it functions have been affiliated to universities. Academics are concerned about not wasting research resources and thus not revisiting what has been done before. Doctoral research degrees have to be original. It is not enough to repeat a study previously performed elsewhere.

Originality which is a corner stone of academic excellence cannot easily be achieved without knowing what has already been established. Thus knowing what has been accomplished and being able to add to this knowledge is fundamental to academic research. This is where the expression attributed to Newton relating to standing on the shoulders of giants encapsulates the spirit of the need to read the literature reporting prior research findings.

Having built on the knowledge created by others academics, researchers then need to offer their own theoretical contribution[110]. This is seldom a new theory but rather an extension or a refinement to an existing theory. The extent of this theoretical contribution can be quite modest but nonetheless it has to be present to justify a doctoral degree.

The importance of theory is that it is required at the outset of academic research and it is necessary to present the findings of the research as a contribution of value to the body of theory.

Summary

Care needs to be taken when using the word theory. It is often used too freely without adequate concern for the meaning it is conveying to others. There are a number of words which are similar to the word theory

---

[110] Standing on the shoulders of giants is the term used by academics to describe how they add to or build on to the knowledge created by others. It has been said that when Newton was complimented for his remarkable discoveries in the fields of gravity, optics etc., he used the expression, "I was standing on the shoulders of giants". Newton may have been referring to Galileo, Descartes and others. As Newton was not known for his modesty some commentators say that it was in fact unlikely that he ever said such a thing.

and it is important to be able to distinguish their different meanings or nuances.

Academic research is traditionally built on already accepted theory or if not then a grounded theory method needs to be employed. When the research is complete the dissertation should point to a contribution to the body of theoretical knowledge.

Not all theories are useful nor do all theories last for long. Some are short lived and are shown to be of little or no value. With respect to ethical considerations theories are normally neutral. But theories are ubiquitous in life in general and especially in academe. Theories, both substantive and formal, play a central role in business and management studies and it is important that the research degree candidate understand what they are and the role they play.

Appendix 4
A short note on positivism

Positivism is a concept which is hard to define, but which lends itself to description. Even in its description there are challenges and it is useful to recall the tale of the Six Blind Men from Hindustan[111] who each describe an elephant by feeling six different part of its body. One man reports that to him an elephant is like a tree, while to another states is like a snake, another like a rope and another a wall, and so forth. Thus it is necessary to be careful when exploring the meaning or meanings of positivism, which is much like the elephant. Furthermore it needs to be remembered that the context of this note is the use of positivism in academic research within the business and management studies field.

Positivism is one of several different research traditions or approaches to academic research. Other traditions include rationalism, a number of variations on interpretivism, and critical theory driven research, to name only a few. These approaches may differ considerably, but they all have in common a set of objectives which are to:-

- contribute to solving a problem by answering a research question;
- achieve this by following a clearly articulated research design;
- be able to offer new insights[112] to both the academic and the practitioner communities as a result of the research.
-

Taking a positivist approach to research requires the researcher to subscribe to the notion of realism as the way of understanding the world. Realism asserts that there is a world which is composed of physical artefacts as well as people, organisations and concepts which have an existence beyond that which is in the mind of the observer. Realism requires

---

[111] This story exists in a number of different Eastern religious traditions including Jain, Buddhist, Sufi and Hindu. John Saxe wrote the English version at the end of the 19th Century and this may be found at URL
http://homepage.usask.ca/~wae123/misc/prose/hinustan.htm
[112] Some researchers would argue that a theory needs to facilitate prediction. In physical and life sciences this is usually one of the main reasons why theory is developed. In social science this need not be the case.

a belief that the researcher can find explanatory mechanisms which will allow the him or her to understand the objective of his or her enquiry. One of the most important aspects of this is an understanding of causation. Causation explains how change has been brought about and what its results are. It identifies a situation or a system and considers what inputs have been made to the system under study and what the outcomes have been. Cause and effect is a central issue and researchers are interested in this so as to improve their ability to predict and control the environment they are studying. In addition a researcher taking a realist position/stance will look for regularities or patterns and will expect to see these patterns elsewhere in similar contexts. These regularities or patterns will sometimes be formalised and expressed as theories which may have some general applicability.

Appendix 5

Research Participants' Information Document

The purpose of this document is to explain to potential research participants the nature of the proposed research and the role which he or she is being invited to play in that research.

	Issue	Detail (the following is a fictitious example)
1	Name of researcher & contact details	Jamie Cassidy jamie.c@thc.com
	Affiliation of researcher	School of Business Studies (Part-time) and The Hi-Tech Corporation
2	Title of Research Project	Cloud Computing, What is in it for us?
3	Purpose of the Study	The purpose of this research is to find out if Cloud Computing can advance the following: - In Business: to sell and supply products or services into the cloud and the considerations of business strategies and processes to do this - In IT: acquiring, and using IT/IS services provided by the cloud to do business – will it be good for ICT strategy, the IT Organisation, and the company as a whole? - In the Hi-Tech sector we operate in: can the sector overall benefit by supplying to, and/or using the services of the cloud?
4	Description of the Study	The research will take the form of Interviews (external participants) and Interviews & Questionnaires (internal participants).
5	Duration of the Study	30 months
6	What is involved?	Send participants an overview of the areas they will be asked questions on when partaking in the interview.
7	Why you have been asked to participate?	You have been asked to partake in this study due to your experience in conventional and Cloud Computing, and have worked in an environment where they have been used.

248

	Issue	Detail (the following is a fictitious example)
8	What will happen to the information which will be given for the study?	The information will be held in a confidential manner while the work is being collated. Following the successful completion of the project all material collected as a result of the interviews and questionnaires will be destroyed. Data will be traceable back to you until it is anonymised.
9	Can you review the data after it has been written up by the researcher?	The data may be reviewed at any time before it is anonymised after which it will not be easy to identify which data came from whom.
10	What will be done with the results of the study?	The results of the interviews and questionnaires will be reported in the findings section of the research dissertation. This will be done in a completely anonymous manner.
11	What are the possible disadvantages?	I foresee no negative consequences for participants in this research.
12	In what way will the study be beneficial and to whom?	This study will provide a useful basis for companies to understand Cloud Computing (private, hybrid, or public) as an option for business initiatives, IT Service delivery (part or whole), and any associated application in the ICT sector. The study will investigate, conclude and recommend what's required (or not) to achieve this.
13	Who has reviewed this Study to ensure that it complies with all the requirements and ethical standards of the university?	The Ethics Committee of The School of Business Studies have approved this research proposal and granted permission for this research.
14	Can permission be withdrawn having previously being granted?	Yes all informants shall retain the right to have their contributions to the research withdrawn up until the data has been anonymised at any time. In addition the contributor has the right to refuse to answer any question asked during the interview. They may also ask to end the interview at any time.
15	Can you refuse to answer any question?	Yes. The contributor has the right to refuse to answer any question on either the questionnaire or as part of the interview and you may terminate the interview at any time.

Appendix 6
Letter of Informed Consent

I, <informant>, agree voluntarily to take part in the research project being conducted by Joe Blogs as part of the requirements for his Degree Research at <XYZ>. I have read the Research Participant's Information Document and I understand the contents thereof. Any questions which I have asked have been answered to my satisfaction.

I understand that the information which I will supply is confidential and that it will be anonymised and will only be used in the findings of the research. I agree that the data may be used both in a masters/doctoral dissertation and also in papers arising from this research which may be published in peer reviewed journals.

I understand that I do not have to answer all the questions which may be put to me. The information which I provide will be held securely until the research has been completed (published) after which it will be destroyed.

The information which I provide will not be used for any other purpose.

I understand that I am entitled to ask for a de-briefing session or a copy of the research at the end of the project.

I have been informed that I may withdraw from this study at any time and that any information which I have supplied will not be used and any records held relating to my contribution will be destroyed. I do realise that this is only possible before my data has been anonymised.

Informant

Date

Researcher

Date

Appendix 7
Research Concept Note

	Dimensions of your research	Your current thinking
1	Field of study	
2	Topic	
3	Source of research question/s	
4	Main question	
5	Sub-question	
6.	Why is this research important	
7	To whom will the findings be important	
8	Main journals for researching this question?	
9	Types of evidence data ? Quantitative ? Qualitative ? Mixed methods Explain why	
10	Options for data or evidence analysis	
11	Possible findings of the research	
12	How will your research findings improve practice?	
13	List any terms that are new to you and their definition	
14	What do you think will be the three most important challenges you will	

	Dimensions of your research	Your current thinking
	face during your research?	
15	Do you know a working paper series to which you can send a paper on your work in progress?	
16	Has an Ethics Protocol been submitted and how long is it likely to take to be approved?	
17	What is your expected date of completion of the proposal/ dissertation?	

Appendix 8
The Doctorate versus the Masters

The following illustrates the difference between a Doctoral Degree and a Masters Degree, as perceived by one university.

The examination criteria for a doctoral degree are as follows: Clear evidence of *originality*, *creative thinking*, and *problem-solving*. The University Report requirement regarding a doctorate states:

> *"In dissertations students must provide proof of original and creative thinking and problem solving, and make a real contribution to the solving of a particular problem in the industry to which their research applies".*

As far as a Masters is concerned, the requirement is that:

> *"In their thesis students must prove that they understand a particular problem in the industry in which they have done their research, are able to analyse and set it out logically, are able to arrive at logical conclusions or a diagnosis, and are then able to make proposals for the improvement/the elimination of the problem".*

Appendix 9

The Monograph Dissertation versus the Papers Approach

Some universities offer a number of different routes to a doctorate. The approach discussed in this book is described as gaining a doctorate by completing a material research project under supervision[113]. At the conclusion of this process the candidate has to demonstrate clearly that he or she has added something of value to the body of theoretical knowledge and that the findings will lead to improved practice. In addition it needs to be shown that the research has been conducted to a high standard of scholarship.

There are different ways in which these objectives may be realized. The two most significant are the Monograph Dissertation and the Papers Approach[114]. Most universities offer both these routes, although the Monograph Dissertation route is by far the best known and is thus regarded by some academics to be the better way of conducting and reporting academic research at doctoral level. It is also often regarded as being less risky. This note compares these two approaches and considers their relative advantages and disadvantages.

The Monograph Dissertation

In a Monograph Dissertation the research is reported in one book, by one author[115] and the completed work is of substantial length. The maximum length of a Monograph Dissertation is often limited to 80,000 words. The work is examined as a single entity, with one set of examin-

---

113 Some universities are now allowing work which was not conducted by the research degree candidate under supervision to be included in their doctoral dissertations. This could be papers written and published before the candidate considered registering for a doctorate. The term Professional PhD has been coined by some universities and business schools to denote such a degree.

114 The Paper Approach is also called the Article Approach. The term paper is normally regarded as being more academically formal than article.

115 In certain parts of the world universities allow research degrees to be undertaken jointly by multiple individuals who may produce only one dissertation. Some academics believe that this is against the spirit of doctoral research while others do not see any problem with it.

ers, only when it is complete. The structure of the Monograph Dissertation has been described in preceding chapters. Most dissertations completed in universities today are presented or structured in this way, and although there is currently an increase in interest in the Papers Approach many academics are not even aware of this method.

Papers Approach

The Papers Approach to doctoral research requires the research degree candidate to undertake a number of related pieces of research which will be written up and 'published' individually as well as being included in the final submission for examination. It is important that these pieces of research can be viewed as addressing a coherent topic. Unrelated pieces of work would not be acceptable. Universities normally require three such papers, although there are some institutions which demand four or even five. The different pieces of research need to address a common research problem and thus they have to display a high degree of coherence. The papers included are thus seen as a portfolio of work which addresses a particular research problem. In addition to this portfolio, most universities which allow this method also require from the candidate two accompanying narratives[116]. These are bound together with the papers into one final product or book which is presented for examination. The first narrative introduces the research problem, discusses some aspects of the extant literature[117] and comments on the methodological issues involved. This narrative will also cover any ethics issues which may arise during the research. The second narrative presents a summary and conclusion as well as a discussion of the limitations of the work and suggestions for further research.

The rationale for the two different approaches

The outcome of a doctoral degree is that the research degree candidate has to show that he or she has added something of value to the body of theoretical knowledge and that he or she has developed themselves into a competent scholar. The degree is about the acquisition of these research and scholarship skills and competencies. This being the case there is no reason why the two objectives mentioned here have to be

---

[116] Because the Paper Approach is 'new' to some universities or academics there is a significant degree of variation in the way a researcher can be allowed to work using this approach. For example some universities have not required accompanying narratives.
117 There will also be some literature discussion within the individual papers.

demonstrated by producing a single piece of work. Therefore it is reasonable to offer research degree candidates a choice as to how they go about developing a case to demonstrate their skills and competencies.

There is another perspective which points out that the choice between the Monograph Dissertation and the Papers Approach is only concerned with the way the research is reported. The same research activity could be written as one large piece of work or it could be reported as three or more activities. For example, a research project involving multiple case studies could be reported as separate case studies which address different dimensions of a research question. A research project involving one case study could be written up as a project concerning the establishment of a research protocol including a field test with the case study; then the case study itself could be presented in such a way that it could be published alone. Then there could be a separate paper of the analysis of the case study and what the finding mean to the community. But in the end the finally compiled work which is submitted for examination has to represent a cohesive body of research.

Do the Papers need to be published?

The Papers need to be 'published' or near 'published'. Originally this route to the doctorate required the Papers to be published in well regarded peer reviewed journals[118]. However, it soon became apparent that waiting for the appearance of the papers in print took too much time. Peer reviewed journals can take several years to process a paper before it finally appears in print. As a result of such delays universities began to allow papers to be included in the portfolio of the research degree candidate's work which had only been accepted by a journal for publication. In some universities papers which have only been submitted, but not yet reviewed, are deemed acceptable. However, it is always better for the credibility of the research if the papers have been published in respected, peer reviewed academic journals.

In general, the submission of a paper to a peer reviewed academic journal is the minimum, although papers that have been internally reviewed or submitted and accepted by a working paper series are sometimes accepted. Internally reviewed papers need to be assessed by competent

---

118 Some universities may have a list of acceptable journals and the papers submitted for the Papers Approach will normally need to have been accepted for publication by one of these journals. However there is a large variation in practice among universities.

internal reviewers (senior members of the school or faculty, perhaps) and confirmed to be of a 'publishable' standard.

Some universities require these papers to be written by the research degree candidate alone, i.e. as a single authored paper[119]. Others allow co-authored papers to be included in the portfolio. When a co-authored paper is used the university may require a certificate from the co-author/s to the effect that the majority of the work conducted and reported in the paper was undertaken by the research degree candidate. Even where such a certificate is provided, examiners may not be entirely comfortable with such papers. A particular case of joint authorship occurs when the supervisor is involved. It is not unusual to find the supervisor's name as a co-author on these papers. The presence of the supervisor's name on such a paper presents problems to some academics who argue that there should be some distance between them (the student and the supervisor) as otherwise their respective contributions to the research may be unclear.

Some universities still strongly prefer single author papers and where co-authored papers are allowed it is normally required by the university that at least one solely published paper is included in the portfolio.

Another reason that single author papers are preferred is that if there are jointly authored papers then these papers could be presented by the different authors for different degrees and possibly at different universities.

If some or all of the papers in the portfolio are as yet unpublished, they will have to comply with the style requirements of the journal to which they will eventually be sent. They also need to comply with the maximum length of paper which the journal will accept. This is typically in the region of 8,000 words. This can lead to a dissertation being formatted in different typefaces or with different referencing conventions. The two narratives leading into the papers and summarising the contribution claimed by the research degree candidate may be in yet another style mandated by the university. As with the monograph, it is important to be clear on the university's rules with regard to presentation and formatting.

---

119 It would be unusual if there were no single authored papers in the portfolio of research work although it is understood that certain universities do allow this.

The research topic and the individual research

Having set out these two different routes to a doctorate it is important to be aware that it may be more appropriate to address some research topics through the Monograph Dissertation rather than the Papers Approach. Research involving a large scale survey may not lend itself to appropriate divisions suitable for separate publishing.

In the wrong circumstances, the Papers Approach can result in three pieces of research with three data sets, three different collection exercises, three different methodologies and three different structures. Some researchers will find the Monograph Dissertation more congenial to their mind set than the Papers Approach and, of course, vice versa. Besides the question of the suitability of the research topic and the researcher's own orientation there is the question of whether there is a suitable supervisor available who feels competent in assisting the researcher with the Papers Approach. There are not many such supervisors available as the Papers Approach has not been the approach of choice in many schools or Faculties in universities.

A rushed decision as to which approach to take, may well lead to a number of problems later.

Leading and Ending Narratives

The Leading and the Ending Narratives are material pieces of work and may constitute a considerable amount of the effort required to obtain the degree, especially if the candidate is drawing on his or her existing portfolio [120] for the papers. When the Leading and the Ending Narratives and the three to five papers are bound for presentation for examination, they may constitute nearly as many pages as a Monograph Dissertation on the same research topic.

The Leading Narrative

The Leading Narrative effectively takes the place of the first three chapters of the traditional Monograph Dissertation. This narrative explains what the research problem is and why it is important. Like the Introduc-

---

120 In theory all the research presented for a doctorate should have been conducted under supervision. However, sometimes universities allow some parts of the final portfolio of the researcher to have predated the research degree candidate's registration. It is important to point out that many academics would be uncomfortable with this.

tory Chapter in the Monograph Dissertation it will also state how the research has been divided among the number of papers required. The title of each of these papers and a two or three sentence description of the paper needs to be supplied. Then the literature has to be reviewed and the methodology or methodologies used have to be discussed together with the ethical considerations[121]. Examples of Letters of Consent and applications for an ethics protocol and other such documents can be supplied in the Appendices. There will inevitably be some overlap between what is said in this narrative and what will also need to be discussed in the individual papers as any publishable academic papers needs to address these issues in their own right. In the interest of parsimony overlap needs to be kept to a minimum, although in these circumstances some degree of overlap will perhaps be inevitable.

The Ending Narrative

The Ending Narrative draws together the research results described in the individual papers and argues that they may be considered as a cohesive body of research. This involves discussing the conclusions and the application of the results to practice. Limitations and future research challenges are also discussed here.

It is in this section that the research degree candidate needs to argue that the research has made a contribution to the body of theoretical knowledge and that it has application for professional or other performance in practical situations. In addition, it is here that the researcher argues for the authority on which the research is based and this includes the validity, reliability and the generalisability issues or perhaps the credibility, transferability, dependability, authenticity and conformability issues.

This section of the work is of critical importance as the research has to integrate the Leading Narrative and the published papers into a convincing argument and many researchers find this a daunting challenge.

Why undertake a Papers Approach to the Dissertation?

The Paper Approach to the dissertation is sometimes incorrectly believed to be intrinsically less demanding than the Monograph Dissertation. This is seldom if ever the case. The three/four/five papers have to

---

121 With this approach issues such as ethical consideration may well be duplicated.

be assessed and are subject to examiners demanding changes. Then the final dissertation is subject to examination and different examiners may require further changes to be made to the work[122]. The length of the Papers Approach Dissertation may be in some cases a little shorter than the Monograph Dissertation but this need not necessarily be the case.

Probably the main motivation for taking the Papers Approach is that Monograph Dissertations are seldom read by anyone other than the degree examiners. Published papers are the recognised means of communicating the results of research to the academic community and therefore the work undertaken for the degree will have a much higher probability of being seen and cited by other academics. For research degree candidates who wish to follow an academic career these publications may be a fast track route to finding a suitable academic post. Of course many, if not most new doctors will seek to publish a number of papers out of their monograph dissertation research. It is normally possible to publish at least one paper and maybe as many as three or four papers if the research is suitable.

Which route to the doctorate should be preferred?

Like so many questions which are asked concerning doctoral studies there is no simple answer to whether a researcher should take the Monograph Dissertation or the Papers Approach. Both are acceptable routes and both can lead to the two requirements which need to be present for a doctoral degree to be awarded.

The Papers Approach is not, at this time, a popular route to a doctorate degree. This means that not many supervisors have experience of supporting a research degree candidate in obtaining a degree this way. Similarly, there is not much experience in the university system in respect to the examination of these degrees. Academics unfamiliar with this approach to doctoral studies have raised concerns about some of the research being published in advance of the submission of the final dissertation. They have suggested that the appearance of such papers in jour-

---

122 Of course with the Paper Approach a dissertation examiner cannot call for changes to be made to the papers if they are already published or even if they have simply been accepted for publication. One of the interesting challenges the research degree candidate faces as a result of the papers being published is that if the papers have been published in different journals there may well have been quite different advice offered by different reviewers and this would be reflected in papers themselves.

nals could be construed as making their inclusion in the dissertation a form of self plagiarism. It has also been said that if the work has been previously published then it cannot be regarded as original. Fortunately, these are minority views.

The Papers Approach to doctoral studies should not be undertaken lightly and certainly not as an 'easy' option. Both the research degree candidate and the supervisor need to be in agreement as to how this work will be conducted and how examiners sympathetic to this route will be found.

With regard to the examination of a doctorate produced by the Papers Approach it is important to bear in mind that some academics may not feel competent to examine such a document and thus care needs to be taken with the appointment of examiners.

On the other hand, it has been argued that the Papers Approach should, in time, become popular with examiners because if the final dissertation contains papers that have already been reviewed then the examiners may be inclined to think that the research need not be scrutinized in quite as rigorous a manner as would have been necessary if there had been no former review of the work.

Writing of the Paper

The writing of a paper has some similarities to the writing of a dissertation although there are a number of important differences. Although the format of academic papers often follows that of a dissertation there is the important issue of the maximum number of words. As mentioned above journals will normally limit submission to a maximum of 8,000 words and this can be problematic when attempting to report a significant piece of research. Nonetheless, journals are frequently uncompromising about this issue. It is also important that researchers learn the principles of parsimonious writing in order to be able to produce comprehensive and competent work of an appropriately defined length.

Furthermore not all academic papers will follow the same outline of a dissertation and the relative importance of the sections in a paper as opposed to a dissertation may vary considerably. Any research degree candidate wishing to obtain a degree using the Papers Approach will need to be become familiar with the different requirements for an academic paper.

As mentioned above, it is also of central importance that the researcher complies with all the style issues which the journal requires. These will be supplied by the journal and the researcher needs to bear them in mind from the outset of the writing process.

Summary

Every university has its own particular regulations concerning the awarding of a degree. In some universities these regulation will vary from faculty to faculty and even from school to school. This is especially the case when it comes to research degrees. Therefore this note has only been able to provide a general discussion of the subject. Academics who are interested in the Papers Approach will have to take advice with regards to their university's 'house-rules' concerning this matter.

There is increasing interest in the Papers Approach to doctoral degrees and for this reason alone academics and particularly those who are supervising research degree candidate needs to know about this subject and the issues involved. It is an area which is controversial in some circles.

Whichever approach is taken, Monograph Dissertation or Papers Approach, to doctoral research the criteria for awarding the degree remains the same. Excellence in research and scholarship is the objective in both cases. It is not possible to argue that the Monograph Dissertation or the Papers Approach is intrinsically better or more difficult. However there are fewer academics who are experienced with the Papers Approach and therefore it is more challenging to find experienced supervisors and examiners.

Appendix 10
A note on preparing for your viva

This is a list of questions which are typically asked during a viva voce and which the supervisor may wish to discuss with a student before this event.

Set 1: Questions used to warm up, i.e. related to the degree objectives

Why did you undertake a doctorate?

What did you think a doctorate was when you started out on your studies and what do you think it is today?

Who are the main stakeholders in this research? In which way will they be able to benefit from the results of your research?

What will a doctorate do for you personally and for your business career?

Set 2: Questions related to the personal development

What do we know now that we did not know before you started your doctorate studies?

What would you say were the most important things that you learnt from your research both in terms of personal development and from a contribution to the body of knowledge point of view?

What would you do differently if you were starting now?

Set 3: Questions related to the research question

What was the original problem/research question?

In which theoretical frame of reference were you able to place this research question?

How was the research question modified as a result of the literature review?

Why was it changed?

Specifically which authors most influenced you thinking about your research question?

In what way does your research question seek to establish a new theory, refute an old theory or develop an extension of an old theory?

How do you describe your theoretical conjecture and how did you derive your hypotheses, empirical generalisations or propositions for testing?

Set 4: Questions related to the research methodology

How would you describe your research methodology?

What influenced you to choose this approach to your research?

What other research methods did you give serious consideration to and why did you reject them?

What would you say were the central methodological difficulties you experienced whilst doing your research and how did you overcome these challenges?

What are the philosophical assumptions underlying your methodology?

Set 5: Questions related to the field work

What was your primary method of evidence collection?

How did you acquire an appropriate measuring instrument?

Did you undertake a pilot study and if so how would you describe its outcome?

How did you locate a suitable sample of informants?

How do you know the informants/sample that you used are/is representative? If is it not representative, how do you defend its use?

What sort of research protocol did you use?

How did you decide when you had enough evidence to proceed with your analysis?

How would you describe the achievements of your field work?

What, on reflection, are the limitations, if any, of the approach you used in your field work?

Set 6: Questions related to the analysis of the evidence

What analytical techniques did you use to help you understand the evidence you collected?

Why did you choose these specific tools?

What other tools did you consider and why did you reject them?

What were the biggest surprises you encountered and can you give an account of what was occurring?

Did your analysis of the evidence support your theoretical conjectures and if not how did this influence your theory development?

Set 7: Questions related to the results of the research

How would you describe your thesis?

How did you arrive at your final thesis?

In what way does it contribute to the body of theoretical knowledge?

How do you regard your work from the point of view of the validity and reliability of the findings?

How do you regard your work from the point of view of generalisability?

Set 8: Questions related to the value of your results

How have you demonstrated that the new theoretical knowledge you have contributed has practical management validity and utility?

How might the results of this research be converted into a practical application or outcome?

What are the major weaknesses of your research?

What questions have you discovered in your research that still need addressing?

Where might this research go from here?

It is important to point out that it is not likely that all these questions will be raised at one viva examination. It would take too much time. However a substantial number are likely to be asked at any thorough examination.

Appendix 11
Tasks or activities for a doctorate

Every doctoral degree is unique and the process involved in completing each doctorate is different. This is because different topics are being researched, different methodologies are being used and different research degree candidates and their supervisors like to work in their own particular way. Nonetheless it is possible to offer a set of high level guidelines as to the type of tasks or activities which need to be completed and provide some rough idea as to how long it may be expected to take to complete each of these tasks or activities. But remember that you will create your own doctoral experience for yourself.

Research Task or Activity	Effort in time required [123]	Start date	End date	Resources	Comment
Attend Introductory Seminar	2 days				
Library research (some of this work can be done on the web but a visit to the library is also essential).	3 days				Keep detailed references including page numbers right from the very start.
Draft Research Concept Note (RCN) – Part 1.	2 – 3 days				
Library research.	3 – 5 days				Web searching will support this but it will not substitute for the library.
Present RCN at Colloquium.	1 day				Feedback will provide some more ideas and even directions.

---

[123] The number of days is not lapsed time but rather a guide as to the amount of effort required. Part-time doctoral candidates may find it challenging to find a block of time in the way it is suggested here. It is important not to attempt to add up the days suggested here to determine how long it will take to finish your doctorate. Part-time students will find it a challenge to finish their dissertations in three years.

Research Task or Activity	Effort in time re- quired[123]	Start date	End date	Re- sourc es	Comment
Update the RCN - Part 1	2 - 3 days				Have a suitable system of ver- sion control.
Formal Registration.	1 day				Registration should be pro- gressed now.
Ensure that you have sound procedures for capturing references and other useful ma- terial.	1 day				The sooner you get organised in this respect the better.
Early library re- search.[124]	2 – 5 days				
Attend Research Concepts Seminar – Part 1.	2 days				
Draft RCN – Part 2.	3 – 5 days				The RCN is now well on its way to being con- vertible into a research pro- posal.
Read a couple of research methods books.	1 week				
Review who you have included in your community and your network.	1 day				From whom can you get some support and with whom do you want to chat about your re- search as you go along.
Feedback – evalua- tion.	1 day				
Start looking for Knowledge Inform- ants.	2 – 5 days				Try to find Knowledge In- formants who are near home if you can.

---

[124] A doctorate requires continuous reading. So visits to the library and web searches are never finished.

Research Task or Activity	Effort in time re-quired [123]	Start date	End date	Re-sourc es	Comment
File useful quotations and other useful material for the final write up of your dissertation.					
Draft Research Proposal.	5 days				This document should be about 20 pages long.
Present Research Proposal.	1 day				Use about 4 PowerPoint slides and keep presentation to 15 - 20 minutes.
Attend Research Concepts Seminar – Part 2.	2 days				
More work on the research Proposal.	5 days				
Attend Research Design Seminar.	2 days				This seminar will confirm some of the ideas you will already have picked.
More library research.	half day a month				Continued throughout the doctorate on an on-going basis.
Make your choice about the nature of your research strategy and design.					
Finalise the details of the research protocol.	2 – 5 days				The protocol is a detailed plan of how you will conduct your research. It needs to address the ethical implications of your research including who you will seek as knowledgeable informants etc.

Research Task or Activity	Effort in time re-quired [123]	Start date	End date	Re-sourc es	Comment
Sort out your sample if you are using a large-scale survey or make contact with your chosen Knowl-edgeable Informants.	1 week				You should be on the lookout for these people from the outset of your doctor-ate.
Interviews with Knowledgeable In-formants.	20 in-terviews over 10 −12 weeks				
Large Scale Survey using Question-naires.	About 10 −12 weeks				Requires the development and piloting of a questionnaire and choice a sample. Then the distribution of the question-naire and sub-sequent collec-tion
Write up transcript of Interviews.	Maxi-mum of 15 weeks				Try to obtain help from a re-search assistant
Analysis of the Tran-script or of the evi-dence acquired by the use of the ques-tionnaires.	4 to 6 weeks for analysis and re-flection				
Learn software to assist with the con-firmation of the anal-ysis of the evidence.	1 − 2 weeks				This require-ment will de-pend on the strategy and the design you have chosen.
Use the above soft-ware if appropriate.	1 week				

Research Task or Activity	Effort in time re-quired 123	Start date	End date	Re-sourc es	Comment
Theory generation.	2 weeks				This requires a high degree of creativity and imagination and the output should be dis-cussed with peers and su-pervisors.
Start compiling the dissertation.	An on-going process over 4 – 12 weeks				Bring together the material you have been col-lecting – Con-sider a paper or two from your results either for a journal or for a conference.
Limitations of the research.	2 –3 days				This is an op-portunity to an-ticipate criticism and to offer an explanation before the ex-aminer/s asks you the ques-tion.
Suggestions for fu-ture research.	2-4 days				Show a rounded knowledge of the subject area and be able to comment on other aspects of the field of study.
Write Abstract	1 day				Spend enough time on this to make it clear that a special piece of re-search has been done and done well.

Research Task or Activity	Effort in time required [123]	Start date	End date	Re-sourc es	Comment
Binding and presentation of dissertation.	1-2 days				Know the rules of the university with regards the number of copies and what sort of binding is required.
Prepare for Viva Voce.	1 week				Try to arrange for a practice run. Come to the Viva having just reread the most important parts of the dissertation – be well prepared.
Attend Viva Voce.	3 hours				Listen carefully to the questions asked and answer them succinctly. Expect to have to make some changes to the dissertation.
Understand the different options the examiners have and what they mean in terms of the additional work requested.					Pass – no changes. Minor changes required. Major changes required. Fail.
Complete changes and resubmit.	1 to 3 months				Ensure you have specific details and understand the changes you are being asked to make to your dissertation.
Receive letter of acceptance of your dissertation and advice of date of graduation.					Time to start celebrating.
Attend Graduation.	1 day				

Research Task or Activity	Effort in time re-quired [123]	Start date	End date	Re-sourc es	Comment
More celebration.	As long as you like!!!!				
Enjoy and use your doctorate.	The rest of your life				

Appendix 12

Authors' reflections on the contents of this book

This book contains a large amount of information and some advice about how to work as a supervisor of research degree students and also about what to expect if you are a research degree candidate. In writing this we have minimised our opinions. We have rather drawn on our experience and our knowledge of this type of work. We would now like to reflect on some of the more philosophical aspects of this subject which readers may wish to consider.

We are of the view that it is a fundamental responsibility of those who hold academic posts to pass on their knowledge and experience to the next generation. We believe that those of us who have been lucky enough to acquire a university education and privileged enough to also work for a university should pay for this good fortune and privilege by 'paying forward'. The idea of paying forward is that one can never pay back the help one has received over the years from our teachers, mentors, supervisors and intellectual companions. Most of these people have moved on and some of them have indeed passed on. What one can do is to be generous and helpful to these coming up through the university system in the same way as our teachers, mentors and companions have been to us in the past. Unfortunately not all supervisors see their role in this light.

We think it is important that care is taken when admitting an individual to an academic research programme. It is not necessary to have an exceptionally high level IQ or to score in the top 1% of the GMAT results. The following attributes are crucial. A research degree candidate needs to have a powerful sense of curiosity and the determination and dedication to undertake and successfully finish a piece of research which makes a unique and scholarly contribution. A research degree candidate needs to have a thorough understanding of the academic principles underpinning his or her chosen topic. In the USA doctoral degree candidates are put through two years of course work to ensure that there are no major gaps in a candidate's topic or subject knowledge. But we do not do that on this side of the Atlantic. The most that is normally offered this side of the world is generic courses in research methodology and methods such as statistics which in some cases is now being converted into a Masters of Research degree. Here, research degree candidates can be accepted to research topics which they have not studied as an undergraduate. This practice can be problematic and has lead to a number of research degree candidates not completing their research and thus not obtaining their degree.

Alongside the question of the doctoral degree candidate's original undergraduate field of study is the matter of the supervisors' core academic competences. In an ideal world the supervisor/s should have an academic qualification in the subject that he or she is supervising. But this does not always happen. There are just not enough academics with the required qualifications. Academic inflation, which has been fuelled by taught masters degrees, has put too much pressure on the system. Sometimes the university will seek to find one supervisor with subject knowledge and one supervisor with methodology experience. This is perhaps how the idea of having a supervisor committee originated.

Research candidates need to be able to work hard and to sustain this hard work, i.e. they need stamina. They need to be able to cope with a high degree of ambiguity as there will be numerous occasions when different courses of action could be acceptable and they will need to be able to choose. This type of uncertainty does not suit everyone. Some doctoral candidates want to be instructed as to what to do next and this can lead to problems. Doctoral candidates need to be self motivated and be able to work things out on their own. Allowing research degree candidates to register who do not have these qualities wastes their time and money and does nothing for the supervisor and the university. It may even harm the good name and reputation of the university.

There is said to be two types of work which a person may undertake. The first is similar to cutting a branch of a tree while the second is similar to digging a hole. It is a relatively easy task to specify what is required when a branch is to be cut off a tree. But it is much more difficult to specify the requirements when a hole is to be dug. Once the branch is on the ground some claim may be made that the job has been done. Of course, there may be some discussion about whether or not it has been accomplished exactly as the specification required, but it is usually a relatively straight forward matter to establish whether or not the job is satisfactory. When a hole is dug there are far more dimensions to be discussed. Is the hole as deep, as wide, as long as required? Are the sides of the hole as straight as required? What is to be done with the material taken from the hole? In short, how well has the task been done. Is the disposal of the material taken from the ground to create the hole part of the job of digging the hole?

Academic research resembles more the digging of a hole than the cutting of a branch. It is difficult to specify what is required in a doctoral dissertation. Most doctoral dissertations uncover additional interesting aspects of the research topic which could have been incorporated in the study. The research could have delved deeper into various aspects of the subject. Other techniques could have been used to explore the topic. In short no piece of research is ever perfect and academics in the role of examiners need to treat the work of others with respect. But this does not mean that there are no standards to be applied. There is a paradox here because one of the hallmarks of quality academic research is the ability to be critical, but it is essential that the criticism is offered in a positive way. Regrettably this is not always done.

The fact that the doctoral degree process is an apprenticeship in academic research is sometimes lost sight of. At the same time inadequate thought is often given to what can reasonably be expected from a new graduate. In the traditional crafts, and academic research is a craft, the move from apprentice to journeyman is only one step on the road to becoming a master craftsman. Some academics do not like the comparison of academic pursuits with the crafts, but we find the apprenticeship analogy useful. By the way recognising the doctoral process as an apprenticeship is in no way intended as an excuse by which to lower standards. The standard of doctorates is an issue which should be addressed. The current approach to maintaining academic quality is built on the view that the presence of an external examiner is an appropriate safe guard of quality and this is not always the case.

Furthermore, if the result of an examination is questioned, academic institutions raise the defence that academic judgement cannot be challenged. Again this is paradoxical as academic judgement is continually challenged in public and private debate. One needs to look no further than the great controversy of our times, i.e. global warming to see how important academic challenges can be. More modest intellectual conflicts occur every day especially with regard to the value of a particular contribution of an academic paper. Here is a typical example taken from a real situation of two different academic judgements.

Referee 1: The paper is timely, terse and rather forcefully presented. I regard it as of far-above-average value to PJP readers.

Referee 2: A large segment of the paper is historical. The remaining part is speculative, verbose and not well written.

Peer review does not mean impartiality and neither does having two examiners.

We are of the view that too much time is devoted to the argument concerning whether quantitative or qualitative research is the most appropriate approach with which to answer a particular research question. So much is made of the differences between quantitative and qualitative research and individuals who support quantitative or qualitative approaches often engage in inappropriate acrimonious debate. The reality is that virtually all academic research projects in the social sciences require both quantitative and qualitative data. A simple example of this is that even when a questionnaire is to be used to acquire the data, the form and the content of the questionnaire can only be finalised after some qualitative discussion in terms of the data requirements and how it will fit into the process of answering the research question. Furthermore, when the analysis of the data obtained from the questionnaire is complete, the process of understanding and interpreting the findings is essentially a qualitative research activity. Thus in a sense it may be said that there is some element of mixed methods thinking in all academic research. We are not arguing that the distinction between quantitative and qualitative research be abandoned, but that we encourage the understanding and appreciation of the similarities between these two approaches instead of always focusing on the differences. Combining qualitative and quantitative data can produce synergies in understanding.

There are numerous other issues which deserve contemplation, but time does not allow for that at this stage. The subject of how to conduct rigorous and relevant academic research is certainly like digging a hole. As a child I was told that if I dug far enough I would get to Australia. This is not the way we want to go to Australia and thus I hope that readers will understand if I stop at this point.

We hope that readers will find this book useful and interesting.

Dan Remenyi and Arthur Money
January   2012.

A Final Word or a Final Fable

The Thesis[125]

One sunny day a rabbit came out of her hole in the ground to enjoy the fine weather. The day was so nice that she became careless and a fox sneaked up behind her and caught her.

"I am going to eat you for lunch!", said the fox. "Wait!" replied the rabbit, "You should at least wait a few days." "Oh yeah? Why should I wait?" "Well, I am just finishing my thesis on 'The Superiority of Rabbits over Foxes and Wolves.'"

"Are you crazy? I should eat you right now! Everybody knows that a fox will always win over a rabbit." "Not really, not according to my research. If you like, you can come into my hole and read it for yourself. If you are not convinced, you can go ahead and have me for lunch." "You really are crazy!" But since the fox was curious and had nothing to lose, it went with the rabbit. The fox never came out.

A few days later the rabbit was again taking a break from writing and sure enough, a wolf came out of the bushes and was ready to set upon her.

"Wait!" yelled the rabbit, "you can't eat me right now." "And why might that be, my furry appetizer?" "I am almost finished writing my thesis on 'The Superiority of Rabbits over Foxes and Wolves.'" The wolf laughed so hard that it almost lost its grip on the rabbit. "Maybe I shouldn't eat you; you really are sick in the head. You might have something contagious." "Come and read it for yourself; you can eat me afterwards if you disagree with my conclusions." So the wolf went down into the rabbit's hole and never came out.

The rabbit finished her thesis and was out celebrating in the local lettuce patch. Another rabbit came along and asked, "What's up? You seem very happy." "Yup, I just finished my thesis." "Congratulations. What's it about?" "The Superiority of Rabbits over Foxes and Wolves.'" "Are you sure? That doesn't sound right." "Oh yes. Come and read it for yourself." So together they went down into the rabbit's hole. As they en-

---

[125] See http://www.cs.umbc.edu/www/graduate/fable.shtml

tered, the friend saw the typical graduate abode, albeit a rather messy one after writing a thesis. The computer with the controversial work was in one corner. And to the right there was a pile of fox bones, on the left a pile of wolf bones. And in the middle was a large, well-fed lion.

The moral of the story:

The title of your thesis doesn't matter. The subject doesn't matter. The research doesn't matter. All that matters is who your advisor is.

References and readings

Alvesson, M. and Deetz, S. (2000) *Doing critical management research*, London: Sage Publications.

Aristotle, (1976) *Ethics.* London: Penguin Books.

Ashall, F. (1994*) Remarkable discoveries*, Cambridge: Cambridge University Press, p62.

Becker, H. (1986) Writing for social scientists: How to start and finish your thesis, book, or article, Chicago: University of Chicago Press.

Becker, H. (1999) Tricks of the trade: How to think about your research while you're doing it, Chicago: University of Chicago Press.

Bell, J. (1993) Doing your research project: A guide for first-time researchers in education and social science, 2nd edition, Milton Keynes: Open University Press.

Black, D. Brown, S. Day, A. and Race, P. (1999), 500 tips for getting published: A guide for educators, researchers and professionals, London: Kogan Page.

Booth, W. Colomb, G. and Williams, J. (1995), *The craft of research*, Chicago: University of Chicago Press.

Brookfield, S. D. (1987) Developing critical thinkers: Challenging adults to explore alternative ways of thinking and acting. San Francisco: Jossey-Bass.

Burke Johnson R and A Onwuegbuzie, (2004), Educational Researcher, Vol. 33, No. 7, pp. 14–26, October

Cantor, J. (1993), *A guide to academic writing*, Greenwood Publishing Group.

Carlile P and C Christensen, (2005), The Cycles of Theory Building in Management Research,

Checkland, P. (1981), *Systems thinking, systems practice*, Chichester: Wiley.

Christensen C and M Raynor, (2003), Why Hard-Nosed Executives Should Care About Management Theory, Harvard Business Review, p67-74, September 2003

Code of Good Practice: Boards of Examiners for Degrees by Research http://www.ex.ac.uk/admin/academic/tls/tqa/resrcexa.html , 21 April ,2002

Collins, H. (1994) A broadcast video on science matters entitled *Does Science Matter?,* Open University, BBC, UK.

Collopy, F. and Armstrong, J. (1992) 'Expert opinions about extrapolation and the mystery of the overlooked discontinuities', *International Journal of Forecasting,* 8 (4) Dec.: 575–82.

Creswell J. W, Plano Clark, V. L., Guttmann, M. L., & Hanson, E. E.(2003). Advanced mixed methods research design. In A. Tashakkoriand C. Teddlie (Eds.), Handbook of mixed methods in social and behavioral research (pp. 209–240). Thousand Oaks, CA: Sage.

David, G. and Parker, C. (1997), *Writing the doctoral dissertation*, New York: Barrons.

Doctoral Information Handbook - Chapter 7: Thesis and examination matters,http://www.monash.edu.au/phdschol/docprog/handbook/chap7g.html , 21 April , 2002

Easterby-Smith, M., Thorpe, R. and Lowe, A. (1993), Management Research An Introduction, London: Sage Publications.

Ewing, A.C. (1965) *Ethics.* New York: The Free Press.

Feyerabend, P. (1993), *Against method*, 3rd Edition, London: Verso.

Feynman R, Six Easy Pieces, p2, Penguin Books, London (1995)

French, W.L. and Bell, C.H. Jr. (1978) *Organisation development: Behavioral science interventions for organisation improvement.* 2nd edition, Englewood Cliffs, NJ: Prentice-Hall.

Galliers, R. (1992) *Information systems research. Issues, methods and practical guidelines*. Henley on Thames, Alfred Waller Information Systems Series.

Ghoshal S, (2005), "Bad Management Theories Are Destroying Good Management Practices"

Giddens A, (1990), The consequences of Modernity, Polity Press, p39, Cambridge.

Glaser B and Strauss A, (1967) *The Discovery of Grounded Theory*, Sage, Thousand Oaks, CA.

Goldfisher, K. (1992) 'Modified Delphi: A concept for new product forecasting', *Journal of Business Forecasting,* 11 (4) Winter: 1–11.

Gould SJ, (1980), 'An early start' in The Panda's Thumb (W.W. Norton and Co., New York) p. 225

Gould SJ, (1984),'Evolution as fact and theory' in *Hens Teeth and Horses Toes* (Penguin Books, 1986) p. 255 and in Lectures on Evolution delivered at Cambridge University

Gould, S. J. (1980a) *Ever since Darwin,* Harmondsworth: Penguin Books.

Gould, S. J. (1988) *The mismeasure of man.* 4th Edition, London: Penguin Books.

Gribbin J, (2002) *Science a history*, London: Alan Lane.

Guardian Weekly (1988) 'The mathematician who turned down a $150,000 prize' in the 'Le Monde' section, 15 May p.17.

Gummesson, E. (1991) *Qualitative methods in management research.* London: Sage Publications.

Honerich, T. (1995) *The Oxford Companion to Philosophy*, Oxford: Oxford University Press.

Huff, A, (1998) *Writing for scholarly publication*, Altamira Press.

Jenkins, T. (1996) A discussion with Professor Trefor Jenkins of the South African Institute of Medical Research in Johannesburg, December.

Jocher, C. (1928/29) 'The case method in social research', *Social Forces Journal.*

Jung C G, (1995), Memories, Dreams, Reflections, p 174, Fontana Press, London

Kant I, (1948) *The moral laws.* London, Hutchinson.

Keynes K, (1936), The General Theory of Employment, Interest and Money, ch. 24, "Concluding Notes"

Kuhn T, (1962), The Structure of Scientific Revolutions, Chicago, IL, University of Chicago Press.

Lacey A, (1982) *Modern philosophy*. Boston, Routledge & Kegan Paul.

Lewin K, (1952). Field theory in social science: Selected theoretical papers by Kurt Lewin, London: Tavistock

Liverpool John Moores University, Regulations and Procedures, http://cwis.livjm.ac.uk/research_and_graduate/regulations/examproc.html 21 April , 2002

Maital, S. (1993) 'Oracles at work', *Across the Board,* 30 (5) June: 52–3.

Marx K, (1844) 'Economic and Philosophic Manuscripts of 1844' repr. in *Karl Marx and Friedrich Engels: Collected Works,* vol. 3, (1975).

Mauch, J. and Birch, J.W. (1983), Guide to the successful thesis and dissertation : conception to publication : a handbook for students and faculty, New York, Marcel Dekker.

McCarthy, K. (1992) 'Comment on the "Analytic Delphi Method"', *International Journal of Production Economics,* 27 (2) May: 135–6.

Medawar P, (1986), The Limits of Science, p41,p 101, Oxford University Press, Oxford, 1986.

Mill, J. (1863) *Utilitarianism.* London: Everyman, London.

Morgan D, (2007), Paradigms Lost and Pragmatism Regained, cited in Plano V and Creswell J, The Mixed Methods Readers, Sage, (2008).

Morgan, G. (1980) 'Paradigms, metaphors, and puzzle solving in orgaflisation theory', *Administrative Science Quarterly:* 9 (4): 605–20, December.

Oppenheim, A. N. (1966) Questionnaire design and attitude measurement., New York: Gower.

Parsons G, (1983), 'IT – a new competitive weapon', Sloan Management Review, Vol 25, No 1, Fall, p3-12.

Parsons, H. (1992) 'Hawthorne: An early OBM experiment', *Journal of Organisational Behaviour Management,* 12 (1): 27–43.

Patton, M. (1990) *Qualitative evaluation and research methods.* Newbury Park, CA: Sage Publications.

Popper K R, (1959). The logic of scientific discovery. New York: Routledge.Tashakkori, A., & Teddlie, C. (Eds.). (2003). Handbook of mixed methods in social and behavioral research. Thousand Oaks, CA: Sage.

Porter M (1980) *Corporate Strategy*, The Free Press, New York.

Preparing for the oral examination of your thesis (the *viva voce*) http://www.ioe.ac.uk/doctoralschool/info-viva.htm, 21 April, 2002

Pugh D and Phillips E, 2000, How to Get a PhD : A Handbook for Students and Their Supervisors , Open University, Milton Keynes.

Quinn, J. B. (1988a) cited in J. B. Quinn, H. Mintzberg, and R. M. James (eds), *The Strategic Process, Concepts, Context and Cases.* New Jersey: Prentice Hall.

Redpath, T. (1990) Ludwig Wittgenstein – A student's memoir. London, Duckworth.

Remenyi D (2011, Field Methods, Academic Publishing International, Reading

Remenyi D, Williams B, Money A and Swartz E, (1998), Doing Research in Business and Management Studies, Sage, London

Remenyi D, Swan N and B Van Den Assem, (2011), Ethics, Academic Publishing International, Reading

Remenyi, D. (1995) 'So you want to be an academic researcher in business and management studies! – Where do you start and what are the key philosophical issues to think about?' *Working Paper Series, Henley Management College,* Henley-on-Thames.

Remenyi, D. (2002) 'Research strategies – Beyond the differences', *Proceedings of the European Conference on Research Methods, University of Reading,29-30 April*, Published by MCIL, Reading.

Remenyi, D. and Williams, B. (1996) 'Some aspects of ethics and research into the silicon brain', *International Journal of Information Management*, 16 (6): 401–11.

Ritchie J and J Lewis Eds. (2003) Qualitative Research Practice, Sage Publications, London

Rosenthal, R. and Rosnow, R. L. (1991*) Essentials of behavioral research methods and data analysis,* 2nd Edition, New York, McGraw-Hill.

Russell, B. (1946) *A history of Western Philosophy*, London, Unwin Hyman.

Russell, B. (1976) 'A free man's worship and other essays', cited in *Columbia Dictionary of Quotations*, 1995, New York: Columbia University Press.

Sanders, M. and Lewis, P., (1997) 'Great ideas and blind alleys? A review of the literature on starting research', *Management Learning*, p283-299.

Sekaran, U. (1992) *Research methods for business – A skill-building approach.* Second Edition, New York: John Wiley & Sons.

Silverman D, (2000), Doing Qualitative Research, Sage Publications, London

Smith, N. (1990) 'The case study: a useful research method for information management', *Journal of Information Technology,* no. 5: 123–33.

Strauss, A. L., and Corbin, J. (1998) 2nd ed., Basics of Qualitative Research: Techniques and Procedures for Developing Grounded Theory, London: Sage Publications.

Sutrick, K. (1993) 'Reducing the bias in empirical studies due to limit moves', *Journal of Future Markets,* 13 (5) Aug.: 527–43.

Sutton R and B Staw, (1995), What theory is not, ASQ 40 p 371-384

Tashakkori A and C Teddlie, (1998), Introduction to Mixed Method and Mixed Model Studies in the Social Sciences, Sage Publications, cited in The Mixed Methods Readers, Sage, (2008).

Trevelyan G M, (1993), 'English Social History, Introduction' in *The Columbia Dictionary,* Columbia University Press.

Tung, L. and Heminger, A. (1993) 'The effects of dialectical inquiry, devil's advocacy, and consensus inquiry methods in a GSS environment', *Information and Management* 25 (1) July: 33–41.

References and readings

Varadatajan P, (1996) 'From the Editor: Reflections on research and publishing', *Journal of Marketing*, Vol. 60, October, p 3-6

Wadeley A. (1991) *Ethics in Psychological Research and Practice.* Leicester: British Psychology Society.

Wadham B, (2009), Qualitative Research, Website, URL, http://web.me.com/benwadham/QualitativeResearch/induction-deduction-abducti.html [7 January 2012]

Wells H G, (1905) 'A Modern Utopia', chapter 2, section 5 (repr. in *The Works of H. G. Wells,* vol. 9, 1925).

Wheatley M, (1992) *Leadership and the new science.* San Francisco: Berrett-Koeler Publishers.

Weick K, (1995), What Theory is Not, Theorizing Is, ASQ,No 40, p 385-390

Wilde O, (1891) 'The Picture of Dorian Gray, 'Preface'', reprinted in *The Complete Illustrated Stories, Plays and Poems of Oscar Wilde*, (1992), Chancellor Press, London.

Williams R T, (2003) Personal correspondence with the author.

Wittgenstein L, (1969) *On Certainty,* sct. 378 (ed. by Anscombe and von Wright,).

Yin R, (2009), Case Study Research: Design and Methods, Sage, Thousand Oaks, Ca

Yin R, (1989) *Case study research – Design and methods* Newbury Park, CA: Sage Publications.

Index

www.ingramcontent.com/pod-product-compliance
Lightning Source LLC
Chambersburg PA
CBHW070717280326
41926CB00087B/2401